DISHING UP **VERMONT**

DISHING UP VERMONT

145 AUTHENTIC RECIPES FROM THE GREEN MOUNTAIN STATE

TRACEY MEDEIROS
FOREWORD BY MOLLY STEVENS
PHOTOGRAPHY BY SCOTT DORRANCE

Storey Publishing

The mission of Storey Publishing is to serve our customers by publishing practical information that encourages personal independence in harmony with the environment.

Edited by Margaret Sutherland
Art direction by Dan O. Williams
Cover and text design by Tom Morgan, Blue Design
Map illustration on page 13 by © David Cain
Indexed by Christine R. Lindemer, Boston Road Communications

Printed in the United States by Walsworth Publishing Company
10 9 8 7 6 5 4 3 2 1

Library of Congress Cataloging-in-Publication Data

Medeiros, Tracey.
  Dishing up Vermont / author, Tracey Medeiros.
     p. cm.
  Includes index.
  ISBN 978-1-60342-025-9 (pbk. : alk. paper)
  1. Cookery, American—New England style. 2. Cookery—Vermont. I. Title.
TX715.2.N48M43 2008
641.5974—dc22

                                    2008003237

CONTENTS

Acknowledgments

This book would not be complete without acknowledging the many wonderful people who were so much a part of its creation: Molly Stevens, president of the Vermont Fresh Network, for writing the foreword and enthusiastically offering a mentoring helping hand whenever needed; Meghan Sheradin, executive director of the Vermont Fresh Network, whose valuable advice was very much appreciated; the farmers, chefs, and food producers — their wonderful recipes have made this book a delicious reality; Charles Hays, my recipe tester, whose ideas and suggestions have added a tasteful flair to the project.

My suppliers: Black River Produce, provider of many of the produce and dairy ingredients; Cavendish Game Birds, Inc. (quail and pheasant); Circle W Rabbitry (rabbit meat); LedgEnd Farm (venison); Maple Wind Farm (lamb); Riverside Emus (emu meat); Sweet Clover Market, in Essex Junction, who kindly agreed to be the distribution hub for many of the needed recipe items; and Justin Molson for assisting with pickups and deliveries.

Storey Publishing and its special staff: Pam Art, Margaret Sutherland, Wesley Seeley, Amy Greeman, and Jessica M. Richard, for allowing me the opportunity to bring this labor of love to life. It is with a heartfelt sense of gratitude that I say thank you to all.

Finally, I would be remiss if I did not mention my mother, Sheridan, who offered her endless support, helpful advice, and constant reminder that all things are possible; my sister, Kelley, whom I adore; my caring husband, Peter, for his encouragement, constant love, and discerning palate; and my incredible son, Peter, who is my biggest fan. Thank you.

A portion of the proceeds from the sale of this book will be donated to the Vermont Fresh Network.

Foreword
A Taste of Place

In the 1980s, the whispers of a movement to change the face of American agriculture began in restaurant kitchens across the country. American chefs were waking up to the reality that they could radically improve their cooking by embracing the virtues of local, seasonal, and sustainable ingredients. These same chefs also recognized that these alternative purchasing choices could positively impact the survival of independent farmers. At the same time, farmers' markets began popping up in more and more places, and small farmers began experimenting with the notion of community supported agriculture. Over time, these whispers became audible in every corner of the nation, and a vibrant new regional cuisine was born. One of the most notable examples occurred in the small state of Vermont with the inception of the Vermont Fresh Network.

In the mid-1990s, a number of dedicated Vermont citizens recognized that the best way to counteract the devastating effects of the modern commodity-driven food system on small-scale farming was to develop local markets for Vermont-grown goods. These visionary individuals coordinated a series of events to bring together Vermont farmers, producers, and growers with their neighboring chefs to explore how the two groups could work in partnership to support local agriculture. The result of these dynamic conversations was the creation of the Vermont Fresh Network, the nation's first statewide farm-to-restaurant program.

Today, the Vermont Fresh Network (VFN) serves as a matchmaker, facilitating innovative partnerships between farmers and chefs across the state. By forging and fostering vital links between local farms and local restaurants, VFN helps insure that Vermont residents and visitors can dine on locally grown and raised ingredients when they eat out. From the most elegant fine-dining establishments, to trendy pubs, to cozy bed-and-breakfast inns, to Mom-and-Pop diners, VFN member restaurants offer a dining experience that is uniquely Vermont — a true taste of place. Consumers choosing to patronize VFN partner restaurants are choosing to spend their food dollars in ways that support local agriculture and sustain Vermont's unique food culture and rural landscape.

In just over a decade, the VFN has grown to include over 300 members, and the familiar green logo can be seen on restaurant doors and barn sides across the state. In order to qualify as a partner-member, each restaurant must certify that they have a minimum of three "handshake agreements" with local farmers and/or producers. (Farmers/producers must in turn have at least one "handshake agreement" with a restaurant.) This arrangement insures that farmers are delivering directly to the restaurants and that chefs are making forays to the farms to visit and cultivate their relationships with their growers. As a result, the ingredients that show up on these restaurant tables resonate with the distinct character of that place and connect directly to the hardworking individuals who work the surrounding farmland. Fresh local food feeds the body and nourishes the soul, and thriving working farms enhance the beautiful landscape for this generation and those to follow.

The VFN also offers consumer memberships to individuals and families equally dedicated to its mission of supporting local agriculture. Throughout the year, VFN hosts a number of events to educate the consumer on the significance of their food choices and to celebrate the joys of Vermont's agricultural traditions. While the farm- and chef-partners and consumer memberships are the backbone of the organization, they are only a start. The real success of the effort lies in the grassroots activities and ongoing conversations between the farmers and the chefs, and then between the chefs and their

customers. In the end, these individuals come together to rebuild Vermont's food system by making real connections to the fresh, flavorful, wholesome food on the table.

In *Dishing Up Vermont*, Tracey Medeiros provides a window into the vibrant and vital network of chefs, farmers, growers, and producers that defines VFN. By recording their stories and recipes, she pays tribute to the diversity and significance of their contributions to Vermont's environmental and culinary landscapes. While there are many reasons to celebrate the successes of the Vermont Fresh Network, the organization still faces future challenges. In addition to continuing to support and foster the farmer-chef relationships that bring locally raised food to all Vermonters and visitors, the organization is dedicated to educating the public about the quality, pleasure, and wholesomeness of eating the bounty of the surrounding working landscape. As you read (and, we hope, cook) your way through this book, we invite you to get to know those who grow your food — wherever you may live. We believe that supporting local agriculture helps sustain local businesses, farmers, and our environment, but most importantly, it preserves a vibrant way of life and provides a unique taste of place.

— **Molly Stevens,** *Vermont Fresh Network*

The Pleasures of Eating Locally

When I moved to Vermont, I was immediately impressed by the spectacular snow-covered mountains that framed picturesque valleys, quaint towns, and miles and miles of pristine countryside. Small farms dotted the landscape, giving me cause to wonder why the family-owned farm could survive here and yet be a distant memory in so many other parts of the Northeast. I soon noticed that local cookbooks, newspaper articles on agriculture, and many of the farmers themselves repeatedly used the term "sustainable" when discussing their philosophy of farming. They continually expressed a commitment to producing healthy, pesticide-free crops and products while also striving to maintain the integrity of the land for future use. As the mother of a young son, I could readily support this desire to produce and use only wholesome, nutritional foods in conjunction with preserving the richness of the land.

My culinary school background and passion for good food prompted me to search through the cooking section of local bookstores, hunting for cookbooks that were dedicated exclusively to Vermont products and recipes. They were a rare commodity. The idea of creating a publication that would showcase the people of Vermont and the wonderful products that make this state unique slowly began to take shape. Using my trusty computer, I started researching Vermont-based Web sites, looking for informational pieces on local farms and restaurants. While doing so, I began to familiarize myself with the Vermont Fresh Network, whose name and reputation seemed to be synonymous with healthy eating.

Many local farmers are members of the Vermont Fresh Network; some are certified organic, and all practice sustainable farming. To join the network, farmers must partner with at least one restaurant; restaurants, in turn, must have working connections with at least three farms. The Vermont Fresh Network encourages farmers, food producers, and chefs to work directly with each other to build partnerships. They believe that forging regional connections promotes a sense of pride, as well as an investment in and responsibility for the economic vitality of local communities. The Vermont Fresh Network is dedicated to supporting and celebrating partnerships between Vermont farmers and chefs.

Before launching my project, I knew that it would be necessary to become well acquainted with the practice of sustainable agriculture. The term didn't become well known until the late 1980s, but all of the people involved with my cookbook follow and/or support this philosophy. It is based on the premise of a deep, continuous respect for nature. Plants, animals, and people are treated with concern for their well-being and an appreciation for who and what they are. This approach shuns the premise of mass food production with its emphasis on "more is better." Instead, these farmers strive to use their land in the most productive way possible without depleting its fertile wealth or polluting the environment. They believe that following nature's example will enable them to raise crops and livestock that will benefit not only the consumer, but the land as well.

Sustainable farming practices work well with both small and larger family-run farms. The goal is to have the farmer connect directly with the consumer. This essential link puts a face on food and builds a community that is invested in its agricultural component. These hardworking Vermonters can be found at farm stands and local farmers' markets. Their crops and products are also being incorporated into the menus of local restaurants. Participating restaurants order directly from the farmer and may have their request picked and

delivered the same day — from field to table within hours. These "field fresh" products last longer because they do not sit on a truck for days waiting to reach their destination. The consumer is often familiar with the farm or person who produces his food. This gives the buyer a sense of confidence and security in the quality of what he is purchasing. When the customer is acquainted with the source that is supplying her food, an invaluable connection is created — one that supports Vermont agriculture and protects consumer health.

Farmers who practice sustainable farming treasure the land from which they make their living; they strive to preserve its richness for the generations to come. They believe that this approach to farming will meet their present needs without compromising the future of Vermont farming. Many chefs, restaurateurs, and consumers are realizing the far-reaching benefits of this evolving agricultural movement. Its emphasis on environmental health, economic profitability, and social well-being is a vision that more and more Vermonters are beginning to recognize and embrace. The recipes in this book, which are based on the freshest locally grown ingredients, reflect this philosophy.

Dishing It Up

This book, like the food culture it celebrates, would not have been possible without the goodwill and support of the local community. All of the people involved spent a considerable amount of time discussing their thoughts, ideas, and vision for the book with me. Throughout, the enthusiasm and support were overwhelming. The idea that this Vermont-based cookbook was long overdue seemed to be a universal refrain; people were delighted that it would soon become a reality. These hard-working Vermonters shared treasured family recipes, along with others that they had skillfully created out of a need for and devotion to using locally grown products.

The book is divided into individual chapters that showcase the best of Vermont's locally produced foods and the recipes that were created to bring out the best flavors of these products. It is my hope that the format gives you a user-friendly approach to the best foods Vermont has to offer.

Dishing Up Vermont demonstrates the unique bond between Vermont farmers, chefs, and food producers and is a testament to their combined community. I've included profiles of various farmers, chefs, and food producers who have contributed to this project — my way of introducing you, the reader, to the men and women who so graciously opened their hearts to me and embraced my project with enthusiasm and generosity. Without them, this book would not be a reality.

These informative snapshots will give you a better picture of the people who are actively working to insure the agricultural vitality of the Green Mountain State. In surrounding states, residential developers are busily gobbling up every inch of open space. Farming is becoming a fast-fading way of life; in the years to come, our children and grandchildren will know it primarily through picture books or reference materials and not direct experience. But the farmers, chefs, and food producers who are presented in this cookbook are committed to preserving Vermont's agricultural way of life, along with its rolling fields and pastoral vistas, and the pleasures of its harvest tables. The community understands that producing best-quality, ecologically responsible food and foodstuffs creates a lasting bond between producers and consumers, and that this bond is the key to the survival of their farming lives.

Dishing Up Vermont applauds its contributors for their dedication to producing fresh, healthy, pesticide-free products. Their kindness and support have enabled me to create a cookbook that I hope will bring a slice of Vermont to your table, no matter where you may live. Enjoy!

1 Seasonal Vegetables

Recipe from LET'S PRETEND CATERING

Tomato and Arugula Salad

A wonderful salad, made even more appealing by its versatility. As the season progresses, try fresh peaches, blue cheese, and a honey vinaigrette, or crisp pears, endive, and walnuts with the arugula.

SALAD

8 cups loosely packed baby arugula

½ small red onion, peeled and thinly sliced

3–4 Roma or heirloom tomatoes, sliced into segments

¼ cup pine nuts, lightly toasted

4 ounces chilled soft fresh goat cheese, crumbled, (about 1 cup) or 1 cup grated Parmesan cheese

LEMON-BALSAMIC VINAIGRETTE

1 tablespoon freshly squeezed lemon juice

3 tablespoons best-quality balsamic vinegar

1 teaspoon Dijon mustard

1 tablespoon minced onion

2 garlic cloves, peeled and minced

1 cup extra-virgin olive oil

Salt and freshly ground black pepper

4 SERVINGS

1. Gently toss the arugula, sliced onion, tomatoes, pine nuts, and goat cheese in a medium bowl. Season with salt and pepper to taste.

2. Combine lemon juice, vinegar, mustard, onion, and garlic in a small bowl. Slowly drizzle in the olive oil, whisking rapidly until well combined. Season with salt and pepper to taste. Just before serving, drizzle desired amount of dressing over the top of the salad and lightly toss.

NOLA'S SECRET GARDEN

To Nola Kevra, tabbouleh is more than a healthy Middle Eastern salad. It embodies all the beauty, color, tastes, and magic of her summers growing up in Somerset, New Jersey. On warm July mornings on her grandparents' 75-plus-acre farm in Franklin Township, Nola would head out to the fields with her grandfather to gather several huge bunches of parsley, an armful of mint, and as many absolutely scrumptious, red, ripe tomatoes as the vines were willing to share. They would take them back to the well house, wash them, and take the load to Grandma (Tata) so that she could carry on the magic.

Sitting at her table under a canopy of huge trees, Tata would spend the morning carefully and thoroughly chopping the parsley and mint. Tomatoes were next. Nola often had the task of squeezing the lemons — 12 to 14, maybe 15 — being sure to keep the pits out and the juice and pulp in. The final additions were the precious olive oil, plus lots of chopped fresh scallions, salt, and pepper. They never made "reasonable" amounts of this salad — instead, they prepared giant tubs, which required mixing by hand. The vat (enough for 50 hungry Lebanese and Egyptian friends and relatives) would then be covered with a lid and placed carefully into the chill of the well house to cool until guests arrived.

Nola's desire to re-create the ambience and magic of her grandparents' New Jersey farm encouraged her to acquire 10 precious acres of land in the mountain village of Ripton, Vermont, which is right smack in the middle of the state. This land is at an elevation of 1,850 feet and is surrounded by the Green Mountain National Forest and all of its wild, wonderful inhabitants. Moose, deer, black bears, ravens, turkey vultures, and owls are just a few of the occasional visitors to this quiet retreat. Nola does not limit her visitors to animals. "I want friends, students, relatives, cancer support group members, curious leaf peepers, chefs, little children, and old native Vermonters to feel welcome to smell, to taste, to visit, to explore, and to share my sense of wonder about all things here — plant and animal — summer, winter, spring, and fall," says Nola.

For the past fifteen years Nola has worked with Vermont chefs. Nola uses her resources as a small local grower to help liven up and diversify their menu offerings. The chefs in turn have shown a willingness to understand her crop-size limitation and her insistence on concentrating on quality rather than quantity. Nola's Garden is known for its herbs, greens, and edible flowers.

As her restaurant relationships have matured, Nola has shared some of her ethnic recipes and produce. She recently made a "Big Batch" of tabbouleh for Blueberry Hill Inn to serve for dinner. The guests were treated to a Middle Eastern surprise, and the chef did not have to worry about his salad that evening. Nola's Lebanese squash, stuffed grape leaves, and various ethnic salads have also graced the tables of local restaurants.

Nola has worked with the Middlebury Food Co-op, presenting how-to food demonstrations. It has been a rewarding connection. Nola also often gives Café Provence a heads-up on special produce that may be coming up: baby bok choy, baby Lebanese squash, and other seasonal rarities.

"Community — teaching, learning, empowering, supporting" — this forms the philosophy that Nola lives by. "A win-win situation for all of those who are involved," says Nola.

Tabbouleh Salad

Garnished with nasturtiums or calendula petals, this salad makes a lovely presentation. Serve with fresh pita bread — you can forget the forks and spoons and use the bread instead!

2 cups cracked wheat

4 bunches parsley

1 bunch mint

3 bunches scallions

2½ pounds ripe tomatoes

½ cup freshly squeezed lemon juice

¾ cup extra-virgin olive oil

Salt and freshly ground black pepper

Nasturtiums or calendula petals (optional)

8–10 SERVINGS

1. Rinse wheat in water until the water is no longer cloudy. In a large bowl, cover wheat with boiling water and let soak for 20 minutes. Drain and squeeze dry with hands to remove any excess water; return to bowl. Set aside.

2. Chop parsley, mint, scallions, and tomatoes (reserve any juice from the tomatoes) and place in a large bowl. Add prepared wheat, lemon juice, oil, reserved tomato juice, and salt and pepper to taste. Chill in the refrigerator just long enough to cool, approximately 30 to 45 minutes.

3. Garnish with nasturtiums or calendula petals, if desired.

Recipe from CAFÉ PROVENCE

Beet Salad in Puff Pastry Layers

Cornichons — crisp, tart pickles made from tiny gherkins — give this salad a lively zing. If you can't find cornichons, you can substitute a good baby dill pickle.

PUFF PASTRY

1 sheet (half of a 17.3-ounce package) puff pastry dough

1 egg, beaten

BEET SALAD

5–6 medium red beets, preferably locally grown

⅓ cup balsamic vinegar

1 teaspoon chopped garlic

3 scallions, white and green parts, trimmed and chopped

¾ cup olive oil

Salt and freshly ground black pepper

2 tablespoons peeled and chopped fresh ginger

1 medium red onion, peeled and thinly sliced

2 medium plum tomatoes, cored, seeded and coarsely chopped

¼ cup minced flat-leaf parsley

CORNICHON TARTARE

2 teaspoons olive oil

¼ cup cornichons, rinsed, drained, and chopped

¼ cup capers, rinsed, drained, and chopped

1 teaspoon Dijon mustard

6 cups mesclun greens, preferably locally grown

¼ cup minced flat-leaf parsley

6 SERVINGS

1. Thaw the puff pastry at room temperature according to package directions. Preheat oven to 350°F. Unfold the dough on a lightly floured, clean work surface. Cut dough into 3 strips along the fold marks and then cut each strip into 2 equal rectangles, making 6 in all. Place the 6 rectangles on a parchment-lined baking sheet and brush with beaten egg. Bake until golden and puffed, about 20 minutes.

2. Meanwhile, make the beet salad: Place beets in a large stockpot with cold water, cover, and bring to a boil over high heat. Reduce heat to a gentle simmer and continue to cook until fork tender, about 1 to 1½ hours. In a colander, drain thoroughly and immediately immerse the beets in a bowl of ice water for 30 seconds; drain again. Peel and finely slice or dice the beets.

3. Combine the balsamic vinegar, garlic, and scallions in a large bowl. Slowly drizzle and whisk in the olive oil. Add salt and pepper to taste. Set aside 6 tablespoons of dressing for the greens. Add the beets, ginger, onions, tomatoes, and parsley to the remaining dressing. Gently mix well.

4. Make the cornichon tartare: Pulse the olive oil, cornichons, capers, parsley, and mustard in a food processor, just to combine.

5. To serve, toss mesclun with the 6 tablespoons of reserved dressing and divide onto six salad plates. Split the baked pastry into top and bottom halves. Place the bottom halves on the mesclun and divide the beet salad among them. Place the top halves of the pastry onto the beet salad, at an angle. Garnish with 1 to 2 tablespoons of the cornichon mixture.

CAFÉ PROVENCE

Located in the middle of the hustle and bustle of Brandon, Café Provence is run by husband-and-wife team Robert and Line Barral, natives of the Provence/Languedoc region of France. The restaurant is bright and cheery with its sunflower yellow walls and olive green trim. The chair cushions showcase colorful Provençal prints that complement the tables' white dinner plates and window wreaths of dried flowers. The open kitchen with its inviting counter space gives guests a view of Chef Barral and his staff as they cook up everything from Robert's hearth-oven pizzas to dishes with a stronger Provençal flavor, such as Tournedos of Beef au Poivre and Chicken Cordon Bleu Niçoise. The menu pleases a wide variety of tastes and varies seasonally as the offerings from local farmers change. A pastry case is filled with delectable desserts, including tiramisu and creamy crème brûlée.

On Fridays, Barral gets up at 5 a.m. to drive to Burlington. He tapes a weekly televised morning news cooking spot for WCAX and then heads back to help his staff with lunch. Barral has been busy with one thing or another since graduating from culinary school in France more than 30 years ago. He has opened new restaurants for the Four Seasons Hotel Group, managed cooks for a cruise line, and spent more than 10 years as executive chef for the New England Culinary Institute. Graduates and students of that institute make up the entire kitchen staff at Café Provence — a reflection of his continued commitment to the school.

By purchasing and preparing locally grown products sourced through the Vermont Fresh Network, Chef Barral is able to offer his guests from New York, Boston, and across the country a true Vermont dining experience.

OLIVIA'S CROUTON COMPANY

Francie Williams Caccavo started Olivia's Croutons in April of 1991. Her brother, Larry, actually gave her the idea for the business. He always made homemade croutons for his dinner parties; when Francie suggested selling them, his reply was, "You can't make any money at it." Happily, he was wrong, and she was right on target. Francie knew that people live busy lives but still enjoy eating good food — and they would prefer purchasing a great product in the grocery store to making a stop at a bakery or making the croutons themselves.

When her son, David, was almost two and daughter, Olivia, was three, the family started the business in their own kitchen. It began with the Butter & Garlic flavor, sold in hand-stamped brown bags. In the beginning, it took a long time to hand-cut each loaf of bread and bake the croutons in their conventional home oven. But within a few months, Francie was selling her merchandise to six stores and had signed on with her first "really big" account.

Since then, Olivia's Croutons has grown steadily. A couple of expansions later, in September 2006, Olivia's Croutons moved into 4,500 square feet of renovated space in a 1912 dairy barn, saving the historic building from being torn down.

The newest growth area for the company is in organic ingredients. Responding to many customer requests, Olivia's has introduced a new Certified Organic Crouton. Francie is happy to be able to support organic producers as she searches for the finest crouton ingredients. Her goal is eventually to use organic flour in all of Olivia's products.

Olivia's Caesar Salad

Caesar salad is such a perfect creation — simple romaine lettuce transformed by the combination of dressing, Parmesan cheese, and, of course, croutons. It can be a delicious beginning to a meal, or, with the addition of chicken or shrimp, Caesar salad becomes a complete dinner.

OLIVIA'S CAESAR DRESSING

1–2 medium garlic cloves, peeled and coarsely chopped

3–5 anchovy fillets

2 tablespoons mayonnaise

½ teaspoon freshly ground black pepper, or to taste

Salt

Juice of ½ lemon

½ cup extra-virgin olive oil

SALAD

1 medium garlic clove, peeled

¼ teaspoon salt

3–4 cups romaine lettuce, washed, dried, and torn into bite-size pieces

Juice of ½ lemon

½ cup freshly grated Parmesan cheese, plus more for garnish

Freshly ground black pepper

Croutons, preferably ½ bag of Olivia's Parmesan Pepper Croutons or Butter & Garlic Croutons

6–8 SERVINGS

1. Make the dressing: Combine the garlic, anchovies, mayonnaise, pepper, salt, and lemon juice in a food processor or blender, mixing well. With the processor running, slowly add the oil. Continue mixing until all the oil has been used; you will have about ¾ cup of dressing. It should have a thick and satiny texture. Use or refrigerate immediately.

2. Place garlic and salt into a large wooden salad bowl and mash into a paste with a fork. Add lettuce and lemon juice and toss gently. Gently toss in the dressing ¼ cup at a time until the greens are coated as desired. Add cheese, pepper, and croutons and toss lightly one more time.

3. Divide salad among chilled salad plates or bowls. If desired, grate additional cheese over the top.

HARLOW
FARM
ORGANIC
SWEET
CORN
69¢/EA. $7.99/DOZ.

Mâche Salad with Carrots, Dried Cranberries, and Walnuts

Vermont Herb & Salad Company is a four-season family farm owned and operated by Jared and Heather McDermott. They grow primarily salad greens and culinary herbs, offering their produce to grocery stores, restaurants, and distributors throughout Vermont. The McDermotts are proud to say that "only rich soil, quality seed, and hard work," are used to produce their greens and herbs. "We are a farm that is committed to preserving Vermont's rural landscape as well as working toward Vermont's social, economic, and ecological sustainability."

Mâche, also known as corn salad or lamb's lettuce, is a cool-weather crop. Its greens form a small rosette-shaped head, which has a mild, almost nutty flavor. It combines well with fruit and nuts in this satisfying salad — a bright addition to the dinner plate on those first chilly days of winter. Mâche can be found in most large specialty food stores.

10–12 SERVINGS

- **1 pound mâche, rinsed gently and dried**
- **1 cup shredded carrots**
- **½ cup dried cranberries, chopped coarsely**
- **½ cup walnut halves, chopped coarsely**

Toss mâche, carrots, cranberries, and walnuts in a large bowl to combine. Divide among salad plates or bowls and serve with your favorite honey mustard dressing or other dressing of your choice.

Goddess Primavera Pasta Salad

Annie Christopher began to bottle and sell delicious homemade sauces, marinades, and dressings out of her barbecue shack in Vermont's Green Mountains in the 1980s. Her family company, Annie's Naturals, soon grew into a local phenomenon. In 2005, they were purchased by Homegrown Naturals, the owners of Annie's Homegrown (the pasta producers in California — no relation between the Annies), and are no longer based in Vermont. But Annie Christopher still develops the salad dressings, marinades, and sauces in the same barbecue shack in the Green Mountains where she started the business.

This Primavera Pasta Salad recipe showcases Annie's creamy, tahini-based Goddess Dressing.

8–10 SERVINGS

1 pound rotini, fusilli, or penne pasta

1 tablespoon olive oil

Salt and freshly ground black pepper

1 cup frozen or fresh peas, cooked

1 medium red bell pepper, chopped

1 medium red onion, peeled and chopped

1 cup grape or cherry tomatoes

Florets from 1 large stalk of broccoli, steamed and cooled

1 cup or more seasonal green vegetables, such as zucchini, asparagus, or green beans, steamed al dente and cooled

1–1½ (8-ounce) bottles Annie's Naturals Organic Goddess Dressing

¼–½ cup chopped flat-leaf parsley

1. Bring a large pot of water to a boil, add salt, and cook the pasta according to package directions. Drain pasta and toss with olive oil and salt and pepper to taste. Set aside to cool.

2. Combine the peas, bell pepper, onion, tomatoes, broccoli, and seasonal vegetables in a large bowl. Add cooked pasta and toss to combine well. Season to taste with salt and pepper. Add the dressing and toss again, combining all ingredients thoroughly.

3. Garnish with parsley. Serve at room temperature or chilled.

Note: *Vegetable quantities are approximate and may be increased and varied according to taste.*

Lump Crab Cakes with Vermont Sweet Peppers

Crab cakes are a summertime favorite. Use the freshest and best-quality crabmeat available and this dish will surely be a big hit.

CRAB CAKES

2 tablespoons unsalted butter

¼ cup minced red bell pepper

¼ cup minced yellow bell pepper

8 ounces jumbo lump crabmeat

1 teaspoon Worcestershire sauce

5 dashes Tabasco sauce

1 teaspoon dried thyme

2 tablespoons lemon juice

3 tablespoons chopped chives

¼ cup mayonnaise

⅓ cup plain breadcrumbs

Salt and freshly ground black pepper

4 tablespoons vegetable oil, or as needed

Unbleached all-purpose flour

Lemon wedges

REMOULADE

1 cup mayonnaise

3 tablespoons whole grain mustard

1 tablespoon Dijon mustard

2 tablespoons lemon juice

3 tablespoons heavy cream

1 tablespoon chopped chives

Salt and freshly ground black pepper

8 CAKES (4 APPETIZER SERVINGS)

1. Melt butter in a medium skillet over medium heat. Add the peppers and sauté until soft, stirring often. Remove from heat and let the mixture cool for a few minutes. Add the crabmeat, Worcestershire sauce, Tabasco, thyme, lemon juice, and chives, mixing until well combined. Fold in the mayonnaise and breadcrumbs. Adjust seasonings with salt and pepper to taste.

2. Line a baking sheet with parchment paper. Shape crab mixture into 8 equal cakes and place on prepared baking sheet. Cover with plastic wrap and chill in the refrigerator for at least 1 hour.

3. While the crab cakes are chilling, make the remoulade. Combine mayonnaise, whole grain and Dijon mustards, lemon juice, cream, chives, and salt and pepper to taste in a medium bowl. Cover with plastic wrap and refrigerate until you are ready to use.

4. Heat vegetable oil in a large skillet over medium-high heat. Lightly dredge the crab cakes in the flour, shaking off excess flour. Add crab cakes to the skillet and cook until golden brown on both sides, turning once, adding additional oil as needed.

5. Serve cakes warm with lemon wedges and remoulade.

Apple, Pickle, and Sweet Pepper Tuna Salad

At Izabella's in Bennington, this flavorful salad is a regular special and a hit at catered events. To balance the lively flavors of the fresh vegetables and tart pickles, it is best served with dense artisanal bread. Or stuff it into pita pockets, spoon it into hollowed-out tomato shells, or serve on a bed of baby organic greens. It also makes an excellent tuna melt!

4 SERVINGS

1 (12-ounce) can white tuna in water, drained well and flaked

Juice of ½ lemon, strained

6 tablespoons plain nonfat yogurt

6 tablespoons light sour cream

½ cup drained sweet gherkin pickles, chopped

1 red bell pepper, diced

1 tart apple, cored, peeled, and chopped

4 teaspoons cider vinegar

Salt and freshly ground black pepper

1. Combine the tuna and lemon juice in a large bowl. Stir in the yogurt, sour cream, and pickles. Season with salt and pepper to taste.

2. Combine bell pepper, apple, and vinegar in a separate bowl, and toss gently to combine. Add vegetable mixture to tuna and mix until well combined. Season to taste with salt and pepper.

THE ALCHEMIST PUB AND BREWERY

The Alchemist Pub and Brewery in Waterbury is a pub in the truest sense of the word: a "public house" where members of the community gather to socialize over food and drink. This seven-barrel brewpub specializes in handcrafted beer and casual pub fare. All of the ales are brewed in the basement brewery, which was designed and installed by house brewer John Kimmich. Only the finest imported malts and domestic hops are used to craft an outstanding selection of tasty beers.

In addition to the house-made ales, the pub offers an eclectic menu featuring Vermont products and seasonal produce. The talented chefs serve appetizers, grilled panini, flatbread pizzas, vegetarian fare, and hearty entrées, such as fish and chips, that pair well with the craft brews. The works of local artists decorate the walls of the pub and contribute to the Vermont atmosphere.

Many local farmers have formed friendships with the people at the Alchemist over pints of beer and good food. These farm friends began bringing bags of tomatoes or maybe a dozen organic eggs to the pub. The cooks at the Alchemist always welcomed the farmers' neighborly gestures, and eventually those small offerings led to dedicated plots of farmland set aside for growing produce for the pub. The farmers enjoy a welcoming gathering place and a steady customer for their crops, while the pub benefits from a constant flow of fresh, high-quality produce. It's a give-and-take that works well for both sides.

Celeriac and Green Apple Salad

Celeriac is an ingredient found in most grocery stores but rarely chosen by home cooks. With a few minutes of preparation time and some delicious Granny Smith apples, you can make an unexpected salad that complements any summer barbecue or fall dinner.

1 small sweet onion, peeled and finely diced

1 tablespoon minced garlic

¼ cup mayonnaise

2 tablespoons whole grain mustard

1 tablespoon apple cider vinegar

1 tablespoon organic honey, preferably locally harvested

2 pounds fresh celeriac (see Note)

2 large Granny Smith apples, unpeeled and cored

Salt and freshly ground black pepper

½ cup balsamic vinegar

1 cup organic baby greens, preferably locally grown

3 organic beefsteak tomatoes, cored and sliced ¼-inch thick

12 sweet baby turnips, washed and quartered

Note: *Celeriac — also called celery root, knob celery, and turnip-rooted celery — is grown for its globular root, which has a taste that is similar to a blend of celery and parsley.*

4–6 SERVINGS

1. Make the dressing: In a medium bowl combine the onion, garlic, mayonnaise, mustard, vinegar, and honey. Mix well and set aside.

2. Peel all of the skin from the celeriac with a paring knife. Grate the celeriac coarsely with a box grater (do not use a food processor — a food processor will grate it too finely, and the salad will have very little texture and be too wet). Set aside. Grate the apples with the box grater.

3. Add the celeriac and apples to the dressing and toss gently. Season with salt and pepper to taste. Set aside for at least 30 minutes before serving.

4. Meanwhile, boil the balsamic vinegar in a small saucepan over medium-high heat. Whisk frequently, and continue to boil until the vinegar is reduced by approximately one-third.

5. Taste the celeriac and apple mixture and add salt and pepper if desired. (Celeriac absorbs seasonings very quickly, so always taste the salad before serving to see if more salt or pepper needs to be added.) Place celeriac and apple mixture on a plate garnished with the baby greens, tomatoes, and baby turnips. Drizzle with the balsamic reduction and serve at once.

Creamy Braising Greens Soup

On the southern edge of the Northeast Kingdom in Craftsbury, Pete Johnson grows a wide variety of organic vegetables, specializing in baby greens, root vegetables, and heirloom tomatoes. The farm, Pete's Greens, uses greenhouses, root cellaring, and other season-extending techniques to offer the greatest vegetable diversity for as much of the year as possible, proudly calling itself "Vermont's four-season vegetable farm." Pete's mixed braising greens were the inspiration for this soup.

1 slice thick-cut bacon, preferably not too lean, diced

1 large sweet onion, peeled and diced

1 large carrot, peeled and diced

2 medium garlic cloves, peeled and minced

½ pound sausage, preferably linguiça or chourico, diced (see Note)

6 medium boiling potatoes, peeled and diced

7½ cups chicken stock

2½ cups mixed braising greens, such as kale, Swiss chard, mustard greens, and dandelion greens, preferably locally grown, thoroughly washed, stems removed, and cut into very fine strips

½ cup heavy cream

¼ teaspoon hot sauce (optional)

Coarse salt and freshly ground black pepper

Note: Linguiça and chourico are Portuguese-style pork sausages that can be found in many supermarkets. It should be noted that chourico is spicier than linguiça.

6–8 SERVINGS

1. Sauté the bacon in a large pot or Dutch oven over medium heat until crisp. Remove bacon with a slotted spoon and set aside, reserving drippings in the pot.

2. Add the onion and carrot to the pot and cook over medium heat until soft and translucent, stirring occasionally. Add the garlic and sausage and cook, stirring frequently, until sausage is lightly browned, about 5 to 8 minutes.

3. Add the potatoes and stock, stir to combine, and bring to a boil, uncovered, over medium heat. Reduce heat to a simmer and continue to cook, uncovered, stirring occasionally, until potatoes are fork tender, about 15 minutes.

4. Add the greens and cream and continue to simmer until soup is heated through, about 5 minutes. Season with hot sauce if desired, and salt and pepper to taste.

5. Ladle into soup bowls and garnish with reserved bacon. Serve at once.

Hemingway's Cream of Garlic Soup

In 1982, Linda and Ted Fondulas had a free-form discussion, searching for new ways to use the local Vermont ham found on Hemingway's first menu. This conversation led to the creation of a warm vichyssoise, which was much heartier than the traditional version of the soup. More recent menus call it their "often imitated, never duplicated" cream of garlic soup.

4–6 SERVINGS

2 tablespoons olive oil

1 medium leek, white part only, coarsely chopped and thoroughly washed

10 garlic cloves, peeled

½ pound smoked ham, preferably locally produced, cut into 1-inch cubes

6–7 cups chicken stock or light game stock

1 pound boiling potatoes, peeled and cut into eighths

½ cup heavy cream

Coarse salt and freshly ground white pepper

Fresh chives or flat-leaf parsley, minced

1. Heat the oil in a large stockpot over medium-low heat. Add the leek, garlic, and ham. Cover and cook until vegetables are slightly tender, about 10 minutes, stirring occasionally.

2. Remove cover and add stock and potatoes, stirring to combine well. Bring to a simmer over medium heat and cook until leek, garlic, and potatoes are fork tender, at least 30 minutes, stirring occasionally.

3. Remove from heat. Remove ham with a slotted spoon. Working in batches if necessary, transfer mixture to a blender and purée until texture is smooth. If the mixture is too thick, add more stock. Transfer purée back to stockpot, slowly whisk in the cream, stir in the ham, and heat through. Adjust seasonings with salt and pepper to taste. Ladle into warm soup bowls. Garnish with chives or parsley.

Spinach Vichyssoise

Birdseye Diner was built by Silk City Diners in 1940 and moved to Castleton, Vermont, in 1960. John and Pam Rehlen restored the diner in 1996 and continue to serve breakfast, lunch, and dinner year-round. The diner shows its support of local small farms by featuring their names on the menu. Salad greens and herbs come from the Vermont Herb and Salad Company in Benson, and Thomas Dairy of Rutland receives credit for all the diner's dairy products. The hand-cut French fries, mashed potatoes, and homemade soups appear courtesy of Perry's Potatoes in Hampton, New York (just over the state line). These farmers have been customers of the diner and good neighbors for years.

John Rehlen always looks forward to making this soup in midsummer, when new potatoes are available. It's very easy to make and is a wonderful example of simple elegance in summer soups.

¼ cup unsalted butter

2 pounds Yukon Gold potatoes, peeled and diced

2 small leeks, white part only, thoroughly washed and diced

10 ounces fresh spinach

3 cups whole milk

1 cup heavy cream

3 cups chicken stock

1 tablespoon salt

¼ teaspoon nutmeg

¼ teaspoon freshly ground black pepper

Sour cream, preferably locally produced

10–12 SERVINGS

1. Heat butter in a large saucepan over medium-high heat. Add potatoes, leek, and 1¼ cups water. Bring to a boil, stirring occasionally. Reduce heat to medium, cover, and simmer for about 30 minutes or until vegetables are fork tender. Add spinach and continue to cook until spinach is wilted.

2. Whisk in the milk, scraping the sides and bottom of saucepan. Working in batches if necessary, transfer vegetable mixture to a blender and purée until just smooth.

3. Return purée to the large saucepan and slowly whisk in the heavy cream and stock. Adjust seasonings with salt, nutmeg, and pepper to taste. Heat to serving temperature or chill to serve cold. Ladle into soup bowls or cups and garnish with sour cream.

Curried Carrot and Sweet Potato Soup

This soup is a favorite and can be served hot or cold. If you make a lot of puréed soups, consider investing in a handheld immersion blender. It is the best way to purée liquids that are still in the pot. This is a sweet and spicy "comfort food" soup. You may adjust the amount of orange juice to your liking.

4–6 SERVINGS

2 tablespoons olive oil

3–4 carrots, peeled, ends removed, and cut into small pieces

2 large sweet potatoes, peeled and cut into 1-inch pieces

1 small onion, peeled and chopped

1 garlic clove, peeled and minced

2 tablespoons sweet curry powder, preferably Penzey's brand

1½ cups vegetable broth or water, or as needed

¼ cup orange juice

Salt and freshly ground black pepper

Chopped chives

1. Heat oil in a large stockpot over medium heat. Add the carrots, sweet potatoes, onion, and garlic. Sauté until vegetables are tender and onions are translucent, about 10 minutes, stirring frequently. Stir in the curry powder and continue to cook for 1 minute.

2. Add vegetable broth to cover the vegetables and bring to a boil. Reduce heat, cover, and simmer until the carrots and potatoes are fork tender, approximately 15 minutes.

3. Remove from heat and purée the mixture with a handheld blender, or transfer mixture to a blender or food processor in batches if necessary, and purée until texture is smooth. If the mixture is too thick, add more broth or water.

4. Transfer purée back to stockpot if necessary, and slowly whisk in orange juice. Heat through, and adjust seasonings with salt and pepper to taste. Ladle into soup bowls, and garnish with chives to taste.

Note: If you want to serve the soup cold, chill and top with crème fraîche or yogurt.

Heirloom Split Pea Soup

Izabella's serves this hearty soup, which is a combination of family recipes, often during chilly winter months. It is equally wonderful with or without ham, and with a slice of warm jalapeño cornbread on the side, it makes for a deliciously filling lunch.

1 pound dried green split peas

3 carrots, peeled and coarsely chopped

2 celery stalks, coarsely chopped

2 leeks, white part only, thoroughly washed and coarsely chopped

3 shallots, peeled and coarsely chopped

3 tablespoons olive oil

6 cups vegetable broth

1 meaty ham bone or 2 cups shredded ham (optional)

2 bay leaves

2 tablespoons fresh thyme leaves

3 tablespoons fresh tarragon leaves

Sea salt and freshly ground black pepper

10–12 SERVINGS

1. Rinse peas, place in a 6- to 8-quart stockpot and add water to cover. Bring to a boil, skim the foam, reduce heat, and simmer, partially covered, until peas are just tender, about 1 to 1½ hours. Drain and set aside.

2. Pulse the carrots, celery, leeks, and shallots in a food processor until finely chopped.

3. Heat the oil in a large pot over medium heat. Add vegetables and cook, stirring often, until vegetables are soft and translucent, about 12 to 14 minutes. Add cooked peas and simmer for another minute or so, stirring until well combined.

4. Stir in broth, 3 cups water, ham bone if using, bay leaves, thyme, tarragon, and salt and pepper to taste. Simmer briskly, stirring occasionally, until peas are soft and falling apart and soup is thickened, about 1 to 1½ hours.

5. Remove bay leaves and ham bone if using, transfer half the soup to a food processor or blender, and pulse to purée. Shred meat from the ham bone and return it and the purée back to the pot.

6. Stir to combine, and adjust seasonings with salt and pepper to taste. Ladle into soup bowls.

Butternut Squash Bisque

The Village Inn is an 1899 Victorian mansion that owners David and Evelyn Brey have happily restored to its original grandeur — its rooms are elegantly detailed and filled with period antiques, and the inn is conveniently located in the village of Woodstock, which is brimming with shops, art galleries, and restaurants.

The Breys are self-trained chefs who delight in serving gourmet meals to guests in their graceful dining room. These tasty creations are prepared using locally grown produce, Vermont cheeses, dairy products, and meats, plus fresh herbs from the inn's garden.

6 SERVINGS

1 large butternut squash (about 2 pounds)

½ teaspoon salt

3 tablespoons unsalted butter

2 tablespoons minced fresh ginger

2 tablespoons minced fresh garlic

¼ cup heavy cream

¼ teaspoon nutmeg

White pepper

2–3 tablespoons fresh flat-leaf parsley or minced chives

1. Halve the squash lengthwise. Discard the seeds. Peel the squash with a vegetable peeler or sharp paring knife. Cut the peeled squash into 1-inch pieces.

2. Place the squash, 4 cups cold water, salt, and 1 tablespoon of the butter in a large stockpot. Bring to a simmer over medium-high heat and cook, covered, until squash is just fork tender, 10 to 15 minutes. During the last 3 to 4 minutes of cooking, add the ginger and garlic to the pot.

3. Drain the squash thoroughly in a colander, reserving the cooking liquid. Working in batches, transfer squash to a food processor and purée until smooth. (You can also use a handheld immersion blender; in that case, the squash does not need to be drained.)

4. Transfer purée back to stockpot. Add the reserved liquid and the remaining 2 tablespoons butter and cook over medium heat for about 5 minutes, stirring until well combined. Slowly whisk in the cream and nutmeg, and heat through. Adjust seasonings, adding salt and white pepper to taste. Garnish with parsley to taste.

   Note: *This recipe may be prepared without the heavy cream and frozen to be stored for future serving.*

Recipe from SQUASH VALLEY PRODUCE

Creamy Vermont Winter Pumpkin Soup

Squash Valley Produce is the source for fresh fruits and vegetables in Central Vermont. Their retail store, on Route 100 in Waterbury Center, is like a year-round farmers' market. Squash Valley is a member of the Vermont Fresh Network and loves to promote local growers with a large selection of Vermont-grown fruits and vegetables.

This soup is also delicious with plain yogurt instead of the heavy cream — a much lighter alternative.

8 SERVINGS

1 pie pumpkin (5–6 pounds)

4 ounces cultured butter, such as the Vermont Butter & Cheese Company product (or substitute sweet butter)

2 sweet onions, peeled and diced

1 tablespoon ground cinnamon

2 quarts chicken stock or water

½ cup pure maple syrup, preferably Vermont-made, or more to taste

1 cup heavy cream

Salt and freshly ground black pepper

Unsweetened whipped cream

1. Preheat oven to 350°F. Lightly grease a shallow baking pan; set aside. Cut pumpkin in half lengthwise and scoop out the seeds and strings. Discard the strings. Place seeds in a large bowl of water and rinse well to remove any remaining pulp. Drain well, and set aside.

2. Place the pumpkin in the prepared baking pan, cut side down, and add 1 cup water to the dish. Bake until fork tender, 45 minutes to 1¼ hours, depending on the size of the pumpkin. Remove from oven and set aside to cool. When pumpkin is cool enough to handle, peel and discard skin.

3. Toast the pumpkin seeds: Reduce oven to 325°F. Place reserved seeds in an even layer on an ungreased baking sheet. Season with salt, if desired. Bake for 1 hour, stirring occasionally, until the seeds are dry and crunchy. Remove from oven and allow to cool. Seeds can be stored in an airtight container at room temperature.

4. Meanwhile, melt the butter in a stockpot or Dutch oven. Add the onions and cook over medium heat until soft. Add pumpkin, cinnamon, and stock. Simmer for 30 minutes, stirring occasionally.

5. Purée soup with a handheld immersion blender, or, working in batches, transfer the soup to a blender and purée until smooth, then transfer purée back to stockpot. Cook over medium heat for another 5 minutes. Slowly whisk in maple syrup and heavy cream and continue to cook until heated through. Add salt and pepper to taste.

6. Ladle soup into warm bowls, garnish with a dollop of whipped cream, and sprinkle with toasted pumpkin seeds.

MONUMENT FARMS DAIRY

Founded in 1930 by Richard and Marjory James on 26 acres of land in Weybridge, Monument Farms Dairy is now operated by brothers Peter and Bob James and their cousin Jon Rooney. The dairy is a processor-handler, meaning that all milk production is handled on the farm. The owners milk the cows and package the milk at their own processing plant. Monument Farms Dairy is one of only two processor-handler dairies remaining in Vermont. Peter is in charge of milk production, Bob manages the distribution end, and their cousin Jon oversees the processing plant.

Today, the farm consists of about 1,600 acres and employs 36 people. Of the 800 Holstein cows at the farm, about 400 are involved in milk production at any given time. Each of the Holsteins gives milk for six to seven years. A cow may produce 72 pounds of milk per day! The busy dairy has a daily output of approximately 3,000 gallons. The milk is sold in a three county area to various stores and restaurants, as well as chocolate companies. The people at Monument Farms Dairy work hard to insure the future of the farm, believing that "a family farm is both a way to make a living and a way to live."

Fresh Asparagus Soup

Asparagus soup is a springtime delicacy that combines this early vegetable with the everyday goodness of Vermont milk and cream.

2 bunches of pencil-thin asparagus (about 2 pounds)

2 tablespoons unsalted butter

1 cup finely chopped onion

1 tablespoon minced garlic

1 cup hot chicken stock

Pinch of sugar

⅛ teaspoon ground nutmeg

1 teaspoon salt

½ teaspoon freshly ground white pepper, or to taste

2 cups whole milk

2 cups half-and-half

Lemon juice

6–8 CUPS/SERVINGS

1. Trim asparagus; discard tough ends. Cut off the tips and reserve stalks. Prepare an ice bath and set aside.

2. Bring water to a boil in a medium saucepan over medium-high heat. Add a pinch of salt to the water and add asparagus tips. Cook for 2 minutes. With a slotted spoon, transfer tips to the ice bath until cool. Remove tips and set aside.

3. Meanwhile, dice the asparagus stalks. Melt butter in a medium saucepan over medium heat. Add onions and sauté until soft and translucent, about 7 minutes. Add garlic and cook for 2 minutes longer. Add hot chicken stock, asparagus stalks, sugar, nutmeg, salt, and pepper, and cook over medium heat until tender, about 8 minutes, stirring occasionally. Slowly whisk in the milk and cook for another 2 minutes.

4. Purée stalk mixture with a handheld immersion blender, or working in batches, transfer stalk mixture to a blender and purée until smooth, and return to saucepan. Cook over medium heat for another 5 minutes, then slowly whisk in the half-and-half. Add asparagus tips and continue to cook and stir until heated through. Adjust seasonings with lemon juice, sugar, salt, and pepper to taste; if the soup is too thick, add more chicken stock or water. Ladle into bowls and serve.

Vermont Asparagus with Parmesan Pepper Crumbs

This recipe was sent to Francie Williams Caccavo from one of her customers in Charlotte, Vermont. It is so easy and really delicious. The simple topping is a perfect complement to the fresh springtime flavor of asparagus.

1 pound asparagus, trimmed

¼ cup unsalted butter

1 teaspoon fresh lemon juice

¾ (5-ounce) package Olivia's Parmesan Pepper croutons, lightly crushed

Salt

4 SERVINGS

1. Wash and pat dry the asparagus with paper towels. Cook the asparagus on all sides in a nonstick grill pan or skillet over medium-high heat for 5 to 8 minutes.

2. Meanwhile, melt butter in a medium saucepan over medium heat. Add lemon juice. Remove from stovetop and set aside.

3. Transfer asparagus to a serving platter. Drizzle with lemon butter, sprinkle with crushed croutons, and season with salt to taste. Serve immediately.

HALF PINT FARM

As the name suggests, Half Pint Farm, located in Burlington's Intervale, is small, cultivating less than one acre. The owners, Spencer and Mara Welton, are dedicated to growing high-quality baby vegetables, micro-greens, herbs, and other specialty crops for farmers' markets and restaurants in the Burlington area. Their gorgeous baby vegetables always attract a great deal of attention at local farmers' markets! These dwarf-size versions of new potatoes, eggplant, zucchini, broccoli, Tuscan kale, and cherry tomatoes are a big draw — they are so fresh and tender that those who buy them always come back for more.

Before coming to Vermont, Mara and Spencer had lived and farmed in a variety of climates — the tropical South Pacific, the high plains of Colorado, western Pennsylvania — where they experimented with biointensive methods designed to build healthy soil and to give high yield. They moved to Vermont "because of the opportunity to farm in an urban setting with a business incubator program." They have not been disappointed in the least!

Their partnership is very complementary. According to Mara, "Spencer is the big-picture thinker: He holds the current and future vision of our farm in his head and translates that into seeding plans. Since our crops turn over quickly, this is a very intense schedule. Spencer has managed market gardens before and is quite comfortable in this role." For Mara's part, "I thoroughly enjoy selling our produce and have no problem making a cold call to a new restaurant to sell veggies."

Each spring, Mara writes a letter to all of her chefs to announce new varieties of vegetables and an anticipated timeline for their availability during the season, reestablishing a connection after the long Vermont winter. And Mara and Spencer make a point of eating at the restaurants they supply; this gives them a sense of each chef's style and enables Mara to make suggestions for future use of the farm's vegetables.

The farm's goal is to stay small, with the Weltons doing all of the work themselves. "We have streamlined the specific varieties of produce that are grown for maximum dollar value, using the same one-acre space from year to year. In doing so, we have been able to increase our profits significantly. Being a two-person operation has driven us to increase efficiency and improve our workload." The hardworking couple remains committed to producing and marketing a top-quality product while they work together in the greenhouse, the field, and at the farmers' markets.

Pan-cooked Summer Greens

Serve these greens as a side to any meat or fish dinner, or with roasted summer vegetables for a vegetarian meal. Alternate versions include adding balsamic vinegar instead of soy sauce (especially good with escarole and broccoli rabe) or substituting sesame oil for olive oil. Tossing the greens with sesame seeds before serving is another option. The potential variations to this basic recipe can inspire you all summer long. Generally one bunch of leafy greens will feed two people.

1 to 2 bunches Swiss chard, washed, dried and cut into thin strips, stalks discarded (see Note)

1 tablespoon olive oil

1 medium yellow onion, peeled and diced

2 medium garlic cloves, peeled and minced

2 tablespoons soy sauce (not "lite")

Salt and freshly ground black pepper

Note: Lacinata kale, collard greens, kale, beet greens, escarole, Chinese cabbage such as bok choy, broccoli rabe, turnip greens, dandelion greens, and other chicories also work well for this dish. If you use greens with tougher stalks, such as kale and collards, be sure to cut out and discard the stalks.

2–4 SERVINGS

1. Steam chard until bright, 4 to 5 minutes. Drain. Immediately immerse the greens in a bowl of ice water for 30 seconds and drain again. Set the cooled greens aside.

2. Heat the oil in a skillet over medium heat. Add the onion and cook until soft and translucent, about 7 minutes, stirring frequently. Add garlic and cook for 2 minutes, stirring continuously. Add the greens and toss gently to combine well. Continue to cook for 3 to 5 minutes, depending on the amount of greens.

3. Add soy sauce, and salt and pepper to taste. Gently toss ingredients and cook for 1 to 2 minutes longer. Remove from heat and serve at once.

Roasted Summer Vegetables

High-quality baby vegetables do not need much special attention in the kitchen and are best when minimally handled to bring out their great flavor. Below is one of Half Pint's favorite combinations, but whatever veggies you have on hand will make a delicious roasted summer dinner. Eat the vegetables on their own with a loaf of bread or as a side with meat or fish. They can also be served over rice, couscous, or pasta noodles. Or blend the vegetables with a little water or chicken stock and cook in a saucepan for 10 minutes to make a tasty soup.

2–4 SERVINGS

8 baby eggplants, cut in half lengthwise

8 baby summer squash

10 pearl onions, peeled

5 baby potatoes, washed, scrubbed, and cut in half

8 baby carrots, scrubbed, greens removed

3–4 tablespoons extra-virgin olive oil

Coarse salt and freshly ground black pepper

15 cherry tomatoes

Note: Baby beets, sweet white Hakurei salad turnips, sweet peppers such as cubanelle or Italian sweet, baby fennel, and garlic also work well in this dish.

1. Preheat oven to 450°F.

2. Put eggplants, squash, onions, potatoes, and carrots in a roasting pan and toss gently with the oil, coating all ingredients well. Season with salt and pepper to taste.

3. Put pan in oven and bake for 4 to 5 minutes. Carefully remove pan from oven and gently stir ingredients with a spoon. Return pan to oven and continue this process until vegetables are fork tender, 15 to 20 minutes. Approximately 5 minutes before the vegetables are done, add the tomatoes.

Variation: An alternate cooking method is to wrap all the oiled and seasoned vegetables in a double layer of aluminum foil and place over hot charcoal on the grill. Cook until vegetables are fork tender, about 15 to 20 minutes.

Eggplant Caponata

Wellspring Farm is a five-acre, organic, community supported farm in Marshfield. Members pay the farm an advance sum and receive weekly selections of produce throughout the growing season. The farm grows more than 40 types of vegetables for their 100 members. Participants pick up their produce, flowers, and herbs at the farm once a week.

The New England Culinary Institute is part of this community. Part of their involvement includes giving on-farm cooking demonstrations performed by NECI students using the farm's freshly harvested vegetables. Wellspring's CSA (community supported agriculture) members love the casual cooking classes and go home prepared to put their produce to good use.

This eggplant caponata recipe is an excellent example of how to use farm-fresh produce to its best advantage. Serve it as a bruschetta topping, a dip, or an accompaniment to grilled meats.

2 tablespoons olive oil

1 (1¼-pound) eggplant, trimmed, peeled, and cut into ½-inch dice

Salt

3 garlic cloves, peeled and minced

1 small red onion, peeled and minced

⅓ cup golden raisins

1 tablespoon capers, rinsed and drained

3 plum tomatoes, cut into ¼-inch dice (about 1 cup)

4 ounces orange juice

½ teaspoon curry powder

¼ teaspoon red pepper flakes

1 teaspoon honey, preferably locally harvested

2 tablespoons balsamic vinegar

¼ cup cilantro leaves, chopped

2 tablespoons chopped flat-leaf parsley leaves

2 teaspoons chopped rosemary leaves

Freshly ground black pepper

2–3 CUPS

1. Lightly grease a baking sheet and set aside. In a medium skillet heat 1 tablespoon of the oil over medium-high heat.

2. Season the eggplant with ½ teaspoon salt. Add eggplant to the skillet and brown on all sides, stirring with a wooden spoon, for 10 to 15 minutes or until tender. Remove from pan and transfer to prepared baking sheet. Set aside.

3. In the same pan heat the remaining 1 tablespoon of oil over medium heat. Add garlic and onion and sauté until soft and translucent. Add eggplant, raisins, capers, tomatoes, orange juice, curry powder, red pepper flakes, honey, and ¼ cup water, stirring well after each addition. Simmer for 20 minutes or until eggplant is fork tender.

4. Remove pan from heat and add balsamic vinegar, cilantro, parsley, and rosemary. Adjust seasonings with salt and pepper to taste. Serve at room temperature or chilled.

Recipe from SCOTT WOOLSEY, KILLDEER FARM

Petits Pois à la Français

Lettuce shakes off the predictability of salad in this fresh but warming pea dish.

½ cup chicken stock

1 large head of Boston lettuce, washed, dried, and chopped

1 medium garlic clove, peeled and smashed

3 whole scallions, thinly sliced

4 fresh spearmint leaves, cut into thin strips

1 fresh thyme sprig

1 fresh parsley sprig

2 tablespoons unsalted butter

1 cup fresh English shelling peas

Kosher salt and freshly ground black pepper

4 SERVINGS

1. Combine the stock, lettuce, garlic, scallions, 2 of the spearmint leaves, and thyme and parsley sprigs in a large saucepan. Bring to a simmer over medium-high heat, and continue to cook for about 5 minutes longer, stirring occasionally.

2. Gently drain lettuce mixture in a colander. Set lettuce aside, removing parsley and thyme sprigs.

3. In the same saucepan, melt the butter over medium-high heat. Add peas and sauté, stirring constantly, until peas are bright green, about 5 to 6 minutes. Return the lettuce to the saucepan and add the remaining 2 spearmint leaves and salt and pepper to taste. Continue to cook until lettuce is heated through, stirring constantly, about 1 minute.

KILLDEER FARM

Jake and Liz Guest started Killdeer Farm in 1979 on the banks of the Connecticut River in scenic Norwich, Vermont. Jake named the farm for the Killdeer bird (a winged plover) that returns to their fields early every spring to nest and lay eggs. They take great care to plow around any killdeer nests they find in the fields.

The farm has about 50 acres of workable land; they cultivate around 25 acres at any time, leaving the rest fallow or in rotation with cover crops. All of the farm's vegetables and strawberries are certified organic, except for a portion of their sweet corn that is low-input grown. (Low-input agriculture is an alternative farming system that is based on a reduction but not necessarily an elimination of the use of chemical fertilizers, insecticides, and herbicides.) Killdeer focuses on the quality and taste of its produce, and they have earned a reputation for growing delicious fruits and vegetables. "We test varieties in our location, our microclimate, our fields, our soil, then we select and continue varieties based primarily on taste (as opposed to production or shipability)," say the owners. In addition to their own produce, Killdeer's excellent farm stand offers select organic and naturally raised meat, organic baked goods, organic dairy products, artisanal farmstead cheeses, berries, and heirloom apples — all obtained from local farms. They also offer foraged wild edibles, maple syrup, honey, preserves, and more.

The farm has fostered several relationships with local chefs, and they have a strong relationship with the bakers at the King Arthur Flour Bakery's Baking Education Center and test kitchen. Scott Woolsey (Killdeer's manager) works closely with bakers to use Killdeer Farm's fruits and vegetables in their tarts and pies. The cooking classes, some taught by Scott, also use Killdeer's products, and the King Arthur Bakery Store uses the farm's seasonal vegetables for sandwiches and salads. In their give-and-take relationship, Killdeer reciprocates by selling the bakery's organic artisanal breads at their stand.

Black Trumpets and Sweet Corn in Tarragon Cream Sauce

Pairing fresh corn with the earthy flavor of the black trumpet mushroom makes for a fabulous side dish that goes well with fish.

3 tablespoons olive oil

⅓ cup diced shallots

1 cup fresh sweet corn kernels, cut from 2 ears of corn

¼ pound black trumpet mushrooms, left whole (see Note)

3 tablespoons fresh tarragon leaves, coarsely chopped

1 teaspoon coarse salt

6 squash blossoms, thinly sliced lengthwise (optional)

⅓ cup heavy cream or whipping cream

Salt and freshly ground black pepper

Note: The black trumpet mushroom, otherwise known as the "horn of plenty," is a wild variety that has a deliciously rich and elegant buttery flavor. For the most part, they are imported or harvested wild and are available at many specialty produce markets. The chanterelle mushroom is a great substitute for the horn of plenty.

4 SERVINGS

1. Heat the oil in a medium skillet over medium-high heat.

2. Add the shallots and sauté until soft and translucent, stirring frequently. Add the corn and sauté for 2 minutes, stirring occasionally. Add the mushrooms, tarragon, and coarse salt and continue to cook for another 2 minutes. Add the squash blossoms (if using) and continue to cook for 1 minute.

3. Reduce heat and add the heavy cream. Gently simmer mixture, stirring occasionally, until the cream thickens, about 1 to 2 minutes. Season with salt and pepper to taste. Serve at once.

Recipe from TRAPP FAMILY LODGE

Cabot Cheddar Mashed Potatoes

Mashed potatoes are a classic mainstay that are always a welcome accompaniment to any meal. Here, they are dressed up with ground nutmeg and sharp cheddar cheese for a different twist.

2 pounds Yukon Gold potatoes

½ cup unsalted butter, plus more as needed

¾ cup whole milk, heated

4 ounces sharp cheddar cheese, preferably Cabot, grated

Nutmeg

Salt and freshly ground white pepper

4 SERVINGS

1. Peel and dice the potatoes. Cover with cold, salted water in a large stockpot. Bring to a boil over high heat and cook until potatoes are just fork tender.

2. Drain thoroughly, and place in a large bowl with the butter, milk, and cheese, and add nutmeg, and salt and pepper to taste. Mash with an old-fashioned masher or handheld mixer, mixing thoroughly until desired consistency is reached. Additional butter and milk may be added to taste.

3. Serve with the Rack of Lamb with Maple Walnut Crust, Green Beans, and Merlot Pan Jus recipe on page 156.

Recipe from GRAFTON VILLAGE CHEESE COMPANY

Grafton Squash Casserole

This recipe is deliciously full of local bounty and Grafton cheddar, which adds a robust flavor and creaminess to the squash. Even though the heavy cream is naturally rich on its own, make sure you thicken the sauce a bit before pouring it into the casserole. Chef Kathy Cary of Lilly's and La Pêche, in Louisville, Kentucky, developed this deliciously rich side dish.

1 cup (2 sticks) plus 4 tablespoons unsalted butter

1 medium onion, peeled and chopped

3 cloves garlic, peeled and minced

3 pounds summer squash, roughly chopped

½ teaspoon red pepper flakes

1 teaspoon kosher salt

1½ teaspoons dried oregano

1½ cups heavy cream

1 teaspoon Dijon mustard

6 ounces Grafton 2-year-old cheddar, or other aged sharp cheddar, grated

1½ cups Panko breadcrumbs (see Note)

¼ teaspoon Spanish smoked sweet paprika

Note: Panko are breadcrumbs used in Japanese cuisine for coating fried foods. Panko can be found in Asian and some specialty markets.

8–10 SERVINGS

1. Preheat oven to 375°F. Lightly grease a 9- by 9-inch pan or casserole dish, and set aside.

2. In a medium skillet, heat ½ pound of the butter over medium heat. Add the onion and garlic and cook until soft and translucent, stirring occasionally. Add the squash, red pepper flakes, and salt, and sauté until the squash is wilted and turning golden brown.

3. Add the oregano, cream, mustard, and two-thirds of the cheese. Reduce the heat to low and cook the mixture until it has reduced and thickened. Pour the mixture into the prepared pan.

4. Melt the remaining 4 tablespoons of butter. Gently combine the remaining cheese, the breadcrumbs, paprika, and melted butter in a medium bowl, and sprinkle mixture evenly over the casserole. Bake for approximately 20 minutes, or until the casserole is hot and bubbly and the topping is nicely browned.

5. Let the casserole rest for 20 to 30 minutes before serving.

Beet Gnocchi with Roasted Garlic Butter Sauce

Humidity can play a big factor in making this dish, so you may have to "play around with it a bit" until you have it just right, says Drew Cory, former innkeeper at the Seyon Lodge State Park. Beet gnocchi has Russian, Italian, and French influences and goes brilliantly with a wide array of flavors. Serve as a side dish or add some pan-seared chicken-and-apple sausage or chourico to make it a complete meal.

8 SERVINGS

1 pound beets, preferably locally grown

1 tablespoon olive oil

4 garlic cloves, peeled

Salt and freshly ground black pepper

3 large eggs plus 2 egg yolks, preferably farm-fresh, lightly beaten

3 to 4 cups all-purpose flour, or as needed, preferably King Arthur (see Note)

4 tablespoons unsalted butter

1 tablespoon all-purpose flour

½ cup white wine, preferably Pinot Grigio, or apple wine, preferably Vermont-made

1 tablespoon lemon juice

Chopped chives

1. Preheat oven to 450°F. Lightly grease a roasting pan and set aside.

2. Wash and dry beets. Rub with oil and place in prepared roasting pan. Sprinkle beets with salt, add the garlic, and cover pan tightly with foil. Roast until beets are fork tender, about 45 minutes.

3. Transfer beets to a large bowl and cover tightly with plastic wrap. Mash the garlic with a fork and set aside to cool. When beets are cool enough to handle, slip off and discard skins and stems. Pulse the beets with salt and pepper to taste in a food processor until almost smooth.

4. Return the beets to the large bowl, add the eggs and yolks, and combine with a rubber spatula or wooden spoon. Gradually mix in 1 cup of flour at a time until well combined.

Note: If you prefer a less dense gnocchi, use less flour. The range of textures you can achieve range from a very thick frosting to a doughy consistency.

5. Prepare the gnocchi for shaping depending on the texture of the dough: For denser gnocchi, roll out the dough and slice into 1-inch-long strips about ½-inch wide. For less dense gnocchi, place dough in a pastry bag fitted with a ⅜-inch plain tip and pipe in straight lines on parchment paper. Chill in the refrigerator for at least 1 hour.

6. Meanwhile, make the sauce: In a medium skillet melt 2 tablespoons of the butter over medium-low heat. Stir in 1 tablespoon of flour to create a roux. Continue to cook and stir until roux turns a light blond color.

7. Add the reserved roasted garlic and stir to combine well. Whisk in the wine and lemon juice. Continue to whisk mixture until it begins to thicken, then add the remaining 2 tablespoons butter. Remove from heat.

8. Bring salted water to a boil in a large pot. Flour a baking sheet with about 1 cup of flour and set aside.

9. With well-floured hands, pinch off 1 piece of dough at a time from the strips onto a spoon and roll the piece around from spoon to spoon until a log about 2 inches long and 1 inch in diameter is formed. Continue the process until all the dough has been used. Toss the gnocchi in flour on the prepared baking sheet and gently shake to remove any excess flour.

10. Working in batches, if needed, carefully transfer gnocchi with a spatula to the boiling water and cook until they rise to the surface, about 2 minutes.

11. Return the sauce to the stove and heat through. Add the gnocchi and toss to coat well. Remove pan from heat and pour mixture onto a large platter or into a serving bowl.

12. Garnish with chives.

Swiss Chard Pie

Located just off Church Street Marketplace in Burlington, the Penny Cluse Café has been serving breakfast and lunch since 1998. It is owned by Charles Reeves and Holly Cluse and is named after Holly's childhood dog. The café is a destination restaurant for tourists, but the likes and dislikes of the loyal local clientele determine the food that is served, where it comes from, and how it is prepared.

This recipe is made in the summer, when the chard is tender and fresh. The café has been known to use fresh chard from its wait staff's gardens if that's what looks and tastes the best! Taylor Farm's Gouda cheese gives the béchamel sauce its rich taste.

BÉCHAMEL SAUCE (MAKES 4 CUPS, ENOUGH FOR 2 PIES; SEE PREPARATION NOTES)

1 pint whole milk

1 pint half-and-half

4 tablespoons butter

½ cup all-purpose flour

½ tablespoon salt

1 teaspoon freshly ground white pepper

¼ teaspoon freshly ground nutmeg

2 eggs

½ cup grated Gouda cheese (about 2 ounces), preferably Taylor Farm

PIE DOUGH

2½ cups all-purpose flour

Pinch of salt

1 cup (2 sticks) transfat-free margarine or unsalted butter, cold

¼ cup ice water

ONE 9- OR 10-INCH PIE

1. Make the béchamel sauce: Heat milk and half-and-half in a medium saucepan over medium heat. Melt butter in a separate medium saucepan over medium heat. Add the flour, salt, pepper, and nutmeg to the butter. Cook for 2 minutes on low heat, stirring occasionally.

2. Slowly whisk the milk into the butter mixture until well combined and smooth. Bring to a simmer and continue to stir until the mixture thickens, about 15 minutes. Remove from heat and whisk ¼ cup of the sauce into the eggs. Slowly whisk the egg mixture back into the pan of sauce and continue to whisk until the temperature is about 180°F. Whisk in the cheese.

3. Divide mixture into two 1-quart containers and gently press pieces of plastic wrap down onto the two surfaces of the sauce to prevent skins from forming. Cool in the refrigerator overnight.

4. Make the pie dough: Place the flour and salt in the bowl of a food processor, pulse in the margarine, and process until the mixture resembles coarse meal. Continue to process, and slowly add ¼ cup ice water in a steady stream until a smooth and slightly sticky dough forms. Divide dough into 2 pieces. Turn each dough piece out onto a clean work surface and flatten into a disk. Wrap in plastic and refrigerate for at least 1 hour.

SWISS CHARD

1½ pounds (about 2 large bunches) Swiss chard, picked, washed, roughly chopped, blanched, and wrung out thoroughly (see Preparation Notes)

2 tablespoons unsalted butter

1 tablespoon chopped garlic

½ cup chopped scallions

¼ cup chopped flat-leaf parsley

½ tablespoon salt

½ teaspoon cayenne pepper

EGG WASH

1 egg, beaten

1 tablespoon milk

5. Prepare the chard filling: Place the chard in a large bowl. Melt the butter in a medium skillet over medium heat. Add the garlic, scallions, parsley, salt, and cayenne pepper. Sauté until garlic is tender. Remove vegetable mixture from the heat, pour over chard, and mix well.

6. Assemble the pie: Preheat oven to 375°F. Butter and flour a 9- or 10-inch pie pan; set aside.

7. Lightly dust a clean work surface with flour and roll out the two disks of the dough into ⅛-inch-thick rounds to fit the pie pan. Place the dough into the prepared pan, trimming edges if needed. Lay in the chard, then 1 cup of the béchamel sauce. Wet the outer edge of the bottom crust with a little water and place the other piece of dough on top, crimp the edges with your fingers or a fork, and cut vent holes.

8. Whisk together the egg and milk to make an egg wash. Brush pastry top with egg wash. Place on a baking tray with sides to catch any overflow.

9. Bake until crust is golden brown and cheese is bubbling, about 45 to 60 minutes. The internal temperature should be 165°F. Cool before cutting.

Preparation Notes: *At the café we make the béchamel sauce in this quantity because it is easier than making a smaller batch. The extra sauce works great with other types of dishes, such as any casserole recipe (like moussaka or pastitsio) that needs a browned, creamy top. The sauce will keep in the refrigerator for four to five days.*

To blanche is to plunge food (usually fruits or vegetables) into boiling water for a short time, then transfer with tongs to a bowl of ice and cold water to stop the cooking process.

Basic Pan-fried Tempeh with Onions and Garlic

Rhapsody Natural Foods in Montpelier is a buffet-style natural and organic food restaurant. In addition, it is a producer and distributor of natural and organic foods and beverages, such as tempeh and amazake (a traditional sweet nonalcoholic Japanese beverage made from fermented rice). They buy directly from local farmers, such as Littlewood Farm, Cate Farm, and Two Rivers Farm, as well as other farmers who grow organic produce. The menu offerings vary with whatever is fresh from the farm.

Tempeh can be baked, deep-fried, used in casseroles, or made into a spread or paté. You can use it alone or in salads, on top of rice, pasta, noodles, couscous, or in sandwiches. But after decades of eating tempeh of all kinds, forms, and flavors, Rhapsody's cook still considers this recipe to be his favorite. Serve it with steamed vegetables — it is so simple to prepare that it makes a great choice for everyday dinners.

4 SERVINGS

- **2 tablespoons sunflower oil or vegetable oil**
- **1 medium yellow onion, diced**
- **4 garlic cloves, peeled and minced**
- **1 (8-ounce) tempeh cake (preferably Rhapsody certified organic), sliced or cubed**
- **2–4 tablespoons soy sauce**
- **Chopped scallions or cilantro**

1. Heat the oil in a medium skillet over medium heat. Add the onion and cook until soft and translucent, stirring occasionally. Add the garlic and continue to sauté until soft, stirring often. Add the tempeh, soy sauce, and 2 cups of water, stirring until well combined. Bring to a simmer and cook until all of the liquid has evaporated and tempeh is golden brown on both sides, about 15 to 20 minutes. Garnish with scallions or cilantro.

Variation: Add ginger, cumin, coriander, or curry with the tempeh.

Rond de Nice Squash Stuffed with Potato "Risotto" and Served with Red and Yellow Tomato Sauces

The Perfect Wife Restaurant & Tavern, located in Manchester, is a great mix of formal and casual dining. The upstairs tavern is well known for its burgers, chicken pot pie, meal-sized salads, and live music. Downstairs, in the greenhouse dining room, Chef Amy Chamberlain's freestyle cuisine shines. In the summer, most of the restaurant's organic produce is purchased from Anjali Farm in South Londonderry.

Amy Chamberlain's business relationship with many of the local farmers began when these growers stopped by her restaurant to showcase their products. She met many more farmers at various Vermont Fresh Network functions and during visits to area farmers' markets. Amy loves to feature their locally grown vegetables as daily specials.

This recipe was created for the Chef's Dinner at the Stratton Wine and Food Festival in 2000. The potatoes in this dish are cooked in the style of risotto, giving the filling a creamy, rich consistency.

POTATO-STUFFED SQUASH

6 SERVINGS

3 tablespoons olive oil

1 small onion, diced

3 large potatoes, peeled and diced

2 tablespoons chopped garlic

6 ounces fresh wild mushrooms, such as morel, shiitake, or oyster, cleaned and thinly sliced

3 cups vegetable stock

¼ cup heavy cream

½ cup shredded, sharp cheddar cheese, preferably Cabot

Salt and freshly ground black pepper

Fresh chopped herbs, such as parsley or thyme

6 Rond de Nice squash (see Note)

1. Preheat oven to 350° F. Lightly oil a baking dish.

2. Heat the oil in a medium skillet over medium heat. Add onion and cook, stirring, until soft and translucent. Add the potatoes and garlic and cook with the onions, stirring gently, until potatoes are heated through.

3. Add mushrooms and cook until soft, stirring frequently. Add the stock, 1 cup at a time, stirring often. Allow potatoes to absorb liquid before adding the next cup. Continue adding stock until the potatoes are cooked through, but still hold their shape. Add heavy cream and cheese. Season with salt, pepper, and herbs to taste. Cook until the cheese is melted.

4. Slice the squash in half, scoop out their centers, and place them in the prepared baking dish. Spoon the potato filling evenly into each squash. Bake uncovered until squash is fork tender, about 30 to 35 minutes. While the squash is baking, prepare the sauces.

2 tablespoons olive oil

15 garlic cloves, roasted (see Preparation Note)

2 cups chopped yellow tomatoes, peeled and seeded

¼ cup dry white wine

1 tablespoon pure maple syrup, preferably Vermont-made

Salt and freshly ground white pepper

RED TOMATO AND
HORSERADISH SAUCE

2 tablespoons olive oil

½ small onion, minced

2 cups chopped, ripe, red tomatoes, peeled and seeded

1 tablespoon tomato paste

¼ cup dry white wine

1 tablespoon pure maple syrup, preferably Vermont-made

2 teaspoons horseradish

Salt and freshly ground white pepper

Grated Parmesan cheese

Note: Rond de Nice is a type of round summer squash similar to zucchini in texture and flavor. It is grown exclusively as green summer squash but when grown to maturity is orange.

5. For the yellow tomato sauce, heat the oil in a medium skillet over medium-low heat. Add garlic and tomatoes, cover, and cook, stirring occasionally, until the vegetables soften without browning, about 15 minutes.

6. Add wine and syrup and allow to simmer uncovered for 5 minutes. Transfer mixture to a blender or food processor and blend until smooth. Season with salt and pepper to taste. Transfer the sauce back to the pan and cook until heated through, stirring frequently.

7. For the red tomato sauce, heat the oil in a medium skillet over medium-low heat. Add the onions, cover, and cook until they soften without browning, about 5 minutes. Add tomatoes and paste and cook uncovered, stirring to combine well. Add wine, syrup, and horseradish and allow to simmer uncovered for 5 minutes. Transfer mixture to a blender or food processor and blend until smooth. Season sauce with salt and pepper to taste. Transfer the sauce back to the pan and cook until heated through, stirring frequently.

8. To serve, pool the tomato sauces on plates, place the baked stuffed squash on top, and garnish with a sprinkle of Parmesan cheese.

Preparation Note: *To roast garlic, preheat oven to 350°F. Place a whole unpeeled garlic head on a flat piece of aluminum foil. Carefully cut off the top of the head with a sharp knife, and generously drizzle with olive oil. Sprinkle with salt and pepper to taste. Wrap head in aluminum foil and bake until fork tender, about 45 minutes. Remove from the oven and set aside to cool. Once cool enough to handle, peel cloves.*

Acorn Squash with Wild Mushroom Cranberry Stuffing

Deep Root Organic Cooperative, headquartered in Johnson, Vermont, is a small, farmer-owned marketing cooperative dedicated to healthful living and the preservation of the environment. They promote and sustain small family farms, marketing more than 70 different organic fruits and vegetables throughout the Northeast and Mid-Atlantic states. Member farms are active in their local communities, running CSAs and selling their goods at farmers' markets. The cooperative currently has 18 member farms in Vermont and southern Quebec.

This recipe highlights acorn squash, one of the classic crops of the Northeast, by pairing it with another Northeast staple, cranberries. The sweet and savory combination is truly enjoyable.

1 (about 1½ pounds) acorn squash halved lengthwise, seeded

Salt and freshly ground black pepper

¼ cup dried cranberries or currants

4 tablespoons unsalted butter

4 ounces fresh wild mushrooms such as shiitake, stemmed and chopped

¼ cup chopped onion

1 teaspoon dried sage

¾ cup fresh whole wheat breadcrumbs

2 SERVINGS

1. Preheat oven to 425°F. Place squash cut side down in an 8- by 8- by 2-inch glass baking dish. Cover dish tightly with plastic wrap. Micro-wave squash on high for 10 to 15 minutes, until soft. With a sharp knife, very carefully cut plastic to let steam escape. Remove plastic wrap and discard. Using a pair of tongs, turn squash halves cut side up. Season cavities with salt and pepper to taste.

2. Place cranberries in a small bowl and add ¼ cup hot water; soak 15 to 20 minutes to soften the fruit. Drain and set aside.

3. Meanwhile, melt 3 tablespoons of the butter in a medium skillet over medium heat. Add mushrooms, onion, and sage, and cook and stir until the vegetable mixture begins to soften, about 5 minutes. Add the breadcrumbs and continue to cook, stirring frequently, until the crumbs become lightly brown, about 3 minutes. Add the cranberries and soaking liquid, stirring until well combined. Season with salt and pepper to taste.

4. Mound stuffing into the squash halves, and dot with the remaining 1 tablespoon butter. Bake until heated through and crisp on top, about 10 minutes.

LOCAL

Pittsfield, Vermont

organically grown

OYSTER MUSHROOMS

Tweed Valley Farm

$13.99 lb

Shiitake and Oyster Mushroom Tortellini with Sherry Cream Sauce

This recipe uses two mushrooms — shiitake and oyster — that thrive in Vermont. The sherry and brandy bring the wild mushroom flavor to the forefront, while the combined textures make for a dish suitable for any season.

FILLING

4–6 SERVINGS

1 teaspoon olive oil

10 ounces shiitake mushrooms, quartered

10 ounces oyster mushrooms, roots removed and quartered

3 ounces brandy

Salt and freshly ground black pepper

TORTELLINI DOUGH (OR USE TWO 9-OUNCE PACKAGES STORE-BOUGHT FRESH TORTELLINI PASTA)

2½ cups all-purpose flour

Pinch of salt

1 tablespoon olive oil

2 eggs

2 egg yolks

SHERRY CREAM SAUCE

1 tablespoon unsalted butter

1 teaspoon chopped garlic

¾ cup dry sherry

1 cup heavy cream

2 scallions, chopped

1. Make the filling: Line a baking sheet with paper towels and set aside.

2. Heat the olive oil in a large skillet over medium heat. Add all of the mushrooms and sauté for 1 to 2 minutes, stirring frequently. Carefully add brandy and allow alcohol to flame. Season with salt and pepper to taste. Spread mixture on prepared baking sheet, and set aside to cool.

3. Make the tortellini: Place the flour, salt, and olive oil in a food processor fitted with the metal blade. Combine eggs and egg yolks in a small bowl and add slowly to the running food processor until dough just starts to come together.

4. Transfer dough to a floured surface and knead until smooth, approximately 10 minutes. Cover dough with plastic wrap and set aside at room temperature for 45 minutes.

5. Roll dough through a pasta machine, starting at the widest setting and gradually moving to the thinnest setting, continuing to flour lightly. Cut rolled dough into 4-inch circles with a round cutter.

6. Place 1 tablespoon of filling in the center of each round, moisten the edges lightly with water, fold in half, and seal together, making a half moon. Bring the points together and seal once again. Set aside on a lightly floured tray until ready to use.

7. Bring cold, salted water to a boil in a large pot over high heat.

8. Make the sherry cream sauce: Add ½ tablespoon of the butter and the garlic to a saucepan and cook and stir until golden brown, about 3 minutes. Whisk in the sherry and cream, simmering until sauce reduces and thickens by half, about 15 minutes. Finish with remaining ½ tablespoon of butter, whisking until well combined.

9. Add the tortellini to the boiling water and cook for 1 minute, then drain.

10. To serve, place the pasta in large bowls, spoon the sauce over the tortellini, and top with scallions. Serve at once.

Poached Salmon Fillets with Baby Spinach and Herbs

This stovetop recipe is a light, elegant dish. Accompany the salmon with a crusty French bread, jasmine rice, and a tossed salad of cool mesclun greens. A lightly chilled bottle of Shelburne Vineyard Cayuga White or Lakeview White wine would be a delicious pairing.

4 SERVINGS

8- to 9-inch salmon fillet, center-cut, skinned

3 very thin lemon slices, seeded and halved

Freshly ground black pepper

1½ teaspoons chopped fresh rosemary, plus several whole sprigs for sauce and garnish

2½ tablespoons grapeseed oil or high-quality extra-virgin olive oil

2 large garlic cloves, peeled and thinly sliced

3 shallot cloves, peeled and thinly sliced

1¼ cups Shelburne Vineyard Lakeview White wine

4 scallions, sliced into ¼-inch pieces

½ pound baby spinach, washed and dried

Salt

1. Cut salmon fillet into four 2-inch-wide slices, and place them on a large plate. Rub salmon slices with 2 half slices of lemon, squeezing juices as you go, and season with pepper to taste. Place a half slice of lemon on each slice of fish. Sprinkle with 1½ teaspoons of rosemary, and set aside.

2. Heat 1½ tablespoons of the oil in a large skillet over medium heat. Add the garlic and shallots, reduce the heat to medium-low, and cook, stirring frequently, for about 10 minutes. Increase the heat to medium and continue to cook until the vegetables begin to caramelize slightly, about 2 minutes, stirring frequently, and adding additional oil if necessary. Transfer vegetables to a plate.

3. Reduce heat to medium-low. Add remaining 1 tablespoon oil, making sure the pan is coated evenly. Place the salmon slices in the middle of pan. Transfer the garlic and shallots back to the pan.

4. Add the wine, and 1 or 2 small sprigs of rosemary. Cover the pan and adjust heat so that the liquid remains just below boiling. Poach until fish is opaque, 7 to 10 minutes. (Cooking time may vary depending on the thickness of fillets and desired degree of doneness.) Remove salmon to a platter and keep warm.

5. Increase heat slightly and add scallions and spinach to the poaching liquid. Continue to cook, covered, until spinach has wilted, about 2 minutes.

6. Remove from heat. Transfer the vegetables to a bowl and gently toss together, combining well.

7. Meanwhile, increase heat to high and continue to cook the poaching liquid, stirring constantly, until slightly reduced, 1 to 2 minutes. Season to taste with salt and pepper.

8. To serve, place salmon fillets on a serving platter. Top with reduced poaching liquid, lemon slices, and rosemary sprigs. Place vegetable mixture around fillets and serve.

Note: This dish is also excellent with other types of fish, such as Arctic char. Try it with sautéed shiitake mushroom slices, or substitute arugula for the spinach. You can also add an Asian flare by replacing the rosemary with chopped basil and adding ½ teaspoon of fresh minced ginger, 1 tablespoon of tamari, and 1 teaspoon of sesame oil to the poaching liquid.

SHELBURNE VINEYARD

Founded in 1998 by Ken and Gail Albert, Shelburne Vineyard prides itself on producing fine, handcrafted wines from both vinifera and American grape varieties. The vineyards are located on well-drained soils on the shores of Lake Champlain, where the lake moderates the Vermont winters and prolongs the growing season. The Alberts achieve the fine quality in their award-winning wines through careful selection of grape varieties, meticulous attention to pruning to ensure each grape cluster receives the maximum sun possible, and by crafting and blending the wines in small lots, with minimal handling, in their Shelburne winery. The vineyards have been certified organic by NOFA-VT since 2000; many of the offerings are estate grown and bottled from these plantings. To produce additional choice wines, they also import grape varieties that cannot be grown in Vermont's cold climate.

Shelburne Vineyard has been an active member of the Vermont Fresh Network for many years. Through the network the Alberts have met a number of Vermont's finest chefs; many of those chefs now serve the vineyard's wines in their restaurants. These chefs and Shelburne Vineyard are part of the annual Vermont Fresh Network event held each summer at Shelburne Farms. Here the public can come and taste the fine dishes created using Vermont-grown products and pair those tastes with Shelburne Vineyard wines. Good food, good wine, and a gorgeous waterfront setting — it's a spectacular event!

The winery has also developed a wonderful relationship with the teaching chefs and wine specialists at the New England Culinary Institute. NECI students regularly visit the winery to learn about grape varietals and to taste Shelburne's wines. Ken and Gail have benefited from their feedback. Some of the students have even returned to further their knowledge by helping to bottle the wines.

Moroccan Vegetable Tagine

This Moroccan-inspired vegetable tagine is lightly spiced with the warm flavors of cumin and cinnamon. Serve over couscous or alongside roast chicken or lamb.

1 tablespoon extra-virgin olive oil

2 yellow onions, sliced

1½ tablespoons ground cumin

3 cinnamon sticks

4 cups peeled and diced organic butternut squash, preferably locally grown (about 1½ pounds)

2 (14½-ounce) cans chickpeas, rinsed

2 (14½-ounce) cans diced tomatoes

¾ cup orange or grapefruit juice

2 tablespoons honey

½ cup pitted Kalamata olives

½ cup pitted prunes

4 cups kale, organic lacinata, washed and tough stalks discarded, preferably locally grown

Kosher salt and freshly ground black pepper

1 cup almonds, toasted and lightly crushed

Harissa (optional)

4–6 SERVINGS

1. Heat the oil in a stock pot over medium-high heat.

2. Add the onions and cook, stirring occasionally, until soft, about 5 minutes. Add the cumin and the cinnamon sticks and cook until fragrant, approximately 1 minute. Add the squash, chickpeas, tomatoes, juice, and honey and bring to a boil.

3. Reduce the heat to low and cook, covered, until the squash is tender, approximately 20 minutes. Add the olives, prunes, and kale, and stir to combine.

4. Cover and continue cooking until the kale is wilted and the olives and prunes are softened, approximately 10 more minutes. Season with salt and pepper to taste. Garnish with the toasted almonds and serve Harissa to taste (if using) alongside the tagine.

2 Orchard Fruits and Berries

Awesome Pear or Apple Pancake

This beautiful baked pancake is easy and elegant. A wonderful "company breakfast" dish!

2–4 SERVINGS

3 eggs

¾ cup whole milk

¾ cup all-purpose flour

¼ teaspoon salt

1 teaspoon almond or pure vanilla extract

2 ripe pears or 2 tart peeled apples, cored and thinly sliced

2 tablespoons sugar

¾ teaspoon cinnamon

2 tablespoons butter

Confectioners' sugar or pure maple syrup to taste

1. Warm an iron skillet in a 425°F oven. With a handheld blender, whisk together the eggs, milk, flour, salt, and extract until smooth. In a separate bowl, toss together pears, sugar, and cinnamon.

2. Melt butter in the warm skillet. Arrange the pears in a single layer on the bottom of the skillet. Carefully pour the batter over the fruit.

3. Bake for 25 minutes or until puffed and golden brown. To serve, sprinkle with confectioners' sugar or drizzle with maple syrup.

APPLE FACTS

Vermont's fresh apple crop is a multimillion dollar business, with processed apple products such as cider, applesauce, and hard cider accounting for as much income as the fresh fruit. The state's commercial apple crop is grown on almost 4,000 acres of farmland.

Vermont's leading apple varieties are McIntosh, Cortland, Red Delicious, and Empire. McIntosh apples became the state's leading variety after an extremely cold winter (1917–1918) devastated most other varieties.

In 1999, the Vermont legislature designated the apple as the state fruit, and the apple pie as the state pie.

Autumn apple festivals attract thousands of tourists and locals every year. Among the most popular are:
- Vermont Apple Festival and Craft Show, held around Columbus Day every year in Springfield, Vermont
- Cabot Pie Festival, held in October in Cabot, Vermont
- Pie Fest and Cider House Run, held at Shelburne Orchards in Shelburne, Vermont

From the Vermont Apple Marketing Board

Maple Apple Waffles with Ben & Jerry's Ice Cream

The Birds Nest Inn, tucked away in the Green Mountains in the Stowe/Waterbury area of Vermont, is an elegantly restored 1832 farmhouse. The inn offers five unique, cozy guest rooms, each with a beautiful view of the countryside, plus a scrumptious full candlelight breakfast and tempting afternoon culinary delights. Over the years the owners have seen that one of the best ways to make their full breakfasts extra special is by featuring local produce, often picked at the farm and served to the guests on the same morning. Many of the inn's delicious creations include local products from Cold Hollow Cider Mill, Cabot Dairy, and Ben & Jerry's. The Vermont-fresh products ensure that guests enjoy a memorable dining experience.

If you don't have a waffle iron, use this batter to make pancakes.

MAPLE APPLES

4 SERVINGS

- 2 tablespoons unsalted butter, preferably Cabot
- 2 tablespoons sugar
- ¼ teaspoon ground cinnamon
- 4 medium apples, peeled, cored, and cut into thin wedges
- ¼ cup pure maple syrup, preferably Vermont-made

1. Make the maple apples: Melt the butter in a large skillet over medium heat. Add sugar and cinnamon and cook, stirring often, until the sugar begins to dissolve (the mixture may clump together). Add the apples and syrup. Cook, stirring occasionally, until the apples are tender yet firm, about 5 minutes. Reduce heat to low and cover with foil until waffles are done.

2. Make the waffles: Preheat an electric waffle iron according to manufacturer's instruction. Preheat oven to 200°F.

3. Sift together the flour, baking powder, sugar, and salt in a large bowl.

4. In a separate medium bowl, whisk together egg yolks, milk, butter, and vanilla extract until blended. Pour into dry mixture and combine well.

5. In a medium bowl, beat the egg whites until stiff and gently fold them into batter with a rubber spatula.

WAFFLES

2 cups all-purpose flour, preferably King Arthur

2 teaspoons baking powder

1 tablespoon sugar

⅛ teaspoon salt, or to taste

4 eggs, separated, room temperature

1 cup (2%) milk, room temperature

¼ cup unsalted butter, preferably Cabot, melted and cooled

1 teaspoon pure vanilla extract

TOPPING

Vanilla ice cream, preferably Ben & Jerry's

Whipped cream

6. Ladle about ⅓ cup of batter onto each section of a deep-pocketed waffle grid and bake until cover opens easily, about 3 to 5 minutes. Continue to make waffles; transfer cooked waffles onto a lightly greased baking sheet and place in the oven until all the batter is used.

7. After all the waffles are done, place them on an oven rack to crisp the outsides only.

8. Transfer to warm plates to serve. Spoon maple apples on top of the waffles and add big scoops of Ben & Jerry's ice cream and whipped cream. Serve immediately.

Blueberry-stuffed French Toast

Susanne Heinzerling, the owner of Bittersweet Farm, has been an active member of the Vermont Fresh Network since its inception. She visits many local farms and restaurants, attends Vermont food-related meetings, and features homegrown food and locally purchased ingredients at her country home B&B.

Bittersweet Farm is an ideal place for a summer vacation. Guests enjoy country walks, bike riding, or just rocking on the front porch with a good book. On rainy days, the B&B offers a small crafts workshop teaching knitting or crocheting. The owner of Bittersweet Farm feels that relaxation needs to be learned; guests are encouraged to stay awhile and enjoy this new lifestyle.

Bittersweet Farm uses their own blueberries and eggs from their chickens for this recipe. Fill the French toast with peaches, plums, or apples when fresh blueberries are not available.

6–8 SERVINGS

1 loaf challah or other egg bread with crust, cut into 1-inch-thick slices

1 (8-ounce) package cream cheese, cut into chunks (optional)

1 cup fresh blueberries

8 farm-fresh eggs

1½ cups whole milk

½ cup pure maple syrup, preferably Vermont-made

½ cup melted butter

1. Preheat oven to 350°F. Lightly coat an 11- by 7- by 2-inch glass baking dish with cooking spray or butter. Layer half of the bread slices into the bottom of the prepared pan. Next, layer the cream cheese (if using) and half of the blueberries evenly over the top of the bread. Top with remaining bread and remaining blueberries.

2. Whisk eggs, milk, syrup, and butter in a medium bowl to combine well; pour over bread mixture. Cover with foil to avoid excessive browning, and bake for 30 minutes. Remove foil and continue to bake for another 30 minutes or until bread mixture is puffed and golden brown.

3. Spoon or cut into portions and serve with warm maple syrup and sausage or ham, if desired.

Cherry Hill Farm's Very Fruity Iced Tea

Cherry Hill Farm's iced tea is popular at farmers' markets and the farm's own fruit stand. It is very refreshing, full of good-for-you ingredients, and appealing to people of all ages. The deep and exciting flavor of the black currants gives this summertime drink a particular zest that takes iced tea to a different level.

9–11 CUPS

6 cups black tea (decaf is fine)

4–5 fresh mint sprigs, or to taste

1 cup black currant purée or 2 cups black currant juice

1 cup raspberry juice

Juice of 1 lemon

Juice of 1 orange (optional)

½ cup honey

1. Prepare tea according to package directions.

2. Place mint in a large heat-proof pitcher and add tea. Set aside to cool.

3. Chill tea in the refrigerator until cold, about 1 hour. Remove mint when the tea has chilled and discard.

4. Stir in black currant purée, raspberry juice, lemon juice, orange juice (if using), and honey.

Recipe from SCOTT WOOLSEY, KILLDEER FARM

Melon Salsa

A quick walk around his farm stand in mid-August gave Scott Woolsey the idea for this refreshing salsa. Sweet, salty, and spicy!

1 large cantaloupe, rind removed, seeded and cubed

1 medium red onion, peeled and diced

6 Roma tomatoes, seeded, cored, and coarsely chopped

2 teaspoons salt

Minced cilantro

4 spearmint leaves

1 jalapeño pepper, minced

1 poblano pepper, chopped

2 Thai peppers, minced (optional)

3 tablespoons fresh lime juice

3 tablespoons white vinegar

6–8 SERVINGS

In a large bowl combine all ingredients and mix well. Cover and refrigerate for 1 hour before serving.

Strawberry Jam

The Whitford House Inn is a spacious, beautifully restored 1790s country home located on a quiet lane in the Champlain Valley. There are three tastefully decorated bedrooms in the main house as well as a lovely guest house. All rooms have full private baths and spectacular views. Amenities include a full hot breakfast, which guests may request at any time of day. This mouthwatering meal is known not only for its quality and freshness but also for its generous portions.

The fabulous breakfasts often feature ingredients from local farmers. The inn purchases seasonal produce from Golden Russet Farm, fruit from Douglas Orchards in Shoreham, and maple syrup from Williams Farm in Cornwall. The owners try to use organic produce whenever possible, buying from the Middlebury Natural Foods Co-op, which receives its produce from local farmers. The inn itself has organic gardens, where rhubarb, tomatoes, onions, carrots, and other vegetables all thrive. Guests might find this just-picked produce in their morning frittatas or on evening hors d'oeuvre trays.

This delicious strawberry jam is the owner's mother's recipe. The owner, Barbara Carson, picks her own strawberries from an organic farm to create this delicious condiment, popular among the inn's guests. It really is more like strawberry syrup than jam, but it may be served with biscuits and toast. When making this jam, cook only one quart at a time so that it does not become too thin.

1 quart strawberries, washed and hulled

4 cups sugar

Juice of ½ lemon

6–7 PINT GLASS JARS

1. Place the strawberries in a large saucepan. Add 2 cups of the sugar and bring to a boil over high heat, stirring only at the beginning of the boil. Boil for exactly 2 minutes. (Refrain from stirring too often unless the jam begins to boil over the top of the pan. Stirring too often causes foam to form on the top.)

2. Slowly add the remaining 2 cups of sugar and the lemon juice. Return the strawberry mixture to a boil, stirring only at the beginning of the boil, and let cook for exactly 3 minutes. Remove from stovetop and pour strawberry mixture directly into a pottery crock or bowl and let stand at room temperature overnight before putting into clean glass jars and sealing.

STEVENS ORCHARD

The Stevens family planted their orchard in Orwell in 1894. When Karen Blair and Bob Fields acquired the 90-acre orchard in 1999, they became only the fourth holders of the stately old standard apple trees surrounded by 220 acres of pebbled shores, bluffs, and mossy woodlands. Rolling up from Lake Champlain, the orchard hills provide spectacular vistas of the lake and the Adirondacks beyond.

The orchard has several microclimates that provide perfect environments for all of its apple varieties. Soon after arriving, Karen and Bob planted many antique varieties of apples to add to the crop of New England standards. They found McIntosh, Cortland, Macoun, and Northern Spy, and not-so-standard Quinte, Hume, Tolman Sweet, Winter Banana, and Fameuse. They added antique favorites like Wolf River, Golden Russet, Esopus Spitzenburg, Sops-of-Wine, Rhode Island Greening, Gravenstein, and Lady, plus two new varieties, Honeycrisp and Zesta.

Today, Stevens Orchard remains a popular destination for Vermonters whose families and relatives have been buying apples from the orchard since its earliest days. Stevens Orchard is also the go-to orchard for the best Honeycrisp around. Through word of mouth, apple fanciers, retailers, and chefs have learned of the unparalleled quality and flavor of the fruit that the orchard grows and sells. Stevens Orchard does not pick their fruit early in order to beat others to the market, nor does it allow apples to ripen off the tree in cold storage. Karen and Bob pick their fruit when it is ripe, even if that means going through a block of trees numerous times to get the color and the flavor that their customers will love. The look of amazement on the face of someone tasting a slice of Gravenstein or Tolman Sweet at a local farmers' market for the first time is a wonderful reward!

Recipe from STEVENS ORCHARD

Fantastic Applesauce

With fall comes a bounty of apples. This simple sauce is a delicious way to enjoy the fresh fruit.

12 apples, preferably Northern Spy

2 tablespoons sugar, or more to taste

ABOUT 9 CUPS

1. Core and cut the apples into small or large chunks.

2. In a large pot, combine the apples, sugar, and ½ cup of water. Bring to a simmer over medium heat. Reduce heat to a low simmer, cover, and cook until the apples are tender, about 30 to 35 minutes, stirring occasionally to bring cooked apples to the top and uncooked apples to the bottom of the pot.

3. Coarsely mash the apples with the cooking juice and adjust taste with sugar if desired. Store in an airtight container in the refrigerator for up to 4 days.

Recipe from BAILEY'S RESTAURANT AT BOLTON VALLEY RESORT

Blueberry Mint Relish

Blueberries and mint combine beautifully in this salad. It works very well as a garnish or relish for the Rosemary Seared Lamb Loin on page 159.

1½ tablespoons fresh mint leaves, cut into thin strips

Juice of ½ lemon

1 teaspoon pure maple syrup, preferably Vermont-made

2 teaspoons extra-virgin olive oil

Salt and freshly ground black pepper

1 pint blueberries, rinsed

4–6 SERVINGS

In a medium bowl whisk together mint, lemon juice, syrup, oil, and salt and pepper to taste. Add blueberries and gently toss to combine all ingredients well. Adjust seasonings as needed and serve immediately.

Field Greens with Candied Apples, Roasted Walnuts, and Apple Vinaigrette

The orchard owner's mother, Audrey Suhr, created this recipe. The warm apples and walnuts add a nice contrast to the bed of cool field greens. The salad is lovely served as a first course for company or special occasions.

1 cup cider, preferably locally made

¼ cup apple cider vinegar

½ cup hazelnut or walnut oil

2 tablespoons minced fresh chives, or to taste

Salt and freshly ground black pepper

1 cup walnut halves

1 tablespoon sugar, or to taste

2 tablespoons extra-virgin olive oil

3 crisp apples, such as Gala or Cortland, peeled, halved, cored, and cut lengthwise into ⅛-inch-thick slices

1 (12-ounce) bag field greens

1 cup crumbled blue cheese or Gorgonzola

6–8 SERVINGS

1. Bring apple cider to a boil in a medium saucepan over medium heat. Lower heat and simmer for an additional 10 minutes or until juice is reduced by half and appears slightly syrupy. Remove from burner, set aside to cool. Once cooled, vigorously whisk in vinegar, oil, chives, and salt and pepper to taste.

2. Preheat oven to 350°F. Place walnuts on a baking sheet and toast stirring frequently, until crisp and lightly browned, about 8 minutes. Coarsely chop walnuts.

3. Meanwhile, melt sugar in a heavy skillet over medium heat, stirring often, until it just begins to turn golden and melt. Carefully add oil and then apples. Sauté apples, stirring constantly, until they are slightly soft but still crisp. Remove from pan and transfer to a plate until you are ready to use.

4. Place greens in a large bowl and drizzle with the vinaigrette, lightly coating all ingredients. Add the walnuts, candied apples, and cheese. Season with salt and pepper to taste. Drizzle additional vinaigrette over the top to taste, and serve at once.

Apple–Butternut Squash Soup

Let's Pretend is a catering company in Burlington, Vermont, that offers fresh, delicious food and professional service. The co-owners, Daniel Samson and Liane Mendez, both graduates of the New England Culinary Institute, were drawn to catering because they love the challenge of listening to customers' concepts and then designing memorable affairs that more than meet expectations.

The owners believe that fresh seasonal foods, simply cooked, have a universal appeal that works for a catering company. They are committed to using locally grown produce and working personally with area farms. Samson and Mendez have built a particularly strong business relationship with Half Pint Farm. Once the season begins they communicate by phone every week. They also touch base with Half Pint during the winter to find out what is in store for the upcoming season, as well as to add a few special requests of their own. Many side dishes and salads are tailored to take full advantage of Half Pint's offerings, supporting and promoting the concept of sustainable farming practices.

Try garnishing this soup with maple-glazed toasted squash seeds, sautéed apples, or caramelized mushrooms with fresh thyme and crème fraîche.

3 tablespoons vegetable oil

1 medium white onion, diced small

3 celery stalks, coarsely chopped

1 medium carrot, peeled and finely chopped

1 large Granny Smith apple, peeled, cored, and coarsely chopped

1 tablespoon kosher salt

1 teaspoon freshly ground black pepper

1 teaspoon ground cinnamon

1 teaspoon ground nutmeg

1 teaspoon ground allspice

1 large butternut squash (about 2 pounds), peeled, halved lengthwise, seeded, and cut into 1-inch pieces

2 quarts water or chicken stock

2 cups apple cider, preferably locally made

2 teaspoons freshly squeezed lemon juice

2 cups half-and-half

10–12 SERVINGS

1. Heat the oil in a large stockpot over medium-low heat. Add onion, celery, carrot, apple, salt, pepper, cinnamon, nutmeg, and allspice. Cover and cook until vegetables are slightly tender, 8 to 10 minutes, stirring occasionally.

2. Remove cover and add squash, water, cider, and lemon juice, stirring to combine well. Simmer over medium-high heat for about 40 minutes or until squash is fork tender, stirring occasionally.

3. Working in batches, if necessary, transfer squash mixture to a blender and purée until texture is silky smooth. Transfer purée back to the stockpot, slowly whisk in the half-and-half, and heat through. Adjust seasonings with salt and pepper. Ladle into warm soup bowls.

4. For best results, make one day in advance to allow flavors to meld. Heat through to serve.

Strawberry Soup

This strawberry soup was created one summer when the owners of the Churchill House Inn were a little too enthusiastic in their berry picking. There's nothing like an overabundance of fresh, organic fruit for inspiring new and exciting recipes. This soup is a hit any time of the day. It can also be enjoyed as a delicious smoothie.

1 pint strawberries, stems removed and coarsely chopped

½ cup sour cream or plain yogurt

½ cup sugar

½ cup red wine

Fresh mint

4 SERVINGS

1. Purée strawberries, sour cream, sugar, and red wine in a blender until smooth. Transfer purée mixture to a large bowl, cover, and refrigerate overnight.

2. Stir soup until well combined. Ladle into chilled soup cups or bowls. Garnish with mint and serve at once.

CHAMPLAIN ORCHARDS

Champlain Orchards is a family-owned and family-operated farm located on a lovely hilltop in the Champlain Valley. They grow 25 varieties of apples, plums, peaches, cherries, blueberries, and raspberries, and they press their own sweet cider. The owner, Bill Suhr, cares for the land and the trees using methods that date back to the first American settlers. He also practices integrated pest management, has a transitional organic orchard, and always works to be a responsible steward of the land.

For 11 months of the year Champlain Orchards delivers apples, apple slices for baking, apple cider, and fresh-baked pies three times a week to restaurants, the University of Vermont campus and dining hall chefs, deli chefs, and produce managers at small groceries, food co-ops, and supermarkets throughout the state of Vermont. Their business has grown tremendously since the days when they delivered only to farmers' markets in the fall. They now make refrigerated deliveries of 1,000,000 pounds of fresh apples and 70,000 gallons of cider annually.

Biweekly communication with their customers has helped them to match their apples to specific culinary needs. This direct contact with their customers has helped them tailor their apple varieties to stay current with changing tastes and trends.

Apple, Blue Cheese, and Walnut Pizza

Most people think a pizza must have tomato sauce and toppings on a crust of pizza dough . . . and it usually does, but tomatoes didn't even exist in Italy or Europe until the 1500s, when they were brought from Peru by sea captains. In the sixth century BC, when Persian soldiers of Darius the Great were marching great distances, they baked a kind of flatbread on their shields and then covered it with cheese and dates. While an apple and blue cheese pizza is unusual today, maybe it really is close to the original!

½ package or 1¼ teaspoons active dry yeast

1 cup all-purpose flour

⅔ cup whole wheat flour

1 teaspoon sugar

1 teaspoon salt

⅛ teaspoon white pepper

2 tablespoons plus ⅛ teaspoon olive oil

1 large apple, such as Granny Smith, unpeeled, cored, and cut into ⅛-inch slices

¾ cup crumbled blue cheese (3 ounces)

½–¾ cup shredded Monterey Jack cheese (2–3 ounces)

1½ teaspoons chopped fresh rosemary, or ¾ teaspoon dried

½ cup coarsely chopped walnuts

White pepper

3–4 SERVINGS OR 12 APPETIZER PORTIONS

1. Preheat oven to 450°F. Lightly grease a 15-inch pizza pan. Set aside.

2. Place ¾ cup of warm water in a small bowl. Stir in yeast with a wooden spoon and let rest until yeast begins to bubble, about 5 minutes.

3. Combine the flours, sugar, salt, and pepper in a separate large bowl. Make a well in the flour mixture, and add the yeast mixture and 2 tablespoons of the oil. Stir with a wooden spoon until well combined. Transfer dough to a clean, lightly floured work surface and knead gently 20 times.

4. Lightly oil a large bowl with remaining ⅛ teaspoon of oil. Transfer dough to the oiled bowl and cover with plastic wrap. Leave dough at room temperature and let rise until double in size, about 45 minutes. Punch down the dough. Transfer dough to a lightly floured, clean work surface, and roll out to a 13-inch circle. Transfer to prepared pizza pan; build up edges slightly.

5. Bake the crust for approximately 10 minutes or until it just begins to brown. Cover the crust with apple, cheeses, rosemary, walnuts, and white pepper to taste. Bake an additional 10 to 12 minutes, or until edges are lightly browned.

PICK YOUR OWN

CHAMPLAIN ORCHARDS

6 MILES

WOOD'S CIDER MILL

Wood's Cider Mill and Farm is located on 170 rolling acres in Weathersfield and has been in the Wood family since 1798. Over the years the owners have raised farm animals, produced corn, oats, apples, maple syrup, and honey, as well as run a sawmill.

When the demand for lumber declined in the 1880s, the old sawmill was converted to a cider mill.

Today, the family supplements apples grown on the farm with fruit from several local orchards to make their apple products. McIntosh apples are used for the boiled cider and cider jelly, while a blend of Roxbury Russets and Baldwins are used for the drinking cider. The apples go from a bin or truck through a washer/

brusher, then up a conveyor to a grinder. From the grinder, they go to a hopper, and then to the press cloth. A pressing takes fewer than 30 minutes on the mill's small press and two to three hours on the big press, which produces 200 gallons of cider per pressing. Production is limited to September through November, when apples are ripe and at their peak. The business produces and sells four main products; cider jelly,

maple syrup, boiled cider, and cinnamon cider syrup, which is a delicious blend of half maple syrup and half boiled cider complemented by a stick of cinnamon.

This hardworking family continues to carry on the traditions started by their ancestors so many years ago. They raise and sell lamb, beef, chicken, and garden products as well as hay, making the most of everything the land has to offer.

Harvest Stuffed Squash with Apples and Cranberries

In the fall, the Woods live on the squash that they have grown. They prefer the simple ease of baking the squash but are always looking for ways to dress up the vegetable. Here is baked winter squash, all dressed up!

2–3 small buttercup or medium acorn squash

1 large apple, such as Cortland, peeled, cored, and chopped

¼ cup boiled cider, preferably Wood's Cider Mill (see Note)

½ cup chopped walnuts

⅓ cup golden brown sugar, packed, or pure maple syrup

½ cup fresh or dried cranberries

Salt and freshly ground black pepper

Unsalted butter

4–6 SERVINGS

1. Preheat oven to 400°F. Lightly butter a baking sheet; set aside.

2. Wash and cut squash in half lengthwise and remove the seeds and stringy portions with a spoon. Place cut sides down on the prepared baking sheet and bake until squash is fork tender, about 45 to 60 minutes.

3. Meanwhile, combine the chopped apple, cider, walnuts, sugar, and cranberries in a medium saucepan over medium heat. Simmer mixture. Reduce heat to low and continue to cook for an additional 10 minutes or until apples are tender.

4. When the squash is baked and cooled slightly, keeping skins intact, scoop out the squash flesh and put in a large mixing bowl. Mash with an old-fashioned masher or handheld mixer until desired consistency is reached. Season with salt and pepper to taste.

5. Add the apple mixture to the squash and gently mix together, combining well. Spoon mixture evenly back into squash shells. Place a pat of butter on top of each squash shell, return to the oven, and bake for 5 minutes or until heated through.

Note: Boiled cider is concentrated cider with no sweeteners or preservatives. To make your own, boil 2 cups of unpasteurized fresh cider until reduced to ¼ cup.

late. Milk
$2.95
$4.60
1.00 bottle deposit

Whipping Cream.

STRAFFORD ORGANIC
CREAMERY
at
Rockbottom Farm
Strafford, Vermont
05072

Grade A
Certified Organic Milk
from our cows,
bottled on our farm
in Strafford, Vermont.

"Know Better Milk"

VERMONT
ORGANIC
CERTIFIED

32 fl. oz. (946 mL)
Plant #50-28
Wash & Return for Deposit

STRAFFORD ORGANIC
CREAMERY
at
Rockbottom Farm
Strafford, Vermont
05072

Grade A
Certified Organic Milk
from our cows,
bottled on our farm
in Strafford, Vermont.

"Know Better Milk"

VERMONT
ORGANIC
CERTIFIED

32 fl. oz. (946 mL)
Plant #50-28
Wash & Return for Deposit

Milk
art $3.30

a gallon.... $4.59
1.00 bottle deposit

Chevre $12.00 / lb.

Skim   2%   Creamline
                  (unhomogenized whole)
1%   Whole   ½ & ½

Stuffed French Toast

The Gables is an 18-room country inn located in Stowe, one of the greatest ski and summer resort towns in the United States. The guest rooms vary in size from cozy to special-occasion rooms that include a fireplace and jacuzzi. The Gables Inn is known not only for lovely accommodations but also for the delicious food they serve, especially at breakfast. Breakfast is complimentary to all lodging guests, but the public is also welcome.

At a breakfast restaurant, the most important ingredient in the kitchen is eggs. The Gables Inn is dependent on the incredibly fresh eggs provided by the Adams family of Mt. Mansfield Poultry Farm.

2 (8-ounce) packages cream cheese, softened

¼ cup molasses

½ cup walnuts, chopped into small pieces

6 eggs, beaten

¼ cup whole milk

1 teaspoon ground cinnamon

⅛ teaspoon nutmeg, or to taste

½ teaspoon pure vanilla extract

1 loaf cinnamon raisin bread, cut into ½-inch-thick slices and ends discarded

Unsalted butter

Confectioners' sugar

6 SERVINGS

1. Place the cream cheese in the bowl of an electric mixer. Mix until soft, smooth, and fluffy, scraping the sides of the bowl as necessary. Slowly mix in the molasses; the mixture should end up a mocha color. Fold in the walnuts with a rubber spatula, and set aside.

2. Whisk together the eggs, milk, cinnamon, nutmeg, and vanilla in a large bowl. Set aside.

3. Spread the cream cheese mixture onto 6 slices of bread with a rubber spatula. The cream cheese layer should be ¼- to ½-inch thick, higher in the middle and lower near the edges. Top each with a second slice of bread.

4. Meanwhile, melt a pat of butter over medium heat in a large nonstick skillet or on a griddle. Dip both sides of each sandwich quickly into the egg mixture. Cook on griddle until brown, turning sandwich once, about 3 minutes per side. Stuffing should be warm and oozing slightly from the bread.

5. Wipe out skillet or griddle and continue to make sandwiches in the same way until the bread and batter are used, adding more butter as needed.

6. Slice each sandwich diagonally with a sharp knife. Place 2 half-sandwiches on a plate and sprinkle with confectioners' sugar. Serve at once.

Churchill House Cottage Cheese Pancakes

A specialty of the Churchill House for over 40 years, every ingredient used in this recipe is produced in Vermont.

4 free-range eggs

1 cup cottage cheese, small curd

½ cup all-purpose flour, preferably King Arthur

6 tablespoons unsalted butter, melted, plus more for greasing the skillet

Pure maple syrup, preferably Vermont-made

3–4 SERVINGS

1. Preheat oven to 200°F. Lightly grease an ovenproof platter, and set aside.

2. Beat the eggs in a medium bowl, and stir in cottage cheese. Add flour and mix until just blended but still lumpy. Add butter and stir gently to combine.

3. Meanwhile, melt a pat of butter in a large nonstick skillet or on a griddle over medium heat. Pour batter by ¼ cupfuls onto the skillet, spacing the pancakes apart.

4. Cook pancakes until the edges are light golden brown and bubbles form on top, about 2 minutes. Turn pancakes over and cook until the bottoms are light golden brown. (The pancakes should be crispy outside but creamy on the inside.)

5. Continue making the pancakes in the same way until all of the batter is used. Place cooked pancakes on the prepared platter in the preheated oven to keep warm. Serve with warm maple syrup.

French Toast à la Tucker Hill

Loved by skiers, summer guests, and fall foliage seekers alike, this breakfast classic is one of the inn's most popular entrées. For variation, add 1 teaspoon of cinnamon and serve with warmed apple slices.

4 SERVINGS

3 farm-fresh eggs

1 cup half-and-half

2 tablespoons honey, preferably locally harvested, slightly warm, or pure maple syrup, preferably Vermont-made

Pinch of salt

8 slices of day-old rustic bread (our favorite is La Panciata's Panne Toscano baked in Northfield, VT), cut into ½-inch-thick slices

Unsalted butter

2 bananas, sliced

Chopped walnuts

Confectioners' sugar

Pure maple syrup, preferably Vermont-made

1. Preheat oven to 400°F.

2. Whisk together the eggs, half-and-half, honey, and salt in a medium bowl until well combined.

3. Place the bread slices in a shallow baking dish in a single layer. Pour batter over bread and soak 1 minute. Turn the bread over with tongs, and soak the other side for about 1 more minute. Set slices on a rack for a few moments to drain any excess batter.

4. Meanwhile, melt a pat of butter in a large nonstick skillet or on a griddle over medium heat. Add bread slices and cook until golden brown, turning slices over once, about 3 minutes per side. Place slices directly onto the rack of the preheated oven, and bake for 5 minutes. The slices will turn to a gentle crisp on the outside but remain soft in the center.

5. Wipe out skillet and continue to make slices in the same way until bread and batter are used.

6. Place 2 slices on each plate and top with bananas, walnuts, confectioners' sugar, and a generous drizzle of warm maple syrup, if desired. Serve at once.

One of the Mad River Valley's oldest country inns, the Tucker Hill Inn is quietly nestled on 14 acres of delightful woodland and mature perennial gardens. It was built as an inn in 1948 to service the "new" Mad River Glen and Sugarbush ski areas. The building is full of stone fireplaces, beams, nooks, and crannies. These details were the work of the original owner, the late Francis Martin, whose spirit is said to protect the inn to this day. Beautifully renovated in recent years to retain its charm and character, the inn offers deluxe accommodations, including private baths, wireless Internet, red clay tennis courts, and an outdoor swimming pool. It also offers direct access to a wide range of hiking and cycling trails, including the renowned Long and Catamount Trails.

Searching for appropriately dense bread for the inn's French Toast à la Tucker Hill, one of the cooks happened to use a loaf that had been picked up for another use at a local grocery store. As luck would have it, that batch was the best French toast the inn's kitchen had ever produced. Happily, the loaf had been made just 20 miles away in Northfield by a newly established Italian bakery, La Panciata. The local connection was made. Tucker Hill also works with other area farmers and vendors who deliver everything from local cheeses and maple syrups to fresh fruits and vegetables.

Recipe from LIBERTY HILL FARM

Cheese Scones

Liberty Hill Farm is a working dairy farm that also provides farm-vacation lodging and meals to guests. Three generations of the Kennett family welcome their guests to participate in barn chores, explore the fields and forest, swim in the river, snowshoe across the meadow, or chase kittens in the hayloft! Dinner and breakfast are served in the 1825 farmhouse with local farm-fresh products featured in season.

A guest from England gave this very special cheese scone recipe to the Kennett family. The guest, her husband, daughter, and son-in-law happened upon the farm one evening during fall foliage season. The visitors from England joined guests from Colorado, Connecticut, and Virginia that day. After dinner, the English guest decided that she would share her very special recipe for "proper" British scones. She informed everyone in the household that she would demonstrate how to make them. So they made batches and batches of scones that night. They laughed all evening as each guest rolled and cut out their scones with a jelly glass and topped them with cheddar cheese. When the men came in from the night milking of the cows, the ladies were all sitting around the kitchen table eating scones with butter and jam . . . at midnight! It was a wonderful, fun-filled evening.

2 cups all-purpose flour

½ cup cold unsalted butter, cut into pieces

2 teaspoons baking powder

½ teaspoon baking soda

⅓ cup sugar

Salt

1 cup sharp shredded cheddar cheese, preferably Cabot, plus more for topping (about 5 ounces)

1 egg

¼ cup whole milk

8 SCONES

1. Preheat oven to 425°F. Lightly butter a baking sheet. Set aside.

2. Place the flour, butter, baking powder, and baking soda in a medium bowl, and combine with your fingers until the mixture resembles wet sand. Add the sugar and a pinch of salt and combine well with a fork. Add cheese and continue to mix well.

3. Whisk together the egg and milk in a small bowl, and set aside 1 tablespoon for an egg wash. Slowly add the rest of the egg mixture to the flour mixture in a steady stream, stirring with a fork, until a dough forms and just holds together.

4. Turn the dough out on a clean, lightly floured work surface, and knead it a few times. Roll or pat out the dough to ¾- to 1-inch thick. Do not overwork the dough.

5. Cut out dough rounds using a 3-inch round juice glass or biscuit cutter, lightly dipping the cutter in flour before each cut. Place the rounds on the prepared baking sheet. Brush tops with 1 tablespoon reserved egg wash and sprinkle with additional cheese. Bake until the scones are golden brown, about 15 minutes. Remove from the oven and cool on racks before serving.

Taylor Farm is a 100-year-old family-operated dairy farm located in the Green Mountains of Londonderry, Vermont. The owners, Jonathan and Kate Wright, have retained the name in honor of the family of the original owners, who were very kind to them. Jon was raised in New York City and spent summers in South Londonderry after his parents bought land in the area. He first worked on Taylor Farm when he was 17 years old. In 1989, Jon and his wife settled in the area and purchased part of the Taylor property in 2002. The rest of the land was put into a conservation trust through the hard work of many committed individuals. Realizing that their 45-cow dairy would not support them financially, the Wrights looked for ways to add more value to the milk. Thus began their cheese-making business.

Every morning Jon awakens at 3:30 a.m. to begin pumping milk into the cheese vat. He milks about 40 Holsteins twice a day. Even with his busy schedule, Jon finds time to show visitors around the barn and cheese house. The farm now offers sleigh rides in the winter, a seasonal farm stand, lodging, which is available in a small house on the grounds, and educational presentations for the farm's daily guests.

The Wrights handcraft award-winning Gouda cheeses with milk from their herd, producing 1,200 pounds of cheese every week. After a minimum of two months of aging, the wheels of cheese are ready for the table. During the aging process, the wheels must be turned by hand each week to maintain even texture throughout — no small task! The Gouda is available in a variety of flavors, such as maple smoked, cumin, caraway seed, and chipotle pepper.

The farm is dedicated to raising cows without growth hormones. The animals graze in pastures free from pesticides, herbicides, and chemical fertilizer. The cows feed on hay from the farm's own fields and eat custom blended grain.

Taylor Farm sells its Gouda-style cheese from the farm, as well as at retail outlets in Vermont. Jon has even established an account in midtown Manhattan — the city in which he grew up. Taylor Farm also enjoys long-standing relationships with local chefs, who were early enthusiastic supporters. The Wrights enjoy the close relationships they are able to maintain with smaller accounts. Many of these customers have been to the farm either to visit or to purchase products and have a true understanding of how the business operates. Dedicated to preserving a largely forgotten way of life, Jon and Kate enjoy sharing their cheese-making skills with visitors. They encourage people to visit their farm and cheese business and see firsthand their sustainable farming practices.

Smoked Gouda, Sun-dried Tomato, and Parsley Muffins

Taylor Farm's Maple Smoked Gouda is a first-place winner in the smoked cheese category at The American Cheese Society's competition. Native maple wood gives the cheese, and the muffins, a delicious, mellow flavor.

10 MUFFINS

2 cups all-purpose flour

2 teaspoons baking powder

1 tablespoon dry mustard

½ teaspoon salt

¼ teaspoon freshly ground white pepper

1 cup whole milk

2 eggs

4 tablespoons unsalted butter, melted

3 tablespoons sun-dried tomatoes in oil, drained and minced

¼ cup chopped flat-leaf parsley

1 cup shredded maple smoked Gouda (about 4 ounces)

1. Preheat oven to 375°F. Grease a muffin pan or line it with paper muffin cups.

2. Mix the flour, baking powder, mustard, salt, and pepper in a large bowl. Whisk together milk, eggs, butter, tomatoes, and parsley in a separate large bowl. Add the milk mixture to the flour mixture, stirring until almost combined. Gently fold in the cheese with a rubber spatula; the mixture should still look lumpy.

3. Spoon the batter into the prepared muffin pan. Bake until muffins are golden brown and firm to the touch, about 25 minutes. A toothpick inserted into the center of a muffin should come out clean. Transfer muffins to a rack to cool before serving.

Crowley Eggs au Gratin

Few cheeses originated in the United States; most recipes were brought here by immigrants. Crowley Cheese is one of the few originals. It is similar to cheddar and grouped with cheeses such as Monterey Jack under the cheddar umbrella.

The Crowley Cheese Factory is a small, 30 feet by 30 feet, three-story building built in 1882. Designated as a National Historic Place, it is the oldest continuously operated cheese producer in the United States. The entire production process is completely "human" powered. Only a few hundred pounds of cheese are made each day, and the process is exactly the same as when the factory was established. There is no automatic stirring equipment or other devices. By comparison, Vermont's largest cheddar producer can make 75,000 to 100,000 pounds of cheese a day in their factory.

Crowley Cheese's method of preparation differs from English-style cheddar. Their variations allow for a shorter period of time to develop the cheese's robust flavor — this contributes to a creamier, smoother taste.

This delicious recipe was the brainchild of a friend and was one of the most popular offerings in the Crowley recipe book.

4 SERVINGS

¼ cup unsalted butter

2 tablespoons flour

½ teaspoon salt

⅛ teaspoon freshly ground black pepper

1⅓ cups whole milk

1 cup shredded Crowley cheese (about 4 ounces), or substitute an extra-sharp cheddar

8 farm-fresh eggs

Minced parsley

1. Preheat oven to 350°F. Lightly butter 4 ramekins, and set them aside.

2. In a medium saucepan, melt the butter over medium heat. Whisk in flour, salt, and pepper. Gradually whisk in milk. Continue to cook, whisking frequently, until flour mixture thickens. Add the cheese and continue to cook until cheese has melted and mixture is well combined. Divide the sauce equally into prepared ramekins.

3. Carefully beat two eggs into each ramekin. Cover with foil and bake in the oven for 15 to 20 minutes or until eggs are set in the middle. Garnish with parsley.

Recipe from SIMON PEARCE RESTAURANT

Cheddar Cheese Quiche

This is a great dish to serve as an appetizer or as a light lunch with a mixed green salad. The quiche features one of Vermont's finest local products — cheddar cheese.

CRUST

1½ cups all-purpose flour

⅛ teaspoon salt

½ cup unsalted chilled butter, cut into pieces

1 egg

FILLING

8 eggs

2 cups heavy cream

¾ teaspoon salt

¼ teaspoon freshly ground black pepper

1½ pounds extra sharp cheddar cheese, grated (about 6 cups)

8 bacon slices, cut into ½-inch pieces and cooked crisp

1. Make the crust: Combine the flour, salt, and butter in the work bowl of an electric mixer. Mix on low speed until butter is well incorporated.

2. Add the egg and ⅓ cup of ice water and mix until the dough forms. It should be soft, but not sticky. If the dough becomes crumbly, slowly add a few more drops of water at a time, until dough holds together. Transfer the dough to a lightly floured, clean work surface, and roll out to a 10½-inch round. Transfer to a 9½-inch tart pan, trimming excess dough to leave a ½-inch overhang, and then crimp the edges of the crust. Refrigerate the dough in the tart pan for at least 1 hour.

3. Meanwhile, make the filling: In a large bowl, whisk together the eggs, cream, salt, and pepper. Set aside.

4. Preheat oven to 400°F. Line a baking sheet with parchment paper, and set aside.

5. Remove the pie crust from refrigerator. Sprinkle a third of the cheese evenly into the bottom of the pie crust. Sprinkle the bacon on top of the cheese. Sprinkle the remaining cheese on top.

6. Create a well in the middle of the quiche and slowly fill with the egg mixture. Shake the quiche gently to let it settle.

7. Place the quiche on the prepared baking sheet and transfer to the oven. Bake for 15 minutes, then reduce the oven to 300°F and bake for 1½ hours or until filling is just set. Allow quiche to cool slightly in the pie plate on a rack before serving.

Potato, Bacon, and Egg Tart

The potato, bacon, and egg tart is of Alsatian origin. Served with a salad of bitter greens and a light vinaigrette, it is perfect for a fall or winter brunch. The tart can be made a few hours ahead and served at room temperature. It may also be reheated just before serving.

8–12 SERVINGS

1 package (2 sheets) puff pastry dough

5 medium russet potatoes, peeled, cut into ⅛-inch slices, and placed in cold water

Salt and freshly ground black pepper

12 slices of bacon cut into ⅛-inch pieces, cooked crisp

3 tablespoons chopped parsley

5 hard-cooked eggs, thinly sliced

½ cup crème fraîche

1 egg

2 tablespoons milk

1. Thaw puff pastry at room temperature according to package directions. Once thawed, unfold the dough onto a lightly floured, clean work surface. Roll out 1 piece of puff pastry to ⅛-inch thickness, line a springform pan with the dough, and chill in the refrigerator for 10 minutes. Meanwhile, preheat the oven to 400°F.

2. Drain the potatoes and place on paper towels to dry. Make an overlapping layer of potatoes in the bottom of the pan. Season the potatoes with salt and pepper to taste. Sprinkle the bacon and parsley over the potatoes. Then layer egg slices and spread crème fraîche evenly over the top of the eggs until smooth. Top with a final layer of potatoes and season with salt and pepper to taste. Roll out second piece of puff pastry to ⅛-inch thickness and place on top of the tart.

3. Moisten the edges of dough with water and seal. Whisk together egg and milk to make an egg wash. Vent the top of the tart and brush with egg wash. Bake for 20 minutes and then lower the temperature to 350°F and bake for an additional 40 minutes. Turn off the oven and let the tart remain in the oven for an additional 10 minutes. Remove the tart from the oven and allow to cool for 30 minutes before serving.

THE GRAFTON VILLAGE CHEESE COMPANY

In the beginning, Grafton dairy farmers gathered together to make their surplus milk into cheese. Cooperative cheese-making was used to turn an abundance of fresh, creamy milk into food that could be stored for longer periods of time. Then the Grafton Cooperative Cheese Factory was established in 1892. It was a little wooden two-story building that was located near the edge of the Saxton River. On the first floor was a cheese cooperative and on the second floor there was reportedly a dance hall. Area farmers joined the cooperative and contributed their unsold milk to the cheese-making efforts. The cooperative's cheese makers gave the cheese back to the farmers.

In 1912 the plant burned down. Little is known of the period between the fire and the construction of the new cheese company in the mid-1960s. The Windham Foundation (a nonprofit established in 1963 to support rural indigenous businesses in Vermont and rejuvenate Grafton to its original state) restored the cheese company; steel vats replaced the old wooden versions, and a new era began for the town.

The company buys mostly Jersey cow milk from about 38 Vermont farms, primarily located in southern Vermont. They are all part of the Agri-Mark family of farmers, a cooperative of dairy producers with one of the toughest milk-quality standards on the market; none use rBST or synthetic bovine growth hormone. All of the farmers have a standing invitation to visit and tour the cheese company. Grafton's production manager has come to know most of the farmers and makes an annual trip to the farms with finished cheddar.

Grafton Cheddar is an award-winning, 100 percent natural, handcrafted, small-batch cheese. Scott Fletcher, the head cheese maker at Grafton, has been "teaching milk to be cheese" for almost 40 years. He and his crew make about 5,200 pounds of cheese a day, using about 10 pounds of milk for every pound of cheddar. Scott believes that the Vermont Jersey cow milk is the best there is for cheddar — high butterfat and high protein. Scott believes that the keys to good flavor are time, temperature, and acidity. He regulates the temperature at which the milk is heated, uses a culture that develops slowly during the initial stages to control the acidity, and gives the cheese a nice long aging period. His cheddar ages naturally in cold rooms for one to six years before going to market.

Those at Grafton believe in what the French call *terroir,* or "taste of the earth" — their cheddar has distinct qualities because of where it is produced and where the cows are raised, here in Vermont. Grafton Cheddar is enjoyed at restaurants, cooperatives, colleges, retail outlets, and in healthy snack programs at many area schools. Chefs love to cook with Grafton cheese, enjoying its creamy texture, good melting qualities, and robust cheddar flavor.

Scott Fletcher's Cheese Dream Sandwich

Scott Fletcher, master cheese maker at Grafton Village Cheese Company, has been handcrafting rich Vermont milk into cheddar cheese for more than 40 years. Enjoy one of Scott's favorite snacks; combine with fruit to make a delightfully hearty lunch.

4 slices of rustic country bread

4 ounces of sharp cheddar cheese, preferably Grafton Cheddar, sliced, or enough to cover 2 slices of bread

Freshly ground white pepper

2 farm-fresh eggs

2 tablespoons milk

4 tablespoons unsalted butter

Pure maple syrup, preferably Vermont-made

2 SANDWICHES

1. Arrange 2 bread slices on a clean work surface. Top with cheese, dividing equally. Season with pepper to taste. Top with remaining bread slices.

2. Whisk eggs and milk together in a shallow bowl.

3. Meanwhile, melt the butter in a medium skillet over medium heat. Dip sandwiches in egg mixture and shake gently to remove excess batter. Grill sandwiches until golden brown on each side. Cover the pan for 1 or 2 minutes at the end, to help melt the cheese. Transfer to a cutting board, and cut each sandwich in half or into 4 wedges. Serve with maple syrup for dipping.

Caramelized Onion, Grafton Cheddar, and Apple Tart

This tart recipe was developed by award-winning chef Kathy Cary of Lilly's & LaPeche Restaurant in Louisville, Kentucky, during the 2005 American Cheese Society conference. She is renowned for her support of the local farmers and agriculture in her region of Kentucky.

DOUGH

2 cups all-purpose flour

1 teaspoon salt

1¼ cups cold unsalted butter, diced

FILLING

6 tablespoons unsalted butter

3 large onions, peeled and cut thinly into half-circles

3 Granny Smith apples, peeled and chopped

1 lemon slice, seeds removed

2 teaspoons fresh thyme

¾ cup green pepper jelly, warmed

1½ pounds sharp cheddar cheese, preferably Grafton 4-year-old Cheddar, grated (about 6 cups)

Freshly ground white pepper

20 APPETIZER SERVINGS, OR 60–80 HORS D'OEUVRE PIECES

1. Make the dough: Place the flour, salt, and butter in the bowl of a food processor and process until the mixture resembles coarse meal. Continue to process; slowly add ½ cup of water in a steady stream until dough holds together, about 30 seconds. Turn the dough out onto a clean work surface and form into a ball. Wrap in plastic and refrigerate for 2 hours.

2. Make the filling: Melt 4 tablespoons of the butter in a large skillet over medium-low heat. Add the onions and cook, stirring frequently, until golden brown, about 20 minutes. Transfer to a bowl and set aside.

3. In the same pan, melt the remaining 2 tablespoons of butter over medium heat. Add the apples and lemon slice and sauté until apples are fork tender. Season with thyme, remove from heat, and set aside.

4. Preheat oven to 400°F. Lightly dust a clean work surface with flour and roll out dough into either a large 18- by 12-inch rectangle or two smaller 9- by 6-inch rectangles. Place dough on a parchment-lined baking pan. Brush the crust with the jelly. Layer with half of the grated cheese, all of the onion mixture, and the apple mixture, then sprinkle the remaining cheese over the top. Adjust seasonings with pepper.

5. Bake on the top rack of the oven until the crust is golden brown and the cheese has melted, 16 to 20 minutes. Remove from oven and allow to cool completely before cutting. Garnish with additional grated cheese and thyme, if desired.

Mini Frittatas with Zucchini, Goat Cheese, and Tomatoes

Does' Leap, located in Bakersfield, is a small, certified organic farm that produces a variety of fresh and aged goat cheeses. Their ongoing relationships with many local chefs have grown along with the business. Many restaurants now showcase various Does' Leap cheeses on their menus.

Does' Leap's owners love to eat well from their farm. When the garden is in full swing, this is one of their favorite dishes.

12 MINI FRITTATAS

1¾ cups grated zucchini

Salt

2 eggs

¼ cup whole wheat flour

1 cup grated cheddar cheese (about 4 ounces)

2 garlic cloves, peeled and crushed

⅛ teaspoon salt

⅛ teaspoon freshly ground black pepper

¼ cup fresh goat cheese, crumbled (about 2 ounces), or to taste

¼ cup seeded and minced ripe tomato (about ½ of one medium)

1½ tablespoons minced fresh basil

1. Preheat oven to 400°F. Lightly oil and flour a mini muffin tin; set aside.

2. Place zucchini in a colander and sprinkle lightly with salt. Place colander in a bowl, and set aside to drain for about 15 minutes. Place salted zucchini between double layers of paper towels and gently press down to remove any excess water.

3. Whisk the eggs in a medium bowl. Add zucchini, flour, cheddar cheese, garlic, salt, and pepper, and mix well. Spoon mixture into each muffin cup, just even with the rim, and sprinkle with crumbled goat cheese. Bake in the oven until the edges are crisp and brown and frittatas are set, about 12 minutes. Carefully remove from oven and evenly top with tomatoes and basil. Return to oven and bake until tomatoes have heated through, about 1 minute.

Grafton Cheddar Ale Soup

America loves cheddar for snacking and cooking. This soup is rich in Grafton Cheddar's complex flavors. Croutons, crackers, or crusty breads are a perfect accompaniment.

5 tablespoons unsalted butter

⅓ cup all-purpose flour

1 (12-ounce) bottle of ale, preferably Vermont-made

1½ teaspoons minced garlic

1½ cups low-sodium chicken stock

1 quart heavy cream, or 2 cups milk and 2 cups cream

1 bay leaf

1 tablespoon Worcestershire sauce

½ teaspoon dry mustard

¼ teaspoon white pepper, or to taste

4 cups shredded cheddar cheese, preferably 2- or 3-year-old Grafton Cheddar, (about 1 pound)

Salt

5 bacon slices, cooked and crumbled (optional)

Croutons (optional)

Chopped chives (optional)

8 SERVINGS

1. Make a roux: Melt the butter in a medium stockpot over medium-low heat, sprinkle in the flour, and cook, stirring frequently, until light brown and thickened, about 5 minutes. Do not let the roux burn. Remove from heat.

2. Meanwhile, bring ale to a rapid boil in a medium saucepan over medium-high heat.

3. Return the roux to medium heat and add the ale, whisking constantly until well combined and thickened. Add the garlic, stock, cream, bay leaf, Worcestershire sauce, mustard, and pepper, and bring to a simmer, stirring constantly. Add the cheese by handfuls and continue to simmer, stirring frequently, until the cheese has melted and is well incorporated. Season with salt to taste.

4. Remove bay leaf and discard. Ladle into 8 small soup bowls and garnish with bacon, croutons, and chives, if desired. Serve at once.

Root Vegetable Chowder with Vermont Maple Smoked Cheddar

The Cheese Outlet Fresh Market chooses and sells cheese for every taste, from sheep, goat, and cow's milk cheeses produced by Vermont artisans to an impressive assortment of cheeses from around the world. The head chef, Jonathan, comes from a long line of Vermont chefs. Preparing foods seasonally has never been a challenge to him; his affinity for cold-weather crops is evident in the warmth this root vegetable and cheddar chowder brings to cold winter evenings. Heavenly!

7–9 SERVINGS

½ pound bacon strips, preferably locally produced (optional)

12 thyme stems

6 rosemary stems

6 tablespoons butter, preferably Cabot

1 medium onion, preferably locally grown, peeled and diced

3 medium parsnips, peeled and diced

1–2 small turnips, preferably locally grown, peeled and diced

3 carrots, preferably locally grown, peeled and diced

½ pound fingerling potatoes, preferably locally grown, sliced

1¼ cup all-purpose flour, preferably King Arthur

3 quarts hot vegetable stock or chicken stock

8 ounces Vermont Maple Smoked Cheddar, preferably Shelburne Farms, shredded (about 2 cups)

1 cup cream

Salt and freshly ground black pepper

1. Cook the bacon in a large pot over medium-high heat until crisp, stirring occasionally and draining the fat as necessary.

2. Make a bouquet garni with the thyme and rosemary: Tie the herbs together with kitchen twine, or place them in the center of a piece of cheesecloth, gather the cloth around the thyme and rosemary, and tie with twine.

3. Reduce the heat under the bacon to medium and add the butter, onions, parsnips, turnips, carrots, potatoes, and bouquet garni. Cook for about 10 minutes, stirring frequently. Add the flour and cook for another 5 minutes over medium-low heat. Slowly whisk in the hot stock. Bring chowder to a simmer over medium heat, whisking frequently. Cook until vegetables are fork tender. Remove bouquet garni and discard.

4. Add the cheese slowly, stirring frequently. Slowly whisk in the cream. Season with salt and pepper to taste.

Recipe from HOPE FARM

Hope Farm's Corn and Cheese Chowder

With homage to the chef of the Blue Strawberry Restaurant, Hope Farm adapted his soup to include their cheese.

¼ pound bacon, coarsely chopped

4 tablespoons unsalted butter

2 pounds onions, peeled and sliced thin

2 cups fresh corn

2 tablespoons all-purpose flour

1 cup dry white wine

3 cups whole milk

1½ cups grated Hope Farm's Tomme de Brebis or Pierce Hill cheese (about 6 ounces), or substitute Asiago, fontina, Gruyère, or a combination

½ teaspoon dried sage, crumbled

1 teaspoon salt

½ teaspoon white pepper

Chopped chives

4–6 SERVINGS

1. Cook the bacon in a 5-quart stockpot or Dutch oven over medium heat until crisp, stirring occasionally. Drain the bacon drippings from the pot.

2. Add the butter, onions, and corn. Cook, stirring frequently, until vegetables are tender, about 10 minutes. Add the flour and cook for another 3 to 4 minutes over medium-low heat, stirring frequently. Slowly whisk in the wine and milk. Over medium-low heat, bring chowder to a simmer, whisking frequently. Continue to cook for about 30 to 40 minutes.

3. Add the cheese and sage and continue to cook, whisking frequently, for about 5 minutes or until cheese has melted.

4. Transfer about 3 cups of the soup to a blender and purée until smooth. Transfer the purée back into the stockpot and continue to cook over medium heat until heated through. Adjust seasonings with salt and pepper. If the soup is too thick, add more milk to taste.

5. Ladle into warm soup bowls, garnish with chives, and serve at once.

Smoked Salmon à la Cream Cheese

This is a quick and easy appetizer that can be prepared a few hours in advance.

1 loaf organic whole wheat bread, sliced, crusts removed, and quartered

Olive oil

1 (8-ounce) package cream cheese, softened at room temperature

1 cup sour cream

8 ounces smoked salmon, thinly sliced, cut into ½- by 2½-inch strips

Capers in brine, drained

Freshly ground black pepper

48 HORS D'OEUVRE PIECES

1. Preheat oven to 400°F. Place the bread squares on a baking sheet, lightly brush each side with olive oil, and toast until golden brown, 12 to 15 minutes. Remove from the oven and place on a decorative platter.

2. Meanwhile, stir together cream cheese and sour cream in a medium bowl with a wooden spoon until well combined. Transfer filling to a pastry bag fitted with a small star tip. Just before serving, pipe the cheese mixture onto the bread squares. This can also be done by spreading the mixture thinly with a small knife.

3. Loosely roll up a strip of the salmon to make a rosette (small flower) and place on top of the cheese for each quarter. Garnish with a couple of the capers in the center and sprinkle with pepper to taste.

LA PANCIATA

Glenn Loati and his wife, Lori, opened their bakery in the summer of 1992, running the business out of their home kitchen. The couple remembered how much they loved the classic Italian breads from their childhoods in Barre, Vermont. The bakeries that made those loaves had long since closed, but Glenn and Lori wanted to bring those tastes back to a new audience.

Over the years the two have stayed true to their philosophy of using only the best all-natural and/or organic ingredients to produce the finest breads possible. The bakery now offers not only the traditional Italian breads they began with but also a complete line of sliced and deli breads for retailers, restaurants, delis, and a variety of food services. Over the years, Glenn and Lori have built many relationships with local restaurants. Not only have they provided these businesses with their regular products but in some cases have worked to develop specialty breads. They bake a custom steak roll for The Spotted Cow in Waitsfield, sheet focaccia for a number of restaurants, a cranberry pecan bread for J. Morgan's in Montpelier, and a classic Italian roll made exclusively for the Mutuo Club in Barre. These creations offer customers something delicious and unique.

Crostini with Fresh Figs, Blue Cheese, Sage, and Balsamic Vinegar

The sweetness of the figs is a great counterpoint to the blue cheese. The sage adds a vibrant herbaceous note.

1 crusty baguette, cut into 24 ½-inch slices

¼ cup extra-virgin olive oil

1 pound fresh ripe figs, cut into quarters (about 2 cups)

2 tablespoons balsamic vinegar, preferably fig balsamic, if available

1 tablespoon finely chopped fresh sage

Kosher salt and freshly ground black pepper

5½ ounces blue cheese, preferably Jasper Hill Bayley Hazen (about ¾ cup)

6–8 SERVINGS, OR 24 HORS D'OEUVRE PIECES

1. Preheat the oven to 400°F.

2. Arrange the baguette slices in a single layer on a rimmed baking sheet, brush them with olive oil, and bake until lightly browned and crisped, 10 to 14 minutes. Set aside until cool.

3. Lightly toss the figs with the vinegar and sage in a medium bowl. Season to taste with salt and pepper. Spread the cheese on the baguette slices and top with the figs. Serve immediately.

Vermont-style Hush Puppies

These corn cakes are a classic southern favorite. Made with Butterworks Farm cornmeal, King Arthur flour, milk from Strafford Organic Creamery, and sour cream from Cabot, they transplant very well to Vermont soil!

1¼ cups cornmeal

1¾ cups all-purpose flour

1 tablespoon baking powder

1 tablespoon salt

Freshly ground black pepper

2 eggs

½ cup whole milk

¼ cup sour cream

¾ cup frozen corn

6 scallions, chopped

Chopped parsley

Oil for frying

Maple BBQ sauce

12–15 HUSH PUPPIES

1. Line a baking sheet with paper towels, set aside.

2. Whisk together the cornmeal, flour, baking powder, salt, and pepper to taste in a large bowl. Whisk together the eggs, milk, and sour cream in a medium bowl, then add to dry ingredients and mix well. Add corn, scallions, and parsley, and mix until just combined.

3. Pour oil into a deep skillet until it reaches 2 inches from the rim. Heat oil to 370°F. Drop batter into the hot oil ¼ cup at a time, working in batches to avoid overcrowding. Fry until golden brown, turning occasionally. With a slotted spoon, transfer the hush puppies to the prepared baking sheet to drain.

4. Serve at once with your favorite maple BBQ sauce.

Goat Cheese Cakes with Crab Apples and Cardamom Sauce

The Riverview Café is a casual hometown restaurant overlooking the Connecticut River. It offers stunning, panoramic views from the rooftop and ground-level decks as well as from the bar and the main dining room. It's difficult to find a bad seat at the Riverview Café! Chef Tristan Toleno features fresh seasonal produce and regional products from local farms. As a student at the New England Culinary Institute, he was present at the founding meeting of the Vermont Fresh Network in 1996. Chef Toleno has worked with his farm partners to find fresh ways to feature their products on his menu, which offers casual, eclectic American fare.

A version of these tangy cakes is served at the Riverview Café. The fresh creaminess of the goat cheese is balanced by the spicy, sweet complexity of the compote, while the crumb crust finishes the dish with a tiny bit of texture. The compote alone is delicious with some rustic bread and wedges of fresh goat cheese.

GOAT CHEESE CAKES

2 (8-ounce) packages plain fresh goat cheese, preferably Vermont Butter & Cheese or locally produced

1 cup unseasoned fine breadcrumbs

2 egg whites

2 teaspoons butter

COMPOTE

1 pound crab apples

1 cup pure maple syrup, preferably Vermont-made

15 cardamom pods

Zest of 1 orange

5 black peppercorns

1 tablespoon cider vinegar

½ teaspoon salt

4 SERVINGS

1. Make the goat cheese cakes: Combine the goat cheese and ¾ cup of the breadcrumbs in a medium bowl. Let the mixture sit at room temperature for about 30 minutes. Form into 8 even balls, then shape the balls into 8 round disks, about ¾-inch thick.

2. Whisk the egg whites lightly in a small bowl. Dip each disk into the egg whites and then dredge in the remaining ¼ cup of breadcrumbs, coating evenly.

3. Melt 1 teaspoon of the butter in a large skillet over medium heat. When the skillet is hot, add the cakes and lightly brown on one side. Flip cakes over, add the remaining 1 teaspoon of butter and lightly brown the other side.

4. Make the compote: Simmer apples, maple syrup, cardamom, zest, peppercorns, vinegar, and salt in a large saucepan over low heat for about 1 hour, whisking occasionally.

5. For a smooth texture, pass sauce through a food mill or fine strainer. If you find that the sauce is too watery, transfer to a clean nonstick pan and simmer, whisking constantly, until it thickens slightly. Taste and adjust seasonings.

6. To serve, drizzle the warm compote over and around the goat cheese cakes.

Hemingway's Fallen Soufflé of Vermont Goat and Cheddar Cheeses

Originally, this flavorful soufflé was presented as a cheese course without the greens and vinaigrette, but it didn't meet with much success. When it was transformed into an appetizer and served with a light salad, it became a hit. A salad of baby lamb's lettuce tossed in garlic oil and salt and pepper completes the presentation of this elegant soufflé. Garnish the salad with a few spears of endive drizzled with Hemingway's Honey Balsamic Vinaigrette on page 211.

8 APPETIZER SERVINGS

1 tablespoon ground almonds

¼ tablespoon ground fennel seed

¾ cup plus 3 tablespoons whole milk

2 tablespoons unsalted butter, preferably locally produced

2½ tablespoons all-purpose flour

Salt

7½ ounces soft fresh goat cheese, preferably locally produced, crumbled

2 ounces sharp cheddar cheese, preferably Cabot, shredded (about ½ cup)

3 farm-fresh egg yolks

4 farm-fresh egg whites

1. Preheat oven to 375°F. Lightly butter eight 5- to 6-ounce ovenproof ramekins, sprinkle the insides with almonds and fennel seeds, rotating dishes to coat, and set aside.

2. Bring the milk to a boil in a medium saucepan over medium-high heat. Remove from heat and set aside.

3. Melt the butter in a medium skillet over medium-low heat. Add the flour and cook for 5 minutes, whisking constantly. Increase heat to medium. Slowly whisk in the milk and bring to a boil for 1 minute, whisking often. Remove pan from heat. Add a pinch of salt and both cheeses. Mix until cheese has melted and is smooth. Lightly whisk in the yolks. Set aside to cool.

4. Beat the egg whites in a medium bowl until stiff but not dry. With a rubber spatula, fold half of the whites into the egg yolk mixture. Gently fold in the remaining egg whites. Spoon mixture evenly into the prepared ramekins and place in a large shallow metal baking pan. Add enough warm water to come halfway up the sides of ramekins and place gently in the oven. Bake for 45 to 50 minutes, or until soufflés begin to puff, turn golden brown on top, and softly set in the middle. Serve immediately.

Note: You can store the baked soufflés covered in the refrigerator for a few days. Before serving, use a knife to unmold and bake on a pan in 300°F oven for 10 to 12 minutes.

HEMINGWAY'S RESTAURANT

Hemingway's Restaurant opened its doors in 1982, offering an American interpretation of fine dining in the European tradition. The owners, Linda and Ted Fondulas, work together on the food and wine selections and constantly consult one another on business issues. In the day-to-day running of the restaurant, Ted oversees the kitchen and finances, and Linda manages the dining room, as well as maintenance and marketing. Linda and Ted have developed their own style of modern cuisine, depending on local farmers for indigenous animals and produce at a time when most food products were purchased through major national distributors. They used locally raised rabbits and pheasant and were the first in Vermont to serve farm-raised venison.

When the restaurant opened, the owners knew of no farm in Vermont that raised game birds, one of the items they wanted to include on the menu. Each week the couple would drive an hour and a half to Brattleboro, Vermont, near the border, to meet a farmer from Massachusetts. As the trunk was loaded with pheasants, they would laugh, thinking it looked as if they were smuggling contraband. Several years later, their Massachusetts connection sold breeding stock to a Vermont farmer with whom Linda and Ted continue to do business to this day.

Hemingway's has also served farm-raised venison for many years. Linda and Ted's enthusiasm for the meat helped procure support from the Commissioner of the Vermont Department of Agriculture for the state's venison farmers. During the spring of 1990, Hemingway's hosted their first farmers' dinner. The tasty farm-raised venison they served was very well received. Linda and Ted believe that this gathering was an inspiration for the Agriculture Department to pursue the idea of the Vermont Fresh Network.

Linda and Ted were also early supporters of soft Vermont cheeses, such as Camembert and Brie.

Although it took a few years for the market to catch up with their enthusiasm, today their restaurant uses goat cheese and cultured butter made by the Vermont Butter & Cheese Company daily.

Hemingway's menu continues to feature as many Vermont products as possible, from game birds to lamb, as well as cheeses and, of course, seasonal local organic produce. Many local farmers contribute to their ever-changing menu. Locally grown perfectly fits their style of cuisine, and the restaurant is such a good customer that local farmers often raise or grow special requests for the restaurant's seasonal offerings. Linda and Ted strive to preserve a close relationship with all the hardworking people who produce the food that Hemingway's is proud to serve.

Recipe from BAILEY'S RESTAURANT AT BOLTON VALLEY RESORT

Goat Cheese Bread Pudding

This dish is a delicious accompaniment to the Rosemary Seared Lamb Loin on page 159.

2 cups whole milk

5 farm-fresh eggs

1½ tablespoons fresh, finely chopped rosemary

Salt and freshly ground black pepper

1 loaf of ciabatta bread, cut into ½-inch cubes

1 cup crumbled fresh goat cheese (4–6 ounces)

6–8 SERVINGS

1. Preheat oven to 350°F. Lightly grease a 9- by 9-inch or 11- by 7-inch baking dish. Set aside.

2. Whisk together the milk, eggs, rosemary, and salt and pepper to taste in a medium bowl.

3. Place bread cubes in another medium bowl. Sprinkle with the cheese and drizzle with the milk mixture, making sure to coat all the bread cubes well. Allow the bread cubes to soak for 5 to 10 minutes, until bread is moist.

4. Pour bread mixture into the prepared dish and bake in the oven for 20 to 35 minutes, until the top is golden brown and gives resistance to the touch, or a toothpick inserted into the center comes out clean. Remove from the oven and let cool for a few minutes before serving.

Baked Macaroni and Cheese, Vermont Style

This recipe is the delicious creation of the Putney Inn's nationally recognized chef, Ann Cooper. The culinary secret that makes this dish truly sensational and distinguishes Putney Inn's mac and cheese from others is the high-quality cheddar cheese. A rich tangy cheddar such as Cabot gives this classic casserole a more sophisticated flavor. The nest of onions is another unique addition. Remember to be patient; melt the onions slowly until they become paste-like. The end result is truly worth the wait.

1 pound elbow macaroni

3 tablespoons unsalted butter

1 medium sweet onion, peeled and sliced thin

1 large garlic clove, peeled and minced

¼ teaspoon dry mustard

1 teaspoon Cajun spice, preferably Paul Prudhomme's Poultry Magic

1½ cups heavy cream

Salt and freshly ground white pepper

2½ cups grated extra sharp cheddar cheese (about 10 ounces)

Minced parsley

6–8 SERVINGS

1. Preheat oven to 350°F. Lightly butter a 3-quart shallow baking dish; set aside.

2. In a large pot of salted boiling water, cook macaroni until just al dente. Transfer to a colander and drain well. Toss cooked macaroni with 2 tablespoons of the butter.

3. Meanwhile, melt the remaining tablespoon of butter in a medium pot over medium-low heat. Add the onion and cook until very soft and translucent, approximately 25 minutes, stirring frequently. Add the garlic, dry mustard, and Cajun spice and continue to cook for another 2 minutes, stirring often.

4. Whisk in the cream and bring to a simmer over medium heat. Remove from heat and purée the mixture with a handheld immersion blender. Return to heat and bring to a simmer. Adjust seasonings with salt and pepper to taste.

   Note: If you find that the consistency is too thin, you may thicken the sauce with a cornstarch paste. Mix together 2 tablespoons cornstarch with a little water to form a paste. Add to the purée and continue to whisk until mixture begins to thicken.

5. Stir in the cheese and cook over low heat, stirring constantly until melted, 1 to 2 minutes. Add the macaroni and stir until well incorporated. Transfer to prepared baking dish.

6. Bake until the top is golden and the cheese sauce is bubbling, 25 to 30 minutes. Remove from oven and let cool for 5 to 10 minutes. Garnish with parsley and serve.

CABOT CREAMERY

A dairy farm family produces more than fresh milk. It produces generations of people who know one another and help out when they're needed. They keep community alive, meet neighbors from other farms, enjoy their stories, and share recipes that have survived for generations.

A creamery has operated continuously among the hills of Cabot village since 1893, and it has been cooperatively owned by the dairy farmers who have supplied its milk since 1919. That year the creamery's owner, Mr. F. A. Messer, announced his plans to exit the dairy business. Concerned with finding an outlet for their daily supply of "white nectar," 94 enterprising farmers contributed five dollars per cow plus a cord of firewood each. The $3,600 was enough to buy the business; the firewood was to ensure that its boiler operated all winter long. This was the humble beginning of Vermont's best-known cooperative, recognized today as maker of the "World's Best Cheddar."

The cooperative now includes 1,500 farmers. Hearty home-cooked meals that nourish the soul and delight the palate are a way of life for Cabot dairy farm families. It has been that way for generations. As dusk settles, after the herds have been milked and barn chores completed, family members gather in the kitchen to give thanks and to savor the evening meal. Not surprisingly, these old-fashioned family recipes, handed down across the generations, share one special ingredient: Cabot's award-winning cheeses. Above all, the food is as much about spending meaningful time with friends and loved ones as it is about the pleasures of eating. Enjoy!

Winter Squash Gratin

This is a home-cooked meal that nourishes the soul and delights the palate — Vermont comfort food at its best. This tasty gratin combines Winooski, the local Native American Abenaki tribe's name for wild onion, with one of a number of "good keepers" from the gourd family, plus some tangy Vermont cheddar to liven up the breadcrumbs. The result is a casserole with a subtle caramelized onion flavor and a stick-to-your-ribs goodness.

6 ounces sharp cheddar, preferably Cabot, grated (1½ cups)

1½ cups fresh breadcrumbs (from about 3 slices of firm white bread)

2 tablespoons salted butter, preferably Cabot

2 medium onions, peeled and chopped (about 2 cups)

1 teaspoon sugar

½ teaspoon salt

½ teaspoon dried thyme leaves, crumbled

¼ teaspoon freshly ground black pepper

2 pounds dry-fleshed winter squash, such as Buttercup, Hubbard or Kabocha, peeled, halved lengthwise, seeded, and cut into ⅛-inch-thick slices

¾ cup chicken broth, or as needed

8 SERVINGS

1. Preheat oven to 375°F. Butter a 1½-quart baking dish, and set aside.

2. Combine cheese and breadcrumbs in a medium bowl and set aside.

3. Melt the butter in a large skillet over medium heat. Add the onions and sugar. Cook until onions are soft and golden, about 10 minutes, stirring often. Add salt, thyme, and pepper and combine well. Add the squash slices and all but ½ cup of the breadcrumb mixture to the skillet, tossing to combine well. Spoon the mixture into the prepared baking dish.

4. Pour broth evenly over squash mixture. Cover the dish tightly with a lid or foil and bake for about 1 hour, or until squash is fork tender and broth is nearly all absorbed. If squash appears dry, add another ¼ cup broth.

5. Remove lid or foil from baking dish and sprinkle squash with reserved breadcrumb mixture. Bake until the topping is golden, about 15 minutes longer.

Recipe from THREE MOUNTAIN INN

Creamy Polenta

It's hard to beat polenta as a satisfying comfort food. This recipe is really flexible — you can use it as a template, adding whatever flavors and seasonings will complement the rest of your menu. Serve this with any type of protein — lamb shanks, pork loin, or the wonderful Grilled Cavendish Quail recipe on page 195. Don't hesitate to experiment with herbs and spices that will bring something new to this dish every time you prepare it. A teaspoon of nutmeg or even a pinch of smoked paprika are two interesting possibilities.

6 cups water or stock

1 teaspoon salt

1 cup polenta, medium or coarse

6 ounces (¾ cup) Euro-style butter, preferably Cabot

2 cups aged sheep cheese, preferably Weston Wheel from Woodcock Farm Cheese, coarsely grated, or substitute Asiago, fontina, Gruyère, or a combination (8 ounces)

Freshly ground black pepper

Chopped parsley, chives, tarragon, chervil

4–6 SERVINGS

1. Bring 3 cups of the water to a boil in a medium saucepan over medium heat. Add salt. Bring the remaining 3 cups water to a simmer in another medium saucepan.

2. Whisking constantly, add polenta in a slow steady stream to salted boiling water. Reduce heat to medium-low, whisking until smooth. As polenta thickens, use a wooden spoon to stir. Stir in 1 cup of simmering water and continue to cook on medium-low. Cook until polenta is soft, creamy, tender, and pulls away from pan — this can take up to 50 minutes depending on the coarseness of the polenta. You may need to add more simmering water if the polenta gets too thick.

3. When the desired texture is achieved, remove polenta from stovetop. Add butter and cheese and stir until melted. Season with salt and pepper to taste. Garnish with chopped herbs and serve warm.

4 Beef, Pork, Lamb, and Game

Pepper-seared Filet Mignon with Maple Balsamic Sauce

This dish is easy and delicious!

4 (6-ounce) filet mignons, trimmed

2 tablespoons freshly cracked black pepper

3 tablespoons olive oil

1 tablespoon minced shallot

¼ cup pure maple syrup, preferably Vermont-made

¼ cup balsamic vinegar

½ cup demi-glace or beef stock

2 tablespoons apple brandy, preferably Flag Hill Farm

2 tablespoons unsalted butter

Salt and freshly ground black pepper

4 SERVINGS

1. Preheat oven to 350°F.

2. Lightly coat one side of each filet with cracked pepper.

3. Heat 2 tablespoons of the oil in a large ovenproof skillet over medium-high heat until oil just starts to smoke. Add filets, pepper side down, and sear well on one side, about 3 minutes. Turn filets, sear on the other side for 2 more minutes, and then put in the oven for 5 minutes.

4. Remove steaks from the skillet, set aside on a plate, and tent with foil to keep warm while making the sauce.

5. Heat the remaining 1 tablespoon of oil in the same large skillet used for the steaks, over medium-high heat. Add the shallot and sauté until soft and translucent, stirring frequently. Stir in the syrup and balsamic vinegar and cook, stirring often, until sauce is reduced by half, about 4 minutes.

6. Stir in the demi-glace. Remove the skillet from heat and add brandy. Return pan to the heat. When the sauce begins to boil, slowly whisk in the butter. Adjust seasonings with salt and pepper.

7. To serve, transfer filets to individual plates with any desired sides. Pour sauce over the steaks.

   Variation: For a more affordable variation, use a cheaper cut of beef or pork and serve with a nice side salad for lunch.

Ale-braised Beef Short Ribs

At the Cliff House, this dish is served in the fall with a Yukon gold potato gratin and in the summer months with a potato salad. The tasty short ribs are from the local Wood Creek Farm. The smooth and rich Ridge Runner Barley Wine Ale from Rock Art Brewery brings all the dish's flavors together. Buttermilk onion rings may also be added for a tasty, crunchy garnish.

¼ cup packed dark brown sugar

1 tablespoon paprika

1 tablespoon cumin

1 tablespoon freshly ground black pepper

1 tablespoon salt

2 tablespoons grainy Dijon mustard

4–5 pounds of short ribs, cut so each piece has 2 bones

¼ cup olive oil, or more as needed

1 pound yellow onions, peeled and roughly chopped

4 medium carrots, peeled and roughly chopped

2 stalks of celery, roughly chopped

2–3 bay leaves

5–6 sprigs fresh thyme

6–8 cloves of garlic, peeled and smashed

2 cups veal stock or low-sodium beef broth

1 (22-ounce) bottle Rock Art Ridge Runner Barley Wine Ale, or other dark ale

1 (28-ounce) can diced tomatoes, drained

6–8 SERVINGS

1. Stir together the sugar, paprika, cumin, pepper, salt, and mustard in a small bowl until well combined.

2. Pat the ribs dry with paper towels and layer in a shallow baking dish. Coat all sides of the ribs evenly with the spice mixture. Marinate in the refrigerator for at least an hour.

3. Preheat the oven to 350° F. Heat oil in a large pot over medium-high heat until hot but not smoking. Add the ribs and sear on both sides, in batches if necessary. Transfer the ribs to a plate and set aside.

4. Reduce heat to medium-low and add the onions, carrots, and celery, and cook, stirring often, until soft and translucent, 15 to 20 minutes. Add the bay leaves, thyme, and garlic, and mix until well combined. Whisk in the stock and beer, scraping the bottom of the pot. Add the tomatoes and stir until well combined. Return the ribs to the pot and increase the heat until the liquid reaches a strong simmer.

5. Cover the pot and place in the oven for 2 to 3 hours, until meat is tender and falling off the bone. Skim off any fat and remove short ribs. Strain the broth and continue to cook until sauce reduces and thickens, about 10 minutes. Adjust seasonings with salt and pepper to taste.

BOWMAN ROAD FARM

Since 1977, Joe LaDouceur has bred and raised grass-fed Hereford cattle on his 200-acre, historic family farm in Barnard, Vermont — the first farm settled in Barnard, in 1776. His approach to farming reflects a tender affection and deep understanding for working the land and raising cattle as simply and naturally as possible. He takes great pride in his herd sire (the male parent of the herd) and his small closed herd of 35 cows.

Joe practices the art of intensive pasture rotation for its dual benefits: The animals continually eat high-quality feed and the land is constantly replenished. The cattle change pastures every two to four days, spring through fall. During the winter months they are fed hay that has been baled on the farm. Their feed is organic: free of antibiotics, animal by-products, and growth hormones.

The animals are processed after 18 to 24 months. To minimize stress, Joe delivers them himself to a USDA-inspected facility. The most genetically correct or "prettiest" cows, as Joe would say, stay on the farm for breeding and herd replacement.

New England Pot Roast

Less-than-tender cuts of beef are greatly enhanced when cooked in a long, slow manner. The low heat and extended simmering time in this recipe bring out the natural flavors while tenderizing the meat.

¼ cup olive oil, or as needed

1 (5-pound) beef chuck roast

Salt and freshly ground black pepper

2 onions, peeled and cut into large slices

2 large garlic cloves, peeled and chopped

3–4 cups beef stock, or reduced-sodium canned beef broth, or as needed

1½ tablespoons tomato paste

1 tablespoon Worcestershire sauce

1 pound potatoes, peeled and cut into 1½-inch chunks

1 pound carrots, peeled and cut into 1½-inch chunks, or 1-pound package of petite carrots

2 tablespoons cornstarch

8 SERVINGS

1. Heat the oil in a large pot or Dutch oven over medium-high heat. Season the roast with salt and pepper. Add the roast to the pot and brown on all sides, about 12 minutes. Transfer roast to a platter.

2. Reduce heat to medium and add the onions and garlic, stirring frequently. Cook until soft, about 10 minutes. Return the roast to the pot. Add enough stock to cover ¾ of the roast. Whisk in the tomato paste and Worcestershire sauce. Bring to a boil, cover, and reduce heat to low. Cook for 3 hours on the stovetop.

3. Add the potatoes and carrots and cook until fork tender, about 45 minutes to 1 hour.

4. Transfer roast, potatoes, and carrots to a platter. Skim visible fat from the cooking liquid.

5. To thicken the cooking liquid, whisk together a ladleful of cooking liquid and the cornstarch in a small bowl until cornstarch has dissolved. Add the cornstarch mixture to the pot and bring to a boil. Season with salt and pepper to taste.

6. Cut roast into thick slices and serve with potatoes, carrots, and gravy.

Hungarian Goulash

Serve this dish over egg noodles for a satisfying cool-weather dinner. Add a salad for a complete meal.

4 tablespoons olive oil

2 pounds beef chuck stew meat, cut into 1-inch pieces

¾ teaspoon salt

¼ teaspoon black pepper

2 tablespoons all-purpose flour

1¼ cups chopped yellow onion

1 large green bell pepper, chopped

1 tablespoon minced garlic

2 tablespoons Hungarian paprika

½ cup dry red wine

1 teaspoon apple cider vinegar

1½ cups beef stock

Salt and freshly ground black pepper

Chopped parsley

Egg noodles

4 SERVINGS

1. Heat 2 tablespoons of the olive oil in a large pot or Dutch oven over medium-high heat. Salt and pepper the meat and flour it lightly. Add meat to pot in batches, to avoid crowding, and brown on all sides. With a slotted spoon, transfer meat to a plate and set aside.

2. Reduce heat to medium and add the remaining 2 tablespoons oil to the drippings in the pot. Add the onion and pepper and cook, stirring often, until soft and translucent, about 7 minutes. Add the garlic and paprika and continue to cook for another 2 to 3 minutes, stirring frequently. Whisk in the wine and bring to a boil, scraping the sides and bottom of pot.

3. Return the beef to the pot and add the cider vinegar, stock, and salt and pepper to taste. Cover tightly and barely simmer for 1½ to 2 hours, until meat is tender and sauce has thickened. Adjust the seasonings, adding salt and pepper to taste.

4. Serve over egg noodles, and garnish with chopped parsley.

Otter Creek Vermont Lager Stew

Adding beer to soups and stews adds depth and complexity to the flavor while also helping to tenderize the meat. Otter Creek Vermont Lager uses German-style hops, which add an earthy, slightly peppery flavor. They also use barley malts to impart a full rich body to the beer; this adds a touch of sweetness to the stew and richness and depth to the sauce.

6–8 SERVINGS

2 pounds beef stew meat, cut into 1-inch cubes

Salt and freshly ground black pepper

1 tablespoon all-purpose flour

2 tablespoons olive oil

1 large onion, peeled and diced

1 garlic clove, peeled and minced

1 (12-ounce) bottle Otter Creek Vermont Lager, or other European-style lager

1½ cups fresh tomatoes, chopped, or 14-ounce can chopped tomatoes

1 teaspoon dry mustard

Hungarian paprika, or commercial paprika

2 bay leaves

1 tablespoon Worcestershire sauce

1 tablespoon soy sauce

6 carrots, peeled and cut into 1-inch pieces

3 large white boiling potatoes, peeled and cut into 1-inch cubes

½ cup sour cream (optional)

2 tablespoons minced parsley

1. Pat the meat cubes dry with paper towels and season well with salt and pepper. Add flour and toss to coat.

2. Heat the oil in a large pot or Dutch oven, over medium-high heat. Add the meat in batches if needed, and brown well on all sides. Transfer meat to a bowl with a slotted spoon, and set aside.

3. Reduce the heat to medium and add the onion and half of the garlic; cook, stirring often, until soft and tender, about 10 minutes. Return meat and any accumulated juices to pot. Whisk in the beer and tomatoes, scraping the sides and bottom of the pot. Add the dry mustard, paprika, bay leaves, Worcestershire sauce, and soy sauce, and stir well.

4. Cover and simmer gently for 1¼ hours. Add the carrots and potatoes and continue to simmer gently until the meat and vegetables are fork tender, about 45 more minutes. Remove bay leaves and discard. Add the rest of the garlic and sour cream, if using, and stir well. Season with salt and pepper to taste, garnish with parsley, and serve.

Note: If you find that the stew is too thick, beer or water may be added for a thinner consistency. If it's too thin, thicken it with a thin paste of water and cornstarch stirred into the stew.

OTTER CREEK BREWING

In 1991, Otter Creek Brewing shipped its first keg of Copper Ale from its original location in Middlebury. Four years later, after quickly outgrowing their first site, the brewery built a new state-of-the-art facility just down the street. In 1998, Otter Creek began producing Wolaver's Certified Organic Ales in partnership with the Wolaver family. The partnership was a success, and in May of 2002, the Wolaver family purchased Otter Creek Brewing. Otter Creek remains a family-owned Vermont company and produces all Otter Creek and Wolaver's brands for distribution throughout the country.

Otter Creek and Wolaver's organic beers are brewed in small batches using natural Vermont water, the best domestic malt and hops available, and their own top-fermenting yeast. All Wolaver's beers are made with no less than 98 percent certified organic ingredients and are certified organic by Vermont Organic Farmers.

Otter Creek and Wolaver's beers are made with as many locally grown ingredients as possible. Local farmer Ben Gleason supplies much of the organic wheat for the brews. Over the years the brewery has also developed relationships with various local chefs, collaborating on joint promotions and tastings. Diners in many local restaurants will find Otter Creek and Wolaver's brews featured in various dishes.

SIMON PEARCE

In 1981, seeking independence from European business constraints and high energy costs, Simon Pearce moved his glass-blowing operation from Kilkenny, Ireland, to a historic woolen mill on the banks of the Ottauquechee River in Quechee, Vermont. Today the river still provides hydroelectric power for the glass furnaces, along with electricity for the entire facility. The company is known for its hand-blown glass and handmade pottery, both traditional and contemporary, all demonstrating classic simplicity, elegance, and everyday functionality.

Simon's intention was to make the mill a destination in itself. With that purpose in mind, he opened the Glassblower Café in 1983. The restaurant's introduction to the mill would offer visitors a complete experience: Watch the pieces being made, eat and drink from the handmade glass and pottery at the restaurant, and buy from the retail store.

Simon's mother was a fabulous cook, using simple recipes with local ingredients to make delicious meals. Preparing and sharing simple but delicious food was a family heritage, and that is what the restaurant's cuisine is all about. Having been a member of the Vermont Fresh Network since its inception, Simon Pearce uses local produce whenever possible and continues to develop new relationships with local farmers, growers, and suppliers knowing that these relationships are as important as the relationship between a restaurant and its guests.

Shepherd's Pie

A traditional Irish meal, shepherd's pie is a favorite among hosts and hostesses who enjoy having a large group of friends or family over for a comforting dinner.

2 tablespoons olive oil

2 pounds lean ground chuck or ground lamb

1 large white onion, peeled and diced

2 large carrots, diced

1 cup low-sodium beef broth

1 (6-ounce) can tomato paste

1 tablespoon Worcestershire sauce

1 cup frozen baby peas

1 cup frozen corn

Salt and freshly ground black pepper

2 pounds russet potatoes, peeled and cut into 1-inch pieces (about 4 cups)

4 tablespoons salted butter

½ cup milk, warmed

2 cups grated sharp cheddar cheese (about 8 ounces)

8 SERVINGS

1. Heat the oil in a large skillet over medium heat. Add ground chuck, and stir to break up lumps. Cook until browned, about 7 minutes. Add onion and carrots, and cook for another 2 to 3 minutes. Add the beef broth, stirring until well combined, and bring to a boil over medium-high heat. Reduce heat to medium-low, and add tomato paste and Worcestershire sauce, stirring until well combined. Continue to cook mixture until it begins to thicken, stirring frequently. Add peas and corn, stirring until well combined. Add salt and pepper to taste. Remove from heat and set aside.

2. Add potatoes to large stockpot, cover with water, and bring to a boil over high heat. Cook until potatoes are fork tender, about 20 minutes. Drain well. Add butter, milk, and half of the cheese. Mash with an old-fashioned masher or handheld mixer and mix thoroughly until desired consistency is reached. Season with salt and pepper to taste. Additional butter and cream may be added to taste.

3. Assemble the pie: Preheat oven to 350°F. Spoon the meat mixture into Brookfield Bakeware #2 dish from Simon Pearce or into a round 10½-inch baking dish with 3-inch sides. Spread the potatoes evenly over the top. Sprinkle the remaining half of the cheese on top of the potatoes. Place dish on a baking sheet to catch any dripping. Bake for 30 to 40 minutes, until the pie is hot and the potatoes are golden brown.

Tortellini alla Farmstead Bolognese

This recipe blends traditional Italian flavors with flavorful local ingredients that give the Bolognese a Vermont twist. The secret to exceptional food is to use the freshest ingredients possible. You don't need a culinary degree to produce a delicious dish — anyone can do it with excellent ingredients!

Note: This dish pairs well with a Chianti or any Primitivo.

2 tablespoons olive oil

¼ pound pancetta, diced

1 pound ground beef, preferably local, natural, grass-fed angus

1 pound venison stew meat, preferably farm-raised, chopped

4 celery ribs, diced

2 carrots, peeled and diced

1 large onion, peeled and diced

5 garlic cloves, peeled and minced

4 tablespoons tomato paste

½ cup white wine

½ cup milk

2 (14-ounce) cans whole peeled tomatoes, crushed by hand, with juice

½ cup beef stock

3 tablespoons chopped basil leaves

3 tablespoons chopped marjoram

Salt and freshly ground black pepper

2 (12-ounce) packages tortellini

¼ cup fresh goat cheese, preferably Vermont Butter & Cheese Company, or to taste (about 2 ounces)

6–8 SERVINGS

1. Heat the oil in a large stockpot over medium-high heat and brown pancetta until crisp. Transfer to a plate and set aside. Add beef and venison and brown, stirring frequently, draining fat if desired. Transfer meat to plate with pancetta and set aside.

2. Reduce heat to medium-low and add celery, carrots, onion, and garlic. Cover and cook vegetables, stirring occasionally, until soft and translucent, 15 to 20 minutes.

3. Return pancetta, beef, and venison to the pot. Add tomato paste, wine, and milk, stirring to combine. Add crushed tomatoes and beef stock, stirring to combine. Add basil, marjoram, and salt and pepper to taste. Bring to a gentle simmer, cover, and continue to simmer on low heat for 1½ hours, stirring every 10 minutes.

4. Bring a large pot of water to a boil. Add salt and cook tortellini until al dente. Drain, toss with Bolognese ragu, and garnish with crumbled goat cheese to serve.

Healthy Living Café Meat Loaf

Healthy Living is an independently owned natural foods market in Burlington. Recognized for 18 years of memorable customer service along with a wonderful selection of natural and organic foods, Healthy Living is committed to serving the community. They support local organic agriculture, participate in community outreach, and employ nearly 100 local people. Customers love the local spirit of the store.

The chefs at Healthy Living cook with ingredients from more than 20 Vermont farms and food producers. They use as much organically grown produce and environmentally sustainable foods as possible, taking pride in their neighborly relationships with people who respect the environment and are responsible stewards of the land.

This is a recipe that Paula Myrick Eisenberg created to replicate her mother's meat loaf. Paula replaces her mother's can of Campbell's vegetable soup with fresh vegetables and punches the whole thing up with garlic, but otherwise it's a pretty faithful interpretation of a childhood favorite.

6–8 SERVINGS

2 tablespoons canola oil

1 medium onion, peeled and finely diced

1 green bell pepper, finely diced

1 small zucchini, finely diced

1 medium carrot, finely diced

2 tablespoons minced garlic

½ tablespoon dried thyme

½ tablespoon dried oregano

½ teaspoon ground allspice

1 tablespoon kosher salt

1 teaspoon freshly ground black pepper

4 slices of stale bread or 1½ cups packaged breadcrumbs

2 farm-fresh eggs

3 pounds ground beef

⅓ cup chopped parsley

½ cup ketchup

1. Preheat oven to 400°F. Lightly coat a 13- by 9-inch loaf pan with cooking spray. Set aside.

2. Heat the oil in a large skillet over medium heat. Add the onions, peppers, zucchini, and carrots and sauté until soft and tender, about 10 minutes. Add the garlic, thyme, oregano, allspice, salt, and pepper and cook for 5 minutes, stirring often. Remove from heat and allow vegetable mixture to cool. Drain off any excess liquid.

3. Toast the bread in the oven until slightly browned. Cool, then crumble into the bowl of a food processor. Pulse until fine crumbs form.

4. Lightly beat eggs in a small bowl.

5. Combine the beef, parsley, vegetable mixture, eggs, and breadcrumbs in a large bowl. Mix together thoroughly using your hands.

6. Transfer to prepared baking dish and shape into a 10-inch by 6-inch oval loaf, smoothing the top. Spread ketchup over top to the edges of meat loaf. Bake meat loaf in the oven for 15 minutes. Remove from oven and drain off excess grease. Reduce heat to 350°F and cook for 40 to 45 minutes more, or until a meat thermometer inserted into the middle reads 155°F.

7. Remove from the oven and allow meat loaf to rest for 15 minutes before slicing.

Sweet and Sour Vermont Cheeseburger with Attitude

Westminster Dairy, at Livewater Farm, has reinvented itself. During their cheese-making period, they sold cheeses to many New England chefs. When they suspended cheese making, Westminster established new business relationships with companies that need organic milk, such as Organic Valley and Strafford Organics. A certified organic grass-based dairy farm, Livewater Farm sells certified organic milk, their own maple syrup, maple candy and maple cream, organic garlic, grass-fed beef, corn-fed pork, non-crated veal, free-range eggs, and pickled garlic and beans. The business sells to CSA groups and reaches more consumers at farmers' markets and on their farm. The farm is very proud of the products they produce and the methods they use to market them.

1 cup cranberry juice, or apple or pineapple juice

Scant ¼ cup vinegar

½ teaspoon red pepper flakes, or to taste

¼ teaspoon celery seed, or to taste

¼ cup pure maple syrup

½ teaspoon salt

1 tablespoon cornstarch

3 pounds lean ground chuck

Freshly ground black pepper

6 thin slices Vermont Pinnacle cheese or Asiago, or any good raw milk cheese

2 tablespoons unsalted butter, softened (optional)

6 hamburger buns

Snow pea sprouts

6 SERVINGS

1. Combine ¾ cup of the juice, the vinegar, pepper flakes, celery seed, maple syrup, and salt in a medium saucepan over medium heat. Whisk thoroughly to combine all ingredients, and bring to a simmer. In a small bowl, whisk the cornstarch with the remaining ¼ cup of cranberry juice until dissolved. Add cornstarch liquid and cook, stirring frequently, for another 1 or 2 minutes, until sauce thickens. The sauce can be made ahead of time and stored in the refrigerator.

2. Heat a grill to medium. Divide the meat into 6 equal portions and form into patties, each about 1 inch thick. Season with salt and pepper to taste.

3. Grill patties 5 to 7 minutes per side for medium doneness, or until they have almost reached desired doneness. Place a slice of cheese on top of each patty and grill until cheese is slightly melted.

4. In the meantime, slice open buns, spread with butter, if using, and grill. When burgers are done, remove from grill and place on toasted buns. Top with the sprouts and drizzle with the sauce.

Sautéed Pork Medallions with Honey Rosemary Butter and Apple Salsa

Stevens Orchard supplies the Middlebury Inn with the wonderful variety of apples used in this salsa and in many other dishes served in the inn's dining room. The inn uses crystallized honey from Champlain Valley Apiaries, but you'll want to get yours from your local bees.

APPLE SALSA

1 apple, such as Honeycrisp, Fuji, Pink Lady, or McIntosh, finely diced

2 tablespoons minced red onion

1 jalapeño pepper, minced

1 tablespoon chopped cilantro

Juice of 1 lime

1 garlic clove, peeled and minced

Salt

PORK AND SAUCE

1½ pounds pork tenderloin, trimmed and cut into 8 (3-ounce) coin-shaped pieces

Kosher salt and freshly ground black pepper

1 cup canola oil or olive oil, or as needed

1 cup all-purpose flour

2 fresh rosemary sprigs

½ cup crystallized honey, preferably locally harvested

½ cup cider vinegar

¼ cup bourbon

4 tablespoons cold unsalted butter, cubed

4 SERVINGS

1. Make the apple salsa: Combine the apple, onion, jalapeño, cilantro, lime juice, garlic, and salt to taste in a mixing bowl and mix thoroughly. Cover and refrigerate for 1 hour before serving.

2. Prepare the pork: Place the pork medallions on a sheet of plastic wrap. Place another sheet of plastic wrap on top of the pork and pound to ¼-inch thickness with a meat mallet or rolling pin. Remove plastic wrap and sprinkle with salt and pepper to taste. Repeat with remaining pork medallions.

3. Heat half the oil in a large skillet over medium-high heat. Dredge pork medallion in flour, shaking off the excess. Working in batches, if necessary, add pork to skillet and sauté until just cooked through, adding more oil to the skillet between batches if needed. Transfer to a platter and tent with foil to keep warm while making the sauce.

4. Remove the skillet from heat and drain any fat or excess oil from the skillet.

5. Heat 2 more tablespoons oil in the same skillet, then add the rosemary, honey, and vinegar. Remove the skillet from the stovetop and carefully add the bourbon. Return the pan to heat and stand back. When the sauce begins to boil, slowly and continuously whisk in the butter until fully incorporated.

6. Transfer pork back to the skillet and cook until heated through. Adjust seasonings with salt and pepper.

7. Serve pork medallions with sauce and a little of the apple salsa spooned onto each medallion.

Yucatan Pork Tenderloin with Jicama, Avocado, and Red Onions

Serve with corn or flour tortillas and a simple watercress and grapefruit salad. Guests can roll their own wraps with the tender pork and cool, crunchy vegetables.

2 tablespoons minced garlic

2 tablespoons ground ancho chili powder, or other ground chili powder

1 tablespoon dried oregano, preferably Mexican

½ tablespoon ground cumin

½ cup freshly squeezed grapefruit juice

1 teaspoon kosher salt

1 teaspoon freshly ground black pepper

1 pork tenderloin (about 1½ pounds), trimmed, preferably organic

1 cup jicama, peeled and cut into ½-inch matchsticks

2 ripe avocados, peeled and thinly sliced

1 small red onion, peeled and thinly sliced

Corn or flour tortillas

4–6 SERVINGS

1. Preheat oven to 450°F.

2. Combine the garlic, chili powder, oregano, cumin, ¼ cup of the grapefruit juice, salt, and pepper in a small bowl. The mixture should have the consistency of a paste.

3. Rub the paste all over the pork and set it on a rack in a roasting pan. Roast on the center rack of the oven for about 25 to 30 minutes, until the pork registers medium on a meat thermometer (140–145°F). Nick the tenderloin at the thickest part to check for doneness. Transfer to a clean cutting board to rest.

4. Meanwhile, in a medium bowl, gently combine the jicama, avocado, and red onion. Drizzle with the remaining ¼ cup grapefruit juice and season with salt and pepper to taste.

5. Slice the pork and place on dinner plates, saucing the pork with any pan juices. Top with the jicama salad and serve warmed tortillas on the side.

Roast Rack of Pork Stuffed with Sage, Apples, and Onion

This dish is a delicious choice whenever a hearty roast is called for. The apple and sage provide the sweet and savory notes that bring out pork's best flavors.

½ cup plus 2 tablespoons minced fresh sage

1 shallot, peeled and minced

1 teaspoon minced garlic

1 cup breadcrumbs

4 tablespoons unsalted butter

1 large onion, peeled and chopped

2 Granny Smith apples, peeled, cored, and sliced

Salt and freshly ground black pepper

1 rack of pork (ask the butcher for a 6-rib rack or 1–2 ribs per serving)

Vegetable oil

1 onion, peeled and cut into quarters

1 carrot, cut into large chunks

2 stalks celery, chopped

1 bottle dry white wine

4 cups veal stock

4 tablespoons clarified butter

4 tablespoons all-purpose flour

4–6 SERVINGS

1. Combine 2 tablespoons of the sage, the shallots, garlic, and bread-crumbs in a medium bowl, and set aside.

2. Preheat oven to 350°F. Heat the butter in a large skillet over medium heat. Add the chopped onion, apples, the remaining ½ cup sage, and salt and pepper to taste. Cook, stirring frequently, until mixture is only slightly soft, about 5 minutes. Open the pork roast by carefully cutting along the bones. Sprinkle with salt and pepper to taste. Spread the apple stuffing evenly into the roast, then close. Tie between every other rib with cooking twine and brush the roast with a little oil.

3. Sprinkle with the breadcrumb mixture.

4. Place the onion quarters, carrot, and celery in the bottom of a roasting pan, then place the roast on top. Pour in half the bottle of white wine, cover with aluminum foil, and roast for 1 hour.

5. Remove the foil and roast for another 30 minutes, until pork reaches an internal temperature of 160°F, begins to color to a nice bronze, and is very firm to the touch. Remove the pork to a serving platter and tent with foil to keep warm.

6. Add the remaining half bottle of wine to the roasting pan and cook over low heat, scraping up the brown bits on the bottom of the pan. Add veal stock, bring to a boil, and stir until the liquid has reduced a little, about 8 minutes.

7. Meanwhile, combine clarified butter and flour in a small saucepan and slowly cook over low heat, whisking frequently, until it just begins to turn a pale golden color. Add to the roasting pan liquid and continue to cook, whisking until well combined and thickened as desired. Pour sauce through a strainer or a fine sieve.

8. Carve the pork, divide among the plates, and serve with the warm pan sauce.

Preparation Note: *A roux is a mixture of flour and fat (equal parts flour and fat by weight) that, after being slowly cooked over low heat and mixed with a whisk, is used to thicken soups, stews, and sauces. There are three classic roux: white, blond, and brown. The color and flavor is determined by the length of time the mixture is cooked and what the roux is used for. Both white roux and blond roux are made with clarified butter. A white roux is cooked just enough to cook out the raw taste of the flour. A blond roux is cooked a few minutes longer, until it reaches a pale golden color, as for this recipe. Both are used to thicken cream sauces as well as lighter colored sauces and soups. The brown roux can be made with clarified butter, or drippings of pork or beef fat. It is cooked to a deep golden brown and used for richer-flavored, darker-colored soups, sauces, and stews.*

OSTERIA PANE E SALUTE

Osteria Pane e Salute turned ten years old in 2006. The business began as a bakery and pasticceria offering light lunches. As the years passed, they developed into a dinner-only restaurant and enoteca. The owners' mission has been to translate their experiences living, traveling, and tasting in Italy to the table. The menu is a reflection of that mission and features only traditional Italian regional recipes collected and refined over the years. The wine list reflects the same attention, offering more than a hundred regional Italian wines made from indigenous grapes. In 2002, owners Deirdre and Caleb published their first book, *Pane e Salute: Food and Love in Italy and Vermont*, a collection of food and travel essays accompanied by recipes.

The owners use only local, natural, and/or certified organic meats and poultry. The restaurant also offers as much regional produce as possible, developing menus around what is available locally each season. As part of the Vermont Fresh Network, they work with many Vermont farmers. Dairy is from Spragues in Randolph; eggs, from Maple Meadow Farm in Salisbury; honey, from Lissey Hemenway in Bridport; quail, from Cavendish Farms; chicken, from Misty Knoll; sheep's milk cheeses, from Peaked Mountain, to name a few. Deirdre and Caleb also forage leeks, fiddleheads, wild apples, black grapes, mushrooms, and dandelion greens, or purchase them from local foragers. Most herbs are grown at the restaurant or at home.

For a fall menu special of Italian sausages and black grapes, the restaurant used the entire grape harvest from three vines planted the previous year. Deirdre and Caleb used additional black grapes they found growing in a snarl of vine and blackberry canes on their property. Black grapes can be found all over Vermont. Look for them during an afternoon's walk or at the countless small farm stands that dot the countryside. When eating local and wild black, some people spit out the seeds, others just crunch them up as they go along. They have an excellent texture and a hint of anise.

Sausages with Black Grapes (Salsicce con l'Uva)

While this dish makes for excellent dinner fare, it is also wonderful served on a crusty roll for lunch along with a glass of Chianti Colli Aretini. The owners of Osteria Pane e Salute — bread and health, in Italian — once enjoyed just such a meal in the Piazza del Municipio in Arezzo on a brisk and bright autumn day during the monthly antiques fair. Those sandwiches weren't much more than grilled sausage and bread with a little rough local wine in a plastic cup, served by shouting, joking cooks among centuries-old sideboards, headboards, and dressers and surrounded by buildings from the Renaissance — an atmosphere to elevate any meal. If you don't have good crusty bread on hand, make some mashed potatoes while the sausages are roasting in the oven.

4 SERVINGS

- 2 large yellow onions, peeled and slivered
- 2 cups black grapes (Concord, Globe, or any other ripe black variety), rinsed well
- Extra-virgin olive oil
- Salt and freshly ground black pepper
- 4 to 8 sweet Italian sausages (1 to 2 sausages per person)

1. Preheat oven to 375°F.

2. In a large roasting pan or skillet mix the slivered onion and grapes with your hands. Drizzle some oil over them and sprinkle with several generous pinches of salt and pepper. Mix again and spread out the mixture evenly.

3. Nestle the sausages into the onion-grape layer, but don't completely cover them. Roast in the oven for 30 to 40 minutes, until the onions have cooked down considerably, the grapes are soft, and the sausages are plump and browned on top, even a little bit crusty. Pierce one of the largest sausages. They are ready when the juices run clear.

4. Spoon a bed of onions and grapes onto a serving platter or individual plates, top with the sausages, and serve.

Stuffed Focaccia

This recipe is the traditional Italian version of a stuffed focaccia sandwich, but the variations are endless. Try grilled flank steak, roasted onions, and Gorgonzola cheese, or grilled or roasted eggplant with tomato and basil. For the ultimate tomato sandwich, slice vine-ripened heirloom tomatoes, drizzle them with olive oil, and season with salt and pepper. You may also use a sandwich press, instead of heating in the oven, or just assemble the sandwich and serve at room temperature.

1 loaf rosemary and garlic focaccia

6 ounces salami

6 ounces mild ham (not smoked) or mortadella

6 slices prosciutto

4 ounces Italian fontina or Brie

4 ENTRÉE SERVINGS OR 8–12 APPETIZER SERVINGS

1. Preheat oven to 350°F.

2. Slice the bread in half horizontally. Layer salami, ham, prosciutto, and cheese over the bottom half of bread and top with the other half. Place on a baking sheet and bake for about 20 minutes or until the bread is golden brown and the cheese is melted. Transfer to a cutting board, cut into wedges, and serve.

Vermont Croque Monsieur

Croque Monsieur is a fun dish that plays on the French Canadian traditions of Vermont and New England. At the Cliff House, the Croque Monsieur is made with maple cinnamon raisin bread from Elmore Mountain Breads, roast turkey from Misty Knoll Farm, ham from Vermont Smoke & Cure, Gouda cheese from Taylor Farm, and mascarpone cheese from the Vermont Butter & Cheese Company. It makes a great brunch dish or a hearty breakfast sandwich.

1 SANDWICH

- **1 teaspoon pure Vermont maple syrup**
- **1 teaspoon chopped chives**
- **2 tablespoons mascarpone cheese**
- **2 eggs**
- **Pinch of ground cinnamon**
- **Pinch of nutmeg**
- **1 tablespoon brown sugar**
- **Salt and freshly ground black pepper**
- **2 slices of maple cinnamon raisin bread**
- **Unsalted butter**
- **2 ounces roasted turkey breast, sliced**
- **2 ounces smoked and cured ham, sliced**
- **2 ounces Gouda cheese, shredded**

1. Mix together maple syrup, chives, and mascarpone in a small bowl. Preheat oven to 325°F.

2. Whisk together the eggs, cinnamon, nutmeg, brown sugar, and salt and pepper to taste in a medium bowl. Dip bread into egg mixture until well soaked and shake gently to remove excess.

3. Melt a pat of butter in a large skillet over medium heat. Add the bread and cook until golden brown on each side. Remove the bread from pan and spread the mascarpone mixture over one slice. Layer turkey, ham, and Gouda over mascarpone. Top with the second slice of bread and bake in the oven until warmed through and the cheese has melted.

MAPLE WIND FARM

Maple Wind Farm has two giant silver maples that shade its farmhouse; these trees, combined with the unusually strong winds that frequent the area, have given the farm its name. The farm practices rotational grazing techniques, caring naturally for the health of the animals and the fertility of the soil. Animals express natural behaviors in this low-stress environment, resulting in healthier meat products. The farm raises grass-fed and grass-finished beef, lamb, organic pork, and poultry, which they supply to area chefs.

Steve Atkins of the Kitchen Table Bistro in Richmond cooks with Maple Wind's pork and lamb and once prepared a six-course meal featuring Maple Wind's pastured organic pork for a Vermont Fresh Network Farmer's Dinner. Steve Atkins is unique among chefs in that he loves to find ways to use the entire animal in his recipes. Doug Mack, of Mary's at Baldwin Creek, in Bristol, Vermont, has trained his staff to properly prepare grass-fed beef, which is a little denser than the conventional product. The positive response he has received for dishes prepared with Maple Wind's beef supports the idea that good farming practices produce better food.

Maple Wind Farm has a strong environmental ethic. It's not enough to produce healthful, pasture-based, sustainable food; the environment must be preserved and protected, too. Dedication to energy conservation and the production of alternative energy is at the core of their philosophy. They even have a 10-kilowatt wind turbine that produces 500 kilowatt hours of energy per month.

The owners are dedicated to selling their products locally. They hope that as consumers develop a relationship with Maple Wind, they will gain an awareness and appreciation for their sustainable farming methods and naturally raised animals. Better products for better health while caring for the environment — what a wonderful formula!

Moroccan Lamb

This recipe was inspired by a dear friend, Mark Lubkowitz. Mark is actually a molecular biology professor who loves to cook. On the fifteenth of each month, he and his wife host a party for 20–40 people around a theme (usually ethnic or seasonal). Beth and Bruce, the owners of Maple Wind Farm, are the official sponsors of the "15th of the month" in Huntington; this recipe was served at one of these occasions using their lamb.

Mark's claim to culinary fame began with his doctoral studies when he worked on yeast. This led to his great love — making beer and wine. He and his wife have started Huntington's first vineyard and eventually hope to serve their homemade wine at their "15th of the month" events.

8–10 SERVINGS

6 tablespoons unsalted butter, melted

3 teaspoons ground cumin, or to taste

3 teaspoons paprika, or to taste

3 teaspoons ground coriander, or to taste

1 teaspoon salt, or to taste

2 teaspoons freshly ground black pepper, or to taste

Pinch of cayenne pepper, or to taste

4–8 medium garlic cloves, peeled and sliced

1 (8-pound) leg of lamb, bone in and trimmed of fat, preferably grass-fed

1 cup fresh dates

1 cup whole fresh almonds

2 lemons, each cut into 6 wedges

1. Place butter in a medium bowl. Whisk in cumin, paprika, coriander, salt, pepper, cayenne, and garlic.

2. Pierce the lamb leg with a paring knife in 12 to 15 places. Rub the spice mixture into the incisions and over the surface of the leg. Place lamb, fat side up, in a roasting pan. Cover and let marinate in refrigerator for at least 3 hours or as long as overnight.

3. Preheat oven to 350°F. Remove lamb from refrigerator, uncover, and transfer to the oven to roast. Baste lamb with pan juices occasionally. Add dates and almonds to roasting pan 15 minutes before roast is done. Roast until meat thermometer inserted into the thickest part of meat registers your desired doneness (140°F for medium-rare, about 2 hours 15 minutes).

4. Transfer lamb to platter and allow meat to rest for 15 minutes. Serve with lemon wedges.

Rack of Lamb with Maple Walnut Crust, Green Beans, and Merlot Pan Jus

The sweet flavor of the lodge's maple syrup goes very well with nuts and a little bit of rosemary. Serve the lamb with a side of Cabot Cheddar Mashed Potatoes (page 56).

2 (26-ounce) racks of lamb, frenched and trimmed of all but a thin layer of fat

Salt and freshly ground black pepper

2 ounces olive oil

6 ounces Merlot wine

½ cup demi-glace

5 small sprigs rosemary, plus more for garnish

1 tablespoon unsalted butter

1 cup finely chopped walnuts

2 tablespoons pure Vermont maple syrup

3 tablespoons breadcrumbs

1 egg white

8 bacon slices

1 pound green and yellow beans, washed and trimmed

4 SERVINGS

1. Season the lamb with salt and pepper to taste.

2. Heat the oil in a large skillet over medium-high heat. When the oil just starts to smoke, add the racks of lamb and brown on both sides, turning as needed. Transfer lamb onto a high-rimmed baking sheet.

3. Pour the wine into the skillet and cook over high heat until reduced by half, whisking often to loosen the browned bits of food at the bottom of pan. Add the demi-glace and 5 rosemary sprigs, and whisk to combine. Reduce the heat to medium and let the sauce simmer for another 3 minutes, whisking frequently. Strain the sauce through a very fine sieve or strainer. Finish by swirling in the butter and adjusting the salt and pepper to taste.

4. Mix together the walnuts, maple syrup, breadcrumbs, and egg white in a medium bowl to form a paste. Spread the paste evenly onto the racks of lamb and press in with a spoon or a spatula. Preheat oven to 400°F.

5. Prepare the beans: Fill a large bowl with ice water and set aside.

6. Microwave the bacon in a single layer for 1 minute.

7. Meanwhile, bring a medium saucepan of water to a boil. Add the beans and cook until they turn bright green and yellow and are just tender. Drain in a colander and immediately plunge into the prepared ice bath to stop the cooking. When cooled, place a bunch of beans on a slice of partially cooked bacon and wrap the whole slice around the beans. (Start at one end of the bundle and slightly spiral the bacon down.) Repeat this procedure until all of the beans and bacon have been used. Place the bean bundles on the same baking sheet with the lamb.

8. Transfer the racks of lamb and beans to the oven. Roast the racks until the crust is golden brown and a meat thermometer inserted into the thickest part of the lamb registers 130°F for medium-rare, about 20 minutes. Roast bean bundles, flipping halfway through, until bacon is cooked, about 20 minutes. Transfer lamb to a cutting board and let rest for 10 to 15 minutes. Cut each rack into 6 lamb chops.

9. Drizzle the lamb chops with the merlot jus, garnish with rosemary, and serve with bacon-wrapped beans.

Rosemary-seared Lamb Loin

Growing up on a small farm, Andrew LaHaye, executive chef at Bailey's, frequently made this lamb dish with his mother, one of his early cooking inspirations. For a real treat, layer lamb slices over Goat Cheese Bread Pudding (page 126) and top with Blueberry Mint Relish (page 86).

1 tablespoon chopped garlic

2 tablespoons chopped rosemary

4½ tablespoons extra-virgin olive oil

2 pounds lamb loin, preferably grass-fed, cleaned

1 tablespoon unsalted butter

6 ounces fresh spinach, stemmed and washed well

⅛ teaspoon salt

4–6 SERVINGS

1. In a large bowl combine the garlic, rosemary, and 2 tablespoons of the oil, mixing well.

2. Add the lamb and spoon marinade over loins to coat well. Cover and marinate in the refrigerator for at least 30 minutes.

3. Heat the remaining 2½ tablespoons of oil in a large skillet over medium-high heat. When the oil just starts to smoke, add the lamb and cook for 4 minutes on each side for medium-rare meat. Transfer loins onto a cutting board and allow to rest for a few minutes.

4. Make the spinach: Melt the butter in a medium skillet over medium-high heat. Add the spinach and salt and cook until wilted and tender.

5. Cut the lamb into thin slices and serve with the spinach.

VERMONT QUALITY MEATS — FROM FARM TO TABLE

Established in 1999, Vermont Quality Meats is a cooperative of farmers whose goal is to sell beef, lamb, goat meat, pork, pheasant, quail, and eggs direct to discriminating chefs. All of their products are grown on small family farms around New England, processed at USDA-inspected slaughterhouses, and delivered fresh to chefs each week. The animals are raised naturally without the use of growth hormones or antibiotics. Careful consideration to grazing techniques and animal husbandry nourishes the land, lowers the stress on the animals, and yields better-tasting products.

Vermont Quality Meats products have received excellent reviews from top chefs in Vermont, Boston, and New York. Tom Biggs, sales manager of Vermont Quality, delivers to more than 55 high-quality restaurants throughout the Northeast and maintains personal relationships with the chefs. This kind of service sets Tom and Vermont Quality Meats apart from mass-marketed products and contributes greatly to the success of the cooperative. And Tom is also a cook! He can answer any questions that come his way about animal management or how to prepare maple-glazed quail or braised lamb.

Recipe from VERMONT QUALITY MEATS

Lamb Loin Chops with Mustard Butter

Delicious grilled lamb loin chops are topped with a melt-in-your-mouth whipped garlic mustard butter. This dish makes a tantalizing presentation when served with mashed potatoes and asparagus.

½ cup (1 stick) unsalted butter, softened

1 tablespoon Dijon mustard

½ teaspoon fresh lemon juice

2 garlic cloves, peeled and pressed

1 tablespoon fresh rosemary leaves

½ teaspoon freshly ground black pepper

8 lamb loin chops, 1¼-inch thick

Salt and freshly ground pepper

4 SERVINGS

1. In a medium bowl, cream together the butter, mustard, lemon juice, garlic, rosemary, and pepper until fluffy. Set aside at room temperature.

2. Season the chops with salt and pepper to taste.

3. Prepare a hot fire in a gas or charcoal grill. Place the chops on the grill and sear for 3 minutes. Reduce heat, turn chops over with tongs, and cook for 7 to 8 minutes longer or until desired doneness is reached.

4. To serve, place chops on a plate and top with mustard butter; the butter will melt over the warm lamb.

    Note: The mustard butter also works well with lamb sirloin tips.

Long-braised Moroccan-spiced Lamb Shanks

Set in a refurbished depot station in Poultney, the Red Brick Grill is committed to using local products. Their menu features many products from Vermont Quality Meats. Meltingly tender lamb shanks enriched by a Moroccan spice blend are a full-flavored treat. Serve over a bed of steamed couscous.

SPICE MIX

2 bay leaves

1 (3-inch) cinnamon stick

1 teaspoon cumin seed

2 teaspoons coriander seed

3 whole star anise

1 teaspoon black peppercorns

1 dried red arbol or other hot chile

1 teaspoon fennel seed

1 teaspoon whole cloves

⅛ teaspoon saffron

1 teaspoon whole allspice

1 teaspoon paprika

1 teaspoon turmeric

1 tablespoon salt

1 teaspoon ground ginger

4 SERVINGS

1. Make the spice mix: Break up the bay leaves and cinnamon stick into small pieces. Toast the bay leaves, cinnamon stick, cumin, coriander, star anise, peppercorns, chile, fennel, cloves, saffron, and allspice in a dry skillet over low heat, shaking the pan, until fragrant and lightly browned, about 3 minutes. Remove from stovetop and allow to cool.

2. Using a spice or coffee grinder, coarsely grind in batches if necessary. Transfer to a small bowl or jar and add the paprika, turmeric, salt, and ginger and combine well.

3. Prepare the lamb: Toss the lamb shanks with 2 tablespoons of the olive oil, the lemon juice, and 1½ tablespoons of the spice mix. Refrigerate overnight.

4. Preheat oven to 300°F. Heat the remaining 1 tablespoon of olive oil in a large skillet over medium heat, add the lamb shanks, and cook until lightly browned, being careful not to burn the spice coating, about 5 minutes. Remove shanks from pan.

5. In the same pan, combine the carrots, celery, onion, and garlic, and sauté until lightly browned. Season with salt and pepper to taste. Add the white wine, tomato paste, bay leaf, and thyme sprigs and bring to a boil.

6. Transfer vegetable mixture and braising liquid to a roasting pan with a tight-fitting lid, or you may use aluminum foil tightly crimped around the edge of the pan. Add shanks to the roasting pan, cover, and braise in the oven for 3 hours or until meat is extremely tender.

4 (1-pound) lamb shanks

3 tablespoons olive oil

1 tablespoon fresh lemon juice

2 carrots, peeled and coarsely
   chopped into 1-inch pieces

2 celery stalks, coarsely chopped
   into 1-inch pieces

1 large onion, peeled and coarsely
   chopped into 1-inch pieces

1 garlic head, split in half crosswise
   and peeled

Salt and fresh ground black pepper

2 cups dry white wine

2 tablespoons tomato paste

1 bay leaf

6 thyme sprigs

1 tablespoon unsalted butter

2 tablespoons chopped cilantro

7. Carefully remove shanks from the liquid, cover with foil, and set aside in a warm spot. (At this point, the shanks may also be refrigerated in the braising liquid until the following day and then reheated.)

8. Strain the braising liquid through a fine mesh sieve or strainer into a saucepan, and discard the vegetables. Bring the liquid to a boil, skim any fat off the top, and boil until slightly thickened. Reduce heat to low and whisk in the butter and cilantro. Adjust the seasonings with salt and pepper to taste.

9. Serve lamb with the pan sauce.

   Note: The remaining spice mix can be reserved in an airtight jar for future use. It may be used as a spice rub for grilled, roasted, and braised meats.

Lamb Curry

The Clyde River Valley of northeastern Vermont is home to Barbara and Harvey Levin, their sheep, and their cheese-making operation. The owners lamb in April and milk their sheep from mid-May through September, when the pastures are at their best. They do not feed antibiotics or growth hormones to their sheep, and the milk is used to produce artisanal, farmstead cheese.

Hope Farm's raw milk cheese is featured at Highland Lodge in Greensboro, Vermont, Smokejacks in Burlington, and in the acclaimed cheese selection at L'Espalier in Boston. After sampling the farm's offerings, these restaurants ordered the cheeses for their cheese carts and platters. Look for their Tomme de Brebis, Pierce Hill, and Summer Daze.

This recipe was given to the owners of Hope Farm by their friend Kalpesh Shah long before they ever dreamed of owning a sheep farm.

3–4 SERVINGS

1 tablespoon pickling spice

4 whole cloves

2 tablespoons vegetable oil

1 large onion, peeled and chopped

1 medium green bell pepper, seeded and chopped

1 pound boneless lamb, cubed

¼ teaspoon turmeric

2 tablespoons curry powder

1 teaspoon ground cumin

⅛ teaspoon ground allspice

2 tablespoons chopped fresh ginger

1 teaspoon salt

1 teaspoon sugar

Juice of 1 lemon

2 medium tomatoes, seeded and coarsely chopped

Yogurt, optional

1. Grind and combine pickling spice and cloves and combine. Heat the oil in a large pot over medium heat. Add pickling spice mixture and sauté until just browned, stirring frequently. (To avoid grease splatter, partially cover pan during frying.)

2. Add the onion and green pepper to the pot and cook for about 5 minutes, stirring constantly. Add the lamb and continue to cook for about 5 minutes, stirring constantly.

3. Combine the turmeric, curry powder, cumin, allspice, ginger, salt, and sugar in a small bowl, mixing well. Sprinkle over the lamb and cook for 2 minutes longer, stirring well to evenly coat the meat. Add the lemon juice and tomatoes and stir to combine well.

4. Cover the pot tightly and simmer for 2 hours over low heat, stirring occasionally, or cook for 2 hours in a 300°F oven. If ingredients begin to stick to pot, add a little water.

5. Serve over rice with a dollop of yogurt, if desired.

Grilled Marinated Venison Loin

Bittersweet Farm B&B prepares venison from LedgEnd Farm in Middlebury. Serve their delicious loin with a mixed salad, warm French bread, and a good red wine. The best way to cook venison steaks is quickly, on a hot grill. For maximum tenderness, serve venison rare or medium-rare. Overcooked or well-done steaks will be tough and unappealing.

4 SERVINGS

1 (1-pound) venison loin, trimmed and cut crosswise into 4 steaks

½ cup olive oil

½ cup dry red wine

1 small onion, peeled and chopped

¼ cup Dijon mustard

2 tablespoons chopped fresh basil

1 large garlic clove, peeled and crushed

Salt and freshly ground black pepper

1. Place each venison steak on a sheet of plastic wrap. Place a second sheet of plastic wrap on top of each steak and gently pound with a meat mallet to flatten steaks to a ¾-inch thickness.

2. Whisk the oil, wine, onion, mustard, basil, garlic, and salt and pepper to taste in a medium bowl to blend. Place the steaks in a shallow dish and pour the marinade over the meat. Cover and place in the refrigerator for 2 to 3 days, flipping the meat twice a day.

3. Prepare a grill to medium-high heat. Remove meat from the marinade and pat dry with paper towels. Sprinkle steaks with salt and pepper to taste.

4. Grill steaks for about 3 to 4 minutes on each side for rare, turning once, or until they are just springy to the touch. Do not cook through. Meat should be warm and red inside. Serve immediately.

On the Farm Rabbit

Champlain Valley Rabbitry is located on 25 acres of land nestled between the Green Mountains and the fertile Champlain Valley, prime farming country along the shores of Lake Champlain. Langis and Lisa Anctil started raising rabbits part time in 2000. The business began with five does and one buck, and has continued to grow every year. By 2004, the owners knew they had found their niche. Customers were happy and the business had become so successful that both Langis and Lisa were able to devote themselves full time to the rabbitry. Currently, they are marketing their top-quality New Zealand white rabbits through Vermont retail markets as well as cooperatives and distributors in the New York City and Boston areas.

Rabbit meat can be used in very much the same way as chicken. It is fine grained and mild flavored, and it is almost all white meat. Like other lean meats, poultry, and lean fish, rabbit meat is a good source of high-quality protein.

2–4 SERVINGS

1 (2½- to 3-pound) rabbit

Salt and freshly ground black pepper

½ cup all-purpose flour, or as needed

2 tablespoons olive oil

½ cup salt pork, diced small

1 medium onion, peeled and diced

1 small garlic clove, peeled and minced

½ teaspoon minced fresh rosemary

⅛ teaspoon Worcestershire sauce

1. Pat the rabbit dry, sprinkle with salt and pepper, and coat with flour. Heat the oil in a skillet over medium-high heat until hot but not smoking, then brown rabbit on all sides.

2. Place the rabbit, salt pork, onion, garlic, rosemary, and Worcestershire sauce in a slow cooker, cover, and cook on high until tender, turning occasionally, about 1 to 1½ hours. Transfer rabbit to a cutting board and let rest for 5 minutes before carving.

Roasted Rabbit with Parsnip Purée, Pete's Red Cabbage, and Sage Jus

Most entrée preparations use the hind leg and loin of the rabbit. One rabbit will generally serve 2 people. Leftover pieces, such as the forequarters and carcasses, can be used in another preparation or simply to make a stock. Ask your butcher to prepare the meat for you unless you have some free time to practice cutting up rabbits. The Pete's Red Cabbage in the original recipe is from Pete's Greens.

BRINE FOR RABBIT

6 thyme sprigs

1 tablespoon whole black peppercorns

1 tablespoon fennel seeds

2 ounces basil, roughly chopped

Cheesecloth

1 cup kosher salt

Legs and loins from 2 whole rabbits, prepared by your butcher

RED CABBAGE

2 tablespoons salted butter, bacon fat, or duck fat

1 onion, peeled and finely diced (½ cup)

1 tablespoon chopped thyme

1 garlic clove, peeled and minced

2 juniper berries, crushed in a spice grinder or mortar

1 tablespoon sugar

1 cup apple brandy

1 small head of red cabbage, quartered, cored, and thinly sliced

2 tablespoons cider vinegar

1 teaspoon kosher salt

1 teaspoon freshly ground black pepper

4 SERVINGS

1. The rabbit brine will need to be done 24 hours in advance. Place the thyme, peppercorns, fennel, and basil in the center of a piece of cheesecloth; gather the cloth around the aromatics and tie with kitchen twine.

2. Bring a gallon of water to a boil in a large stockpot over high heat. Remove the pot from the heat, add the aromatic package, and stir in the salt. Allow the aromatics to steep until the water has cooled, then add the rabbit and set in the refrigerator for 24 hours.

3. Make the cabbage: Melt the butter in a large skillet over medium heat. Add the onion and cook until soft and translucent, about 6 minutes, stirring frequently. Add the thyme, garlic, juniper berries, and sugar, stirring often. Reduce the heat to medium-low and continue to cook for about 10 minutes.

4. Increase the heat to high and add the brandy. Add the cabbage, vinegar, salt, and pepper, stirring to combine. Reduce the heat to low and continue to cook for about 45 minutes, stirring often.

5. Keep warm until serving, or store in the refrigerator overnight and reheat gently to serve.

6. Make the parsnip purée: Place parsnips in a medium saucepan and cover with water. Add 1 tablespoon of salt. Bring to a boil, reduce heat to a simmer, and cook until fork tender. Drain the parsnips, and place them in a food processor along with the remaining 1 teaspoon salt and the butter, and purée. Cover the purée and keep warm near the oven while you roast the rabbit and finish the sauce.

PARSNIP PURÉE

1 pound parsnips, peeled and cut into large chunks

1 tablespoon plus 1 teaspoon salt

2 tablespoons unsalted butter

RABBIT

Salt and freshly ground black pepper

2 tablespoons olive oil, or as needed

SAGE JUS

2 tablespoons unsalted butter

1 shallot, peeled and diced

½ cup cognac

1½ cups chicken stock

6 branches fresh thyme

8–12 leaves fresh sage

Salt and freshly ground black pepper

7. Roast the rabbit: Remove the rabbit legs from the brine, pat dry with paper towels, and season evenly with salt and pepper. Preheat oven to 425°F.

8. In a large ovenproof skillet, heat the oil over medium-high heat until hot but not smoking. Add the rabbit legs and brown on one side, 3 to 4 minutes. Do not turn the legs; this will help develop a nicely caramelized crust.

9. Transfer the skillet to the oven and roast legs for 10 minutes.

10. Meanwhile, prepare the sage jus: Melt the butter in a medium skillet over medium heat. Add the shallot and sauté, stirring often, until soft and translucent, about 5 minutes. Whisk in the cognac, scraping the bottom of pan. Whisk in chicken stock, thyme, and sage and boil until liquid is reduced to about ½ cup. Remove thyme branches and discard. Adjust seasonings with salt and pepper.

11. About 2 minutes before the rabbit legs are done, season the loins with salt and pepper. Transfer to the oven with the legs and roast for about 2 minutes for medium.

    Note: The loins cook very quickly, so keep an eye on them and do not overcook.

12. Remove the skillet from the oven and allow the rabbit to rest in the hot skillet for about 2 minutes.

13. To serve, place a heaping scoop of parsnip purée in the center of a dinner plate and add a tangle of red cabbage. Place 1 leg and 1 loin on top of the parsnip and cabbage. Top with the jus, and pass any remaining sauce at the table.

Venison Stew

Farmer Hank Dimuzio raises fallow deer in small herds at LedgEnd Farm, and Two Brothers Tavern uses his exceptional venison in this local favorite. The rich and warming stew has a deep, mildly gamey flavor. Hearty beer and winter vegetables complete this meal.

1 cup all-purpose flour

1 tablespoon fresh thyme

¼ cup parsley

3½ tablespoons celery salt

Salt and freshly ground black pepper

2 pounds venison stew meat, cut into 1-inch cubes

6 tablespoons vegetable oil

1 large Spanish onion, peeled and diced small

¼ cup chopped garlic

2 (12-ounce) bottles Otter Creek Stovepipe Porter, or other porter

3 cups venison stock or beef stock

1 (28-ounce) can stewed plum tomatoes

1 bay leaf

1 teaspoon Old Bay Seasoning

2 peeled parsnips, diced small

2 peeled carrots, diced small

4–6 SERVINGS

1. Combine the flour, thyme, parsley, celery salt, and salt and pepper to taste in a medium bowl.

2. Pat the venison cubes dry with paper towels, add to the flour mixture, and toss to coat.

3. Heat 4 tablespoons of the oil in a large pot or Dutch oven over medium-high heat. Add the venison, in batches if necessary, and sauté until browned on all sides. Transfer meat to a bowl using a slotted spoon, and set aside.

4. Heat the remaining 2 tablespoons of oil in the pot over medium heat. Add the onions and garlic and cook, stirring constantly, until soft and translucent. Add the porter to the pot, and boil over high heat, whisking often to loosen the browned bits of food at the bottom of pot, until the liquid thickens.

5. Reduce heat to low and return the meat and any accumulated juices to the pot. Whisk in the stock and tomatoes, scraping the sides and bottom of the pot. Add the bay leaf and Old Bay Seasoning, and simmer, covered, whisking occasionally, for about 1 hour, or until meat is tender.

6. Add parsnips and carrots, cover, and simmer gently, until vegetables are fork tender, about 30 minutes. Discard the bay leaf and season to taste with salt and pepper.

5 Poultry and Game Birds

Recipe from FLAG HILL FARM

Normandy Chicken with Apples and Cream

This version of the famous French dish is perfect for showcasing some of the best ingredients Vermont has to offer: naturally raised meats, crème fraîche from the Vermont Butter & Cheese Company, organic cooking apples, dry hard cyder, and Pomme de Vie, Vermont's own apple brandy from Flag Hill Farm.

Flag Hill Farm grows 87 varieties of organically certified cider apples for their three drinks. After pressing the apples, the juice is barrel fermented, producing a dry still hard cyder. Approximately a third of the still cider is then made into a champagne-method sparkling cyder, and another third is double distilled to produce Vermont's only organic apple brandy know as Pomme de Vie — literally "Apple of Life."

This dish is also great with pork — trim the fat off a tenderloin and cut thick diagonal slices — and can even be adapted as a robust vegetarian meal when made with mushrooms. Serve with new potatoes, or for a winter-friendly version, with a purée of potatoes with root vegetables such as parsnips, carrots, and celeriac.

½ (3½–4 pound) chicken, cut into 4 pieces, or 2–3 chicken breasts (see Note)

Salt and freshly ground black pepper

2 tablespoons unsalted butter

½ large onion, peeled and chopped

2 teaspoons all-purpose flour

2 tablespoons Pomme de Vie (Vermont apple brandy)

2 cups Flag Hill Farm Vermont Still Cyder (about ⅔ of a 750 mL bottle)

½ cup chicken stock

⅓ cup crème fraîche

1–2 tablespoons fresh lemon juice, or to taste

1–2 medium apples, such as Jonagold, Cortland, or Russets, peeled, cored, and cut into thick slices

½ tablespoon sugar

Note: Chicken breast will take far less time to cook than bone-in chicken.

2–3 SERVINGS

1. Rinse chicken and pat dry with paper towels. Season with salt and pepper to taste.

2. Melt 1 tablespoon of the butter in a large skillet over medium heat, add the onion, and sauté until soft. Transfer the onion to a bowl and cover with foil.

3. Return the skillet to the heat and raise temperature to medium-high. Add the chicken and brown on all sides. Sprinkle flour over the chicken and cook a few more minutes. Add the onion back to pan.

4. Remove pan from heat, and stir in the Pomme de Vie. Return skillet to the heat, tilting it to expose the brandy to the burner or igniting it with a match, and cook until the flame dies down and the alcohol burns off.

5. Pour in the cyder and stock, stirring to dissolve any lumps. Partially cover the pan and simmer on medium heat, turning the pieces of meat over occasionally. The chicken is done when the juices run clear.

6. Transfer the chicken to a warm serving dish and tent with foil.

7. Continue to cook the brandy sauce over medium heat, whisking frequently, until it is reduced by half. Add the crème fraîche and lemon juice, and stir to combine, then return the chicken to the skillet. Cook until the chicken is heated through. Adjust seasonings with salt and pepper to taste.

8. While chicken is heating, melt the remaining 1 tablespoon of the butter in a large skillet over medium-low heat. Add the apples and sauté until lightly brown and slightly softened. Raise heat to medium, add the sugar, and cook, stirring often, until sugar begins to dissolve (mixture may clump together) and caramelize. Remove pan from heat and set aside.

9. To serve, place the chicken on a serving platter and arrange the apples around the meat. Top with the brandy sauce.

Maple-glazed Chicken with Roasted Garlic and Lemon Purée

Brining poultry adds moisture and firmness to the meat and an even seasoning throughout. This recipe requires brining a whole chicken, then skinning and deboning the breasts and thighs. However, if you are not up to cutting a whole chicken into parts, boneless pieces will work as well.

Try serving this juicy bird on a bed of millet or couscous, with steamed baby carrots.

4 SERVINGS

1 cup coarse salt, preferably kosher

¼ cup pure maple syrup

1 tablespoon dried rosemary

1 tablespoon dried sage

1 small dried hot chile, such as Serrano, crushed (about 1 teaspoon)

1 (3½- to 4-pound) whole chicken

3 medium garlic heads, preferably a hard-neck variety

1 tablespoon Asian fish sauce

4 tablespoons fresh lemon juice

1 tablespoon grapeseed, walnut, or olive oil

1 tablespoon pure maple syrup

1–2 teaspoons freshly ground black pepper

2 eggs, beaten

1 cup all-purpose flour

3 tablespoons unsalted butter

1. Brine the chicken: Dissolve the salt and maple syrup in 2 gallons of water in a large pot. Add the rosemary, sage, and chile, then the whole chicken. Refrigerate for 2 to 6 hours.

2. Meanwhile, prepare the purée: Preheat oven to 450°F. Place the garlic heads in the middle of a 12- by 8-inch piece of foil. Add the fish sauce, 2 tablespoons of the lemon juice, and the oil. Carefully wrap up the foil into a purse, and bake in the oven until the cloves are soft, about 30 minutes. Remove the purse from the oven, and let it cool slightly. Separate the cloves, and gently pinch each at the top, forcing the garlic out of its skin. Mash all of the cloves with the syrup, the remaining 2 tablespoons of lemon juice, and the pepper, and set aside.

3. Assemble the dish: Preheat the oven to 375°F. Remove the chicken from the brine, rinse well in cold water, and cut into eight pieces. Skin and debone the thighs and breasts; the remainder of the bird can be used to make chicken stock for another use.

4. Dip the chicken pieces in the egg, then in the flour. Melt the butter in a skillet over medium-high heat until it begins to bubble, then arrange the chicken pieces in the pan. Cook each side for about 4 minutes, or until lightly browned. Remove from heat, and spread the purée on each side of the meat. Place in a buttered baking dish, and bake for 20 minutes.

Note: The lemon purée is also delicious spread on toasted sourdough bread to accompany soups, or added to 1 cup of sour cream or yogurt and served as a dip for raw vegetables.

FAT ROOSTER FARM

Fat Rooster Farm is a small, diversified farm located on the second branch of the White River in Royalton, Vermont. Heirloom varieties of vegetables and heritage breeds of livestock are a special priority on the farm. The owners firmly believe that it is necessary to preserve a variety of vegetables and livestock breeds in the United States. The tomatoes may not withstand shipping over 5,000 miles, and the Buff-silver-meat chickens don't grow to 12 pounds in 10 weeks time, but the farm's produce and meats offer customers unique and delicate flavors not found in most mainstream markets.

Both of the owners, Jennifer Megyesi and Kyle Jones, have master's degrees in wildlife biology and conservation. They have worked as biologists, reintroducing endangered species and preserving ecosystems in Hawaii, Maine, Massachusetts, and Vermont. After working for the U.S. Fish and Wildlife service, Jennifer became disenchanted with the bureaucracy and set her sights on learning about farming and sustainable living practices. She and her husband, Kyle, began hands-on farming in 1998. Kyle grew up in rural Ohio, working more than 1,000 acres of family farmland using conventional methods. He left for a time to pursue bird-watching and conservation biology.

Jennifer pretty much dragged Kyle back into farming. Their combination of hands-on experience and book research seems to work. Kyle dreams of someday being able to pursue his interest in woodworking (making bowls, pens, and furniture) and let someone else do the weeding.

Hemingway's Restaurant first approached the couple after meeting Jennifer at a Vermont Fresh Network event. The owners of Hemingway's were very enthusiastic about the farm's tomatoes, many of which are grown from seeds that the couple have saved for decades. Jennifer and Kyle love the restaurant's outstanding cuisine and the fact that much of it begins with locally produced items. By supplying this gourmet restaurant with heirloom vegetables, Jennifer and Kyle are hoping to increase the demand for products that may not travel well or grow quickly but have superior taste and an agricultural history.

Fat Rooster Farm is also involved with the "Good Food Direct Program," which offers locally grown produce to area schools. The program posts the schools' produce needs to the farmers, who respond with the portion of the order that they can supply. The produce is harvested during the weekend and delivered on Monday to the program coordinator, who distributes everything to elementary schools according to their needs. This innovative concept has allowed Jennifer and Kyle to introduce and involve more people in the workings of their busy farm while also offering the freshest produce to schools.

Farming is more than a profession to this dedicated couple. Jennifer and Kyle demonstrate their commitment and expertise to the community through the use of organic farming and sustainable living practices. They bring to the area a love of the land and a desire to preserve the treasure that is Fat Rooster Farm for many years to come.

Organic Roast Chicken

Maple Wind Farm's chickens are pasture raised — they receive 70 percent of their diet from foraging the earth. This natural diet results in a more delicious and nutritious meat, lower in saturated fat, and high in Omega 3s and conjugated linoleic acid (CLA).

1 (4- to 6-pound) roaster chicken, rinsed and patted dry

2 tablespoons minced fresh thyme

2 tablespoons minced fresh basil

4 garlic cloves, peeled and chopped

1½ tablespoons extra-virgin olive oil

Lemon pepper

Salt

1 medium white onion, peeled and quartered

4 SERVINGS

1. Preheat oven to 350°F.

2. Mix the thyme, basil, garlic, and olive oil in a bowl, and blend well.

3. Put the chicken in a roasting pan. Rub the outside of the chicken with the thyme-basil oil and sprinkle with lemon pepper and salt.

4. Sprinkle the main cavity of the chicken with more lemon pepper and salt, and fill with onion. Loosely tent the chicken with aluminum foil.

5. Roast in the oven for 20 minutes, then remove the foil and continue to roast about 60 minutes, until the skin is golden brown, juices run clear, and a meat thermometer inserted into the thickest part of the thigh registers between 170 and 180°F.

   Note: Calculate a total cooking time of 20 minutes per pound.

6. Transfer the chicken to a serving platter and allow the bird to rest for 15 minutes before serving.

THE DORSET INN

The Dorset Inn, one of Vermont's oldest continuously operating establishments, has been offering gracious lodging, fine dining, and traditional New England hospitality for more than 200 years. Located within minutes of ski resorts and Manchester's designer outlets, the facility also offers a relaxing in-house day spa.

Sissy Hicks is owner and chef of the Dorset Inn. Born and raised on a dairy farm in Pennsylvania, Sissy moved to Vermont in 1973. She began her cooking career at the Barrows House. It wasn't long before she was discovered by Joe Allen, proprietor of Joe Allen's Restaurants in London, Paris, Los Angeles, and New York. His influence ultimately determined Sissy's career and shaped her culinary pursuits. A self-taught chef, she has gained her cooking experience from reading recipes and continually experimenting with foods and flavors.

Today, Chef Hicks is most noted for her simple, homestyle American cuisine — comfort food at its best. Her restaurant offers mouthwatering daily specials such as meat loaf and shepherd's pie. Due to continued popular demand, the Dorset Inn's famous sautéed fresh calf's liver recently earned a permanent spot on the menu.

Farmers meet with Sissy regularly to discuss and taste their fresh products. The inn's good relationships with local farms allow the kitchen to serve only the freshest produce and meats. The restaurant's menu changes weekly — and sometimes more often — which enables Sissy to take advantage of everything her farmers have to offer.

Over the years local farmers have often grown specific types of vegetables or provided distinctive cuts of meat exclusively for the Dorset Inn — in this way they are able to showcase their finest specialty items in the restaurant's unique cuisine. There is often a featured "farm of the month" poster on display in the inn's front lobby, and the restaurant also acknowledges specific farms in the menu's food descriptions. Customers have the opportunity to meet these hardworking farmers at the inn's annual Vermont cheese-tasting events, gatherings that have become a welcome tradition at the Dorset Inn.

Brie-stuffed Chicken Breast in Pear and Cider Sauce

Moist chicken breasts from Misty Knoll are topped with the inn's special pear and cider sauce. It's a combination rarely found anywhere else that has become a favorite of the restaurant's frequent diners.

PEAR AND CIDER SAUCE

2 tablespoons unsalted butter

2 shallots heads, peeled and minced

3 ripe Bosc pears, peeled, cored, and cut into small chunks

4 fresh sage leaves

½ cup Applejack or apple brandy

3 cups fresh cider

Salt and freshly ground black pepper

STUFFING

6 ounces Brie cheese, rind removed, and cut into small pieces

¼ teaspoon ground coriander

1 shallot head, peeled and minced

1 teaspoon minced parsley

Salt and freshly ground white pepper

CHICKEN

6 (4-ounce) boneless skinless chicken breast halves

2 tablespoons vegetable oil

½ cup all-purpose flour

Salt and freshly ground pepper

6 servings brown basmati rice, prepared according to package instructions

6 SERVINGS

1. Make the pear and cider sauce: Melt the butter in a medium saucepan over medium heat. Add the shallots and cook for 3 minutes or until soft and tender, stirring often. Add the pears and sage and toss quickly and briefly.

2. Remove the pan from the heat and add the brandy. Ignite with the burner or a match and let the alcohol burn off. When the sauce begins to thicken and reduce, whisk in the cider. Bring to a boil then turn down heat to a simmer, whisking frequently. Simmer uncovered for about 30 minutes, or until sauce thickens and reduces, whisking occasionally. Adjust seasonings with salt and pepper to taste.

3. With a slotted spoon, transfer the pears to a blender or food processor and purée until smooth. Transfer the pear purée back to the sauce and whisk until well combined and heated through. Discard sage. Serve immediately, or place sauce in a container and store in the refrigerator until you are ready to use.

4. Prepare the stuffing: Mix brie, coriander, shallot, parsley, and salt and pepper to taste in a medium bowl.

5. Prepare the chicken: Preheat oven to 350°F.

6. Cut pockets in the breast halves (see Note): Starting at the center of the thicker end of breast, insert a small sharp knife horizontally and cut, stopping about 1 inch from opposite side. Be careful not to cut all the way through. Open the incision with your fingers to create a pocket. Divide stuffing mixture equally and spoon into each pocket. This can be made a day ahead and refrigerated until ready for use.

7. Heat the oil in a medium skillet over medium heat.

8. Combine the flour and salt and pepper to taste in a medium bowl, blending well. Dredge the breast halves in the flour mixture, shaking off the excess, and add to the skillet. Brown the chicken in batches, for about 4 minutes on each side, turning once, then transfer to a small roasting pan. Roast the chicken in the oven for about 10 minutes, until cooked through. Remove from oven and set aside for 5 minutes before serving.

9. Spoon the brown basmati rice onto six plates or bowls. Lay the chicken breast halves on top and spoon pear sauce over the meat.

Note: You can also ask your butcher to cut the pocket in each breast half.

Recipe from BLUEBERRY HILL INN

Apple-stuffed Chicken Breast with Calvados Jus

Blueberry Hill is nestled high in the Moosalamoo region of the Green Mountain National Forest, at the foot of Romance Mountain. The inn, with its early-1800's charm, imparts a sense of traditional country living in a warm and informal atmosphere. The cuisine at Blueberry Hill is always seasonal and always freshly prepared in their open kitchen.

To give their guests a truer Vermont dining experience, the inn regularly buys ingredients from a number of local suppliers. They buy their venison from LedgEnd Farm in Middlebury and potatoes from the Heleba Potato Farm in Rutland. (Mr. Heleba, quite a character, uses only hand tools passed down from his father.) The inn also grows a number of herbs, salad greens, and vegetables on the property.

Vary the ingredients in the filling to suit your taste; walnuts are a nice addition.

4 SERVINGS

4 tablespoons olive oil, or to taste

1 medium onion, peeled and diced

3 apples, such as Granny Smith or whatever is in season, peeled, cored, and thinly sliced

5 medium fresh sage leaves, chopped

1 cup breadcrumbs

Zest of 1 lemon

4 (6- to 8-ounce) boneless chicken breast halves with skin, tenderloins removed

Salt and freshly ground black pepper

1 pint chicken stock or reduced-sodium chicken broth

½ cup apple cider

1 tablespoon Calvados

6 tablespoons cold unsalted butter, cut into small pieces

1. Prepare the stuffing: Heat 2 tablespoons of the oil in a medium skillet over medium heat. Add the onion and sauté until soft and translucent, stirring often. Add the apples and continue to cook until fork tender. Add the sage, breadcrumbs, lemon zest, and salt and pepper to taste, combining well. Continue to cook for about 1 minute, then remove from heat and transfer to a medium bowl.

2. Place each chicken breast skin-side down on a sheet of plastic wrap, cover with another sheet of plastic wrap, and gently pound with a meat mallet to flatten. Remove the plastic wrap and season the chicken with salt and pepper to taste.

3. Place one-quarter of the apple stuffing in the center of each breast. Roll each breast into a cylindrical shape to enclose the stuffing, tie with butcher twine, and set aside. Repeat with the other breasts. If you are making this dish in advance, the stuffed breasts can be refrigerated for up to 24 hours. When ready to cook, allow breasts to reach room temperature.

4. Boil the chicken stock and apple cider in a medium skillet over medium-high heat, stirring often, until liquid is reduced by half. Remove the skillet from the stovetop and add the Calvados. Return to heat. When the sauce begins to boil, slowly whisk in the butter. Adjust seasonings with salt and pepper.

5. Preheat oven to 350°F. Lightly grease a baking sheet and set aside.

6. Heat the remaining 2 tablespoons of oil in a large skillet. Add the stuffed breasts, placing them joint-side down first to seal, then brown on all sides, about 6 to 8 minutes total. Remove the chicken from the skillet and place on the prepared baking sheet. Bake in the oven for 12 to 15 minutes or until the juices run clear.

7. Remove twine and slice the chicken at an angle into thin slices, and serve with a Calvados jus.

Sesame Chicken with Spicy Dipping Sauce

A festive and colorful dish, this sesame chicken offers a hint of Asian flavor and is ideal for a light summer meal. The apricot glaze, or nappage, can be purchased at specialty baking stores. High-quality apricot jelly may be used as a substitute for the glaze.

MARINADE

6 tablespoons lemon juice

6 tablespoons olive oil

3 tablespoons soy sauce

3 tablespoons dark rum

1½ garlic cloves, peeled and minced

½ small onion, peeled and minced

½ tablespoon crushed red pepper

1 tablespoon grated ginger

1 tablespoon sugar

1 tablespoon salt

2–2½ pounds boneless skinless chicken breasts, cut into 2-inch strips

SOY-GINGER VINAIGRETTE

2 tablespoons soy sauce

2 tablespoons lemon juice

1 teaspoon minced ginger

¼ cup olive oil

¼ cup canola oil

SPICY APRICOT SAUCE

1 cup apricot glaze or jelly

½ cup balsamic vinegar

1 tablespoon soy sauce

1 teaspoon red pepper flakes

1 teaspoon grated ginger

2 tablespoons mirin

6–8 SERVINGS

1. Marinate the chicken: Combine the lemon juice, oil, soy sauce, rum, garlic, onion, red pepper, ginger, sugar, and salt, and whisk to mix well. Place chicken in a resealable plastic bag, and add the marinade. Seal the bag and refrigerate overnight.

2. Make the vinaigrette: Combine soy sauce, lemon juice, ginger, olive oil, and canola oil in a food processor or blender, mixing for 30 seconds. Slowly add a tablespoon of boiling water and blend for another 10 seconds. Set aside.

3. Make the spicy apricot sauce: Combine the apricot glaze, vinegar, soy sauce, pepper flakes, ginger, and mirin in a medium saucepan and cook over medium heat until sauce becomes smooth, whisking frequently. If you find that the sauce is too thick, add a little water.

4. Make the chicken: Preheat oven to 400°F.

5. Toast the sesame seeds in a dry skillet over low heat until light brown. Cool and combine with the flour. Dredge the chicken strips in the flour-sesame mixture. Season with salt and pepper to taste.

6. Heat canola oil in a medium skillet over medium-high heat until hot but not smoking. Cook chicken strips on both sides until golden brown. Transfer to a shallow roasting pan and bake in the oven until chicken has cooked through, about 3 to 4 minutes.

CHICKEN

½ cup sesame seeds

½ cup all-purpose flour, or as needed

Salt and freshly ground black pepper

2 tablespoons canola oil

SESAME NOODLES

½ pound angel hair pasta

2 tablespoons chopped cilantro

4 tablespoons chopped scallions

1 tablespoon olive oil

1 tablespoon sesame oil

Fresh greens

Pickled ginger

7. Make the sesame noodles: Cook pasta according to package directions. Drain and rinse with cold water. Add cilantro, scallions, olive oil, and sesame oil. Toss to combine well.

8. Assemble the dish: Drizzle noodles with the desired amount of soy-ginger vinaigrette and some fresh greens. Place the noodle salad on a large platter and top with the chicken. Drizzle chicken with desired amount of the spicy apricot sauce. Garnish with pickled ginger and a side of the apricot sauce.

Hot Chicken Salad in Lavash Bread Bowls

This hot chicken salad is also great for low-carb diets; just leave out the lavash. The balance of textures in this dish makes it a year-round favorite.

4 tablespoons olive oil

2 sprigs fresh thyme

1 medium garlic clove, peeled and crushed

1 medium carrot, peeled and cut into ½-inch matchsticks (about ½ cup)

⅓ medium turnip, peeled and cut into ½-inch matchsticks (about ½ cup)

Salt and freshly ground black pepper

1½ tablespoons butter

8 shiitake caps, trimmed and sliced

2 (10-inch) soft lavash flat breads (see Note)

1 small head Boston lettuce, shredded, washed, and spun-dry (about 3 cups)

1 teaspoon chopped chives

1 teaspoon chopped parsley

1 pound boneless chicken breast, cut into finger-size pieces

All-purpose flour, as needed

2 shallots, peeled and minced

2 tablespoons red wine vinegar

Note: *Lavash is a large flat Middle Eastern bread. It can be found in most grocery stores.*

2 SERVINGS

1. Preheat oven to 350°F.

2. Combine 2 tablespoons of the olive oil, the thyme, and the garlic in a cold nonstick pan. Turn the heat to medium, add the carrot and turnip, and season with salt and pepper to taste. Sauté the vegetables until they become limp, stirring frequently. Transfer mixture to a plate and set aside at room temperature.

3. Heat the butter in the same pan over medium-high heat. Add the mushrooms and sauté, stirring occasionally, until liquid evaporates and they are nicely browned, about 10 minutes. Set aside.

4. Place one flat bread into a 10-inch skillet then cover with another skillet so that the upper pan molds the flat bread into a bowl shape. Bake in the oven until the bread is crisp and holds its bowl shape. Repeat with the second flat bread. Place the bread in 2 large soup bowls.

5. Meanwhile, toss the cooked vegetables, lettuce, chives, and parsley in a large bowl until well combined.

6. Heat the remaining 2 tablespoons of olive oil in a medium skillet over medium heat. Season the chicken with salt and pepper to taste. Lightly dust the chicken in flour and sauté until the meat is golden brown and cooked through. Add the shiitakes and shallots and cook, stirring frequently, until mushrooms are heated through, about a minute. Add the vinegar and cook for another minute.

7. To serve, divide lettuce mixture between the bread bowls and top with the chicken mixture. Season with salt and pepper to taste and serve at once.

Grilled Quail Salad with Maple Vinaigrette and Scallions

This is a simple but delicious appetizer salad. It is great served any time of the year but best in the spring when mixed greens, scallions, and radishes may be purchased from the local farmers' markets. The Weathersfield Inn uses quail from Cavendish Game Birds and cider products from Wood's Cider Mill. A nice wine pairing for this salad would be an organic Pinot Noir.

4 semiboneless quail

3 tablespoons balsamic vinegar

1 tablespoon chopped fresh thyme

1 tablespoon chopped fresh sage

2 medium garlic cloves, peeled and chopped

Salt and freshly ground black pepper

¼ cup maple cider jelly

¼ cup apple cider vinegar

2 tablespoons Dijon mustard

1 tablespoon ginger powder

1 tablespoon ground cinnamon

1½ cups olive oil, plus additional for tossing scallions

1 bunch of green scallions, washed and trimmed

8 ounces spring mixed greens

1 (2-ounce) bunch of radishes, washed and thinly sliced

4 SERVINGS

1. Marinate the quail: Place the quail in a large glass bowl. Meanwhile, whisk vinegar, thyme, sage, and garlic in a small bowl to combine. Season marinade with salt and pepper to taste. Pour marinade over quail and cover with plastic wrap. Place in the refrigerator for at least 1 hour.

2. Make the vinaigrette: Place the cider jelly, vinegar, mustard, ginger, cinnamon, and olive oil in a blender and mix until smooth. Season with salt and pepper to taste and set aside. (You will have more vinaigrette than you need for dressing the salad, but it's a delicious salad accompaniment, so you will be very happy to have an extra supply on hand.)

3. Meanwhile, prepare a charcoal grill or stovetop grill to medium-high. Remove the quail from the marinade, pat dry with paper towels, and sprinkle with salt and pepper to taste. Grill for about 3 minutes per side. (This game bird is best eaten medium or medium rare.) Transfer quail to a platter to rest for a few minutes before serving.

4. Toss scallions in olive oil and season with salt and pepper to taste. Transfer to the grill and cook until lightly charred on the outside.

5. Place mixed greens and radishes in a medium bowl and drizzle with the vinaigrette, lightly coating all ingredients. Season with salt and pepper to taste. Place the grilled quail and scallions on top and serve warm.

THE INN AT WEATHERSFIELD

The Inn at Weathersfield is a classic full-service inn located in Southern Vermont. Set on 21 wooded acres, the original building was built in 1792 as a stagecoach stop. In 2002, the inn was reopened after being shuttered for a year. The new owners, Jane and David Sandelman, have spent four years restoring the building and establishing it as a dining destination.

Executive Chef and owner Jason Tostrup was recruited as the head of the inn's dining operations. After working in Aspen and Napa Valley, he had moved to Vermont to be closer to the seasons, local farmers, and their products. His menu follows the harvest; because winter is a challenge for produce in the Northeast, he has started working with a few area greenhouses to produce herbs and greens year round. Jason also helps plan and tend the inn's herb and vegetable garden, where all of the edible flowers and a good percentage of herbs for the inn are grown. The dinner menu changes weekly based on what ingredients are available in market.

Every week, both an à la carte menu and Chef's Verterra's tasting menu are available. Usually a five-course tasting event, the chef's special showcases the best of the season from local farms. "I created the Verterra menu to show off what is wonderful about the land in Vermont. The intent is to bring our guests closer to the source of their food," says Jason Tostrup. Even on the à la carte menu there is a section that highlights "Food from the Neighborhood."

The Inn at Weathersfield works with a long list of local farms. The relationships vary: raspberries and currants from Cherry Hill Farm; rabbits from Champlain Valley Rabbitry; jelly, syrups, and cider from Woods Cider Mill; naturally raised beef from Black Watch Farms; and local pheasant and quail from Cavendish Game Birds. Most of the farms they do business with are located within a 10-mile radius of the restaurant.

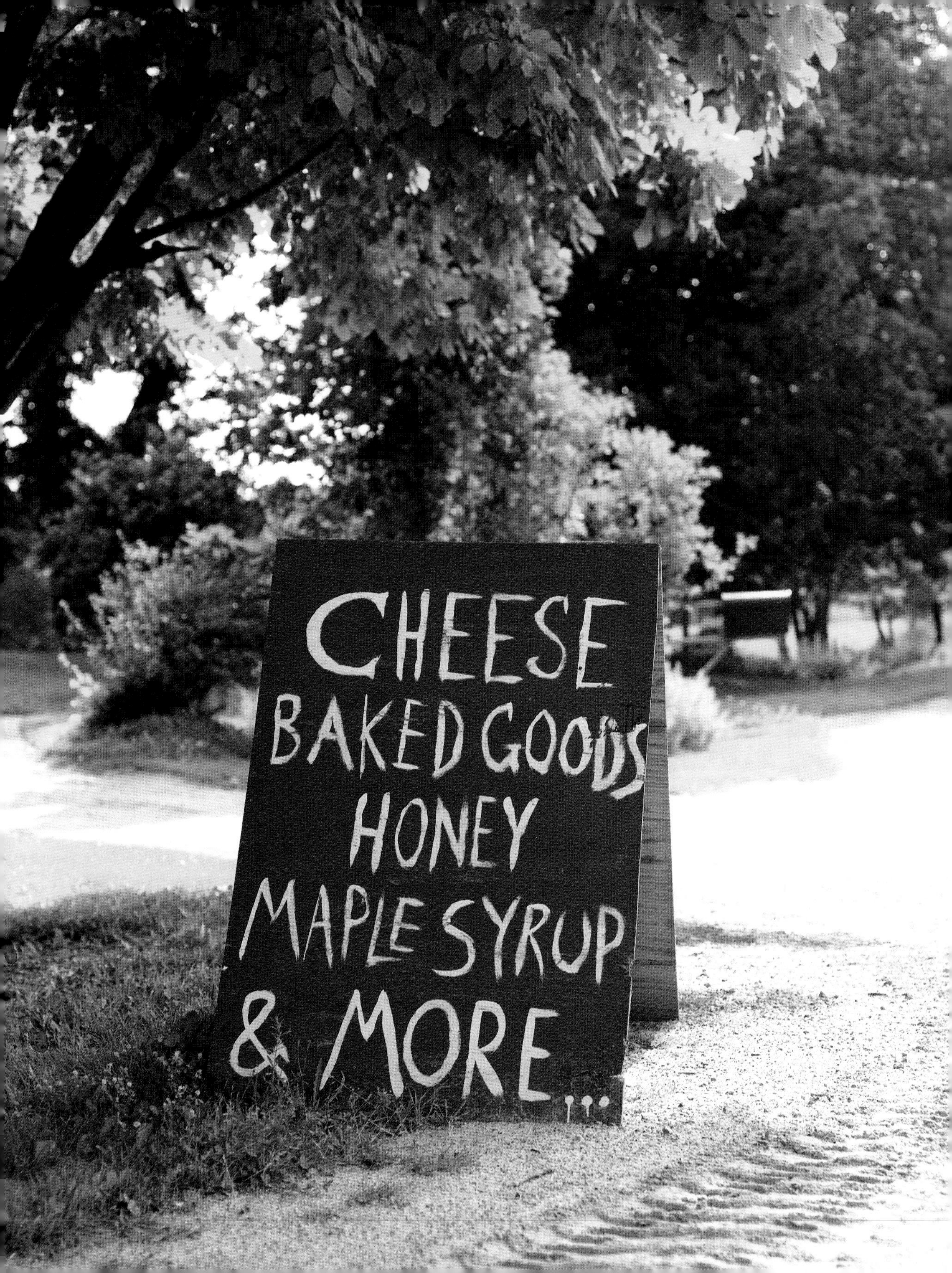
CHEESE
BAKED GOODS
HONEY
MAPLE SYRUP
& MORE...

Recipe from VERMONT QUALITY MEATS

Cavendish Quail with Maple Onion Glaze

A rich maple and onion glaze complements tender local quail from Cavendish Game Birds. This dish goes well with wild rice and steamed sugar snap peas.

12 semiboneless quail

Salt and freshly ground black pepper

2 tablespoons unsalted butter

3 tablespoons olive oil

1 large Spanish onion, peeled and sliced

½ cup dry white wine or dry sherry

½ cup pure maple syrup, preferably Vermont dark amber

6 SERVINGS

1. Preheat oven to 300°F, and place a shallow baking pan on the center rack to warm.

2. Rinse quail inside and out. Pat quail dry with paper towels and season inside and out with salt and pepper.

3. Heat 1 tablespoon of butter and 1 tablespoon of the olive oil in a large skillet until hot. Add 6 quail and brown on each side, about 3 minutes per side. Transfer quail to the preheated shallow baking pan. Add remaining quail and brown in the same manner and transfer to the baking pan with the other quail. Place in the oven to keep warm.

4. Add remaining 1 tablespoon of butter and 2 tablespoons olive oil and the sliced onion to the same skillet, and sauté, stirring constantly, over medium-high heat until the onions brown, about 10 minutes. Add the wine, loosening any browned bits of food on bottom of pan. Cook until liquid is reduced by half, add maple syrup, and heat until liquid thickens. Remove from stovetop, remove the quail from the oven, and toss the quail in the onion glaze. Serve immediately.

MICHAEL'S ON THE HILL

Michael's on the Hill serves innovative European cuisine with a perfect blend of American regional influence. By combining imported products with local ingredients, Michael Kloeti has created a cuisine worthy of the most discriminating palates.

The Vermont Fresh Network has been essential in helping to create strong relationships between Vermont farmers and chefs, and the restaurant has taken full advantage of this special organization. The use of local, fresh products makes all the difference to Michael, who designs new menus around the specialties of area farmers. Before Vermont's growing season begins, Michael discusses his wish list, specialty crops that he would like, and any unique seasonal conditions with his farmer associates. The farmers tailor what they grow to meet the restaurant's needs.

Michael loves to take advantage of specialty products that are available only for the briefest of seasons. Word of mouth has spread and now specialty food purveyors such as local wild mushroom foragers come to Michael to offer him their wonderful earthy treasures. And each spring, Michael, his family, and his staff join in the search for ramps (wild leeks). Delicious sauces and soups are made with the ramps' leaves, while the bulbs are pickled and saved for the fall, when they appear alongside braised rillettes of venison.

The restaurant itself has an on-site garden, and whenever possible, Michael uses his own berries, grapes, herbs, vegetables, and flowers to complement the menu and dècor. For aesthetic purposes, Michael keeps an area of the garden for ornamental use, always keeping in mind that a beautiful view enhances the dining experience.

Raised in a small village in Switzerland, Michael knows firsthand the importance of community support, old-fashioned values, and personal attention. He appreciates the unique opportunity to work intimately with local farmers. "In Vermont, we take advantage of the shorter growing seasons and what these seasons have produced. Following in our ancestors' footsteps, we pick fresh ramps in the spring, herbs and produce in the summer, and flowers whenever possible. This enjoyable process connects us to the traditions and true way of life of the past," says Michael. He believes that we should be grateful for, and take full advantage of, what technology and transportation have to offer — while never forgetting the pure base of where our food has come from. "There is nothing better than using meat, cheese, and eggs produced down the road. Seeing the farmer walk through our doors with beautiful, freshly picked lettuce and vegetables can elicit no greater respect for their hard work and ingenuity."

Roasted Cavendish Quail with Celery Root Purée

This recipe highlights the best of the fall season in Vermont. Michael's uses tender quail from Cavendish Game Birds — look for locally raised fresh quail in your area. Make the purée and sauce well in advance, and you have an impressive dish that's relatively simple to prepare for dinner guests. Garnish with a bouquet of seasonal greens and vegetables wrapped with a cucumber tie.

4 SERVINGS

CELERY ROOT PURÉE

1 pound celery root

¼ cup heavy cream

2 tablespoons truffle butter, (or substitute 2 tablespoons sweet butter)

⅛ teaspoon salt

⅛ teaspoon freshly ground black pepper

SAUCE

2 tablespoons unsalted butter

2 large shallot cloves, peeled and chopped

2 medium garlic cloves, peeled and chopped

1 cup red port wine

2 cups veal stock

Salt

1 tablespoon freshly cracked black pepper

QUAIL

4 semiboneless quail

4 teaspoons apple cider vinegar

⅛ teaspoon salt, or to taste

⅛ teaspoon freshly ground black pepper, or to taste

1 teaspoon vegetable oil

1. Make the celery root purée: Preheat oven to 350°F. Wash the celery root and wrap in aluminum foil. Bake in the oven until fork tender, about 2 hours. Remove from the oven and set aside to cool.

2. Once cool enough to handle, remove from foil. Peel the celery root and purée it in a blender until smooth. Slowly add heavy cream, truffle butter, salt, and pepper. Set aside.

3. Make the sauce: Heat the butter in a large skillet over medium-high heat. Add shallots and garlic and sauté until soft and translucent, stirring often. Whisk in port wine, scraping the sides and bottom of the pan. Continue to whisk until sauce reduces and thickens. Reduce heat to medium. Whisk in the veal stock, salt, and pepper. Continue to cook and whisk the sauce until it has reached desired consistency. Adjust seasonings with salt and pepper, and set aside.

4. Prepare the quail: Rub the quail with vinegar and set aside to marinate for 2 hours, then pat dry with paper towels to remove excess moisture. Season the quail with salt and pepper.

5. Preheat oven to 400°F. Heat the oil in a large ovenproof skillet over medium-high heat. Add the quail, and sear until brown on all sides, about 2 minutes per side, beginning with the breast side down.

6. Transfer to oven and cook for 5 minutes for medium rare or 10 minutes for well done. Serve immediately.

CAVENDISH GAME BIRDS

In 1986, Bill Thompson sold his New Jersey restaurant to move to Vermont and work at an inn. Fresh game birds weren't available locally, so he began raising pheasants and quail in his backyard to feed the inn's guests. Three years later, Bill was delivering fresh pheasant and quail to many of Vermont's finest restaurants, while his brother, Rick, was selling them to his restaurant accounts in Philadelphia and Boston. In 1991, the brothers joined forces to expand the business.

In 1998, they purchased a 75-acre farm in Springfield, Vermont, where they maintain their breeding stock of Coturnix quail and operate a state-of-the-art hatchery that fills their barns with thousands of quail each week. The brothers spent three years selectively breeding Coturnix quail to develop a meatier bird, which is 25 percent larger than

many chefs who were dissatisfied with the small size of commercially raised quail. Originally from Asia, these quail produce a light meat with a well-rounded, slightly sweet flavor, making them a very versatile choice for chefs. This delicate meat can be prepared in a variety of ways, using traditional or contemporary cooking methods.

Ring-necked pheasant, also of Asian origin, are prized by food connoisseurs and sportsmen alike. Cavendish Game Birds' pheasants are reared in open flight pens under a natural cover of corn and sorghum, enabling them to develop a mild game flavor reminiscent of their wild counterparts. The cold fall and winter in Vermont provide an ideal climate for developing a finish, or layer of fat under the skin, which enhances their flavor and keeps them moist

Grilled Cavendish Quail

This is a great meal to serve for a dinner party with Creamy Polenta (page 130); your guests will think you spent days in the kitchen. The recipe is also delightful for a fall or winter offering — it really warms the soul.

4 SERVINGS

3 tablespoons olive oil

½ pound hen-of-the-wood mushrooms, chopped into bite-size pieces (see Note)

2 medium shallot cloves, peeled and minced

2 medium garlic cloves, peeled and minced

1 cup Pinot Noir wine

1 cup chicken stock or reduced-sodium chicken broth

4 ounces unsalted butter

½ cup crème fraîche

Salt and freshly ground black pepper

1 teaspoon fresh, minced parsley, chives, tarragon, or chervil (optional)

4 semiboneless quail

Note: "Hen-of-the-wood" mush-rooms are available in Vermont during the summer and early fall.

1. Prepare a charcoal or stovetop grill to medium-high.

2. Meanwhile, make the sauce: Heat two tablespoons of the oil in a large skillet over medium heat. Add the mushrooms, shallots, and garlic, and sauté until soft, stirring often. Whisk in the wine and reduce by half, whisking frequently, over medium heat. Add stock and continue to whisk until sauce reduces and thickens. Swirl in the butter a tablespoon at a time. Add the crème fraîche, salt, and pepper to taste. Add herbs, if desired, and continue to simmer for another 3 minutes.

3. Prepare the quail: Lightly rub the remaining tablespoon of oil over the quail, and season with salt and pepper to taste.

4. Grill the quail for 3 to 4 minutes on each side. Transfer to a platter and let rest for a few minutes prior to serving.

Crispy Mushroom Strudel with Pheasant, Fresh Herb Cream Sauce, and Cranberries

Chef Juergen says, "I love using native products and incorporating them with Austrian style. I enjoy making strudel in a variety of ways."

Sautéed baby spinach or root vegetable julienne accompany this appetizer very well.

FILLING

4 tablespoons unsalted butter

1 small onion, finely diced

1 pound mixed fresh mushrooms, such as oyster, portobello, shiitake, button, and cremini, chopped

4 cloves garlic, peeled and minced

¼ cup Chardonnay

Salt and freshly ground black pepper

½ cup plain breadcrumbs

2 tablespoons chopped fresh chives

10 ounces pheasant breast meat, diced

STRUDEL

6 tablespoons unsalted butter, melted

10 phyllo dough sheets, thawed according to package

1 egg, lightly beaten

2 STRUDELS (8 SERVINGS)

1. Make the filling: Heat the butter in a medium skillet over medium heat. Add the onion and sauté for 1 minute, stirring often. Add the mushrooms and garlic and sauté for about 3 minutes, stirring often. Transfer the mushroom mixture to a bowl, and set aside to cool.

2. Add the wine to the skillet and cook over high heat for 2 minutes, whisking to loosen the browned bits of food at the bottom of pan. Add the liquid to the mushrooms. Season with salt and pepper. Add the breadcrumbs, chives, and pheasant and combine well.

3. Prepare the strudel: Preheat oven to 350°F. Lightly grease a baking sheet and set aside.

4. Unroll phyllo dough and cover unused portion with damp paper towels to prevent it from drying out. Cover a work surface with a kitchen towel and place a sheet of phyllo on the towel; brush evenly with butter. Cover with another sheet of phyllo and brush again with butter. Repeat this process 3 more times.

5. With the long side of the dough toward you, spoon on half the mushroom mixture in a strip about 2 inches wide. Using the towel, gently roll up the dough to encase the mushroom mixture. Transfer the strudel to the prepared baking sheet and brush with egg. Repeat the above process with the 5 remaining phyllo sheets.

6. Bake in the oven until the dough is golden brown, about 20 minutes.

SAUCE

1 cup low-sodium chicken stock

¾ cup Chardonnay

1 medium shallot, sliced

1 cup heavy cream

2 tablespoons chopped mixed fresh
    herbs, such as parsley, chives,
    rosemary, basil, and thyme

CRANBERRIES

1 tablespoon unsalted butter

¼ cup sliced cranberries

4 fresh thyme sprigs

7. Meanwhile, make the sauce: Combine the stock, wine, and shallot in a stockpot and bring to a boil over high heat, stirring occasionally. Reduce heat to medium and let liquid reduce by about two-thirds, whisking frequently. Whisk in the heavy cream and allow sauce to thicken and reduce by half. Strain the sauce through a fine sieve or strainer and adjust seasonings with salt and pepper. Add the herbs and whisk to combine well.

8. Prepare the cranberries: Melt butter in a small saucepan over medium heat. Add cranberries and cook until heated through.

9. To serve, pour the sauce in the center of a plate, spoon the cranberries across the sauce, and place a 2-inch slice of strudel in the middle of the plate. Garnish with fresh thyme.

Emu Steaks with Soy Ginger Sauce

Emu meat is taken primarily from the back of the emu, not from the breast as with most other birds. The meat is very lean and is an excellent choice for low-fat cooking. Be sure to cook the meat quickly over high heat without overcooking and eat it while hot.

1 pound emu steak, cut into small slices across the grain

1 small onion, peeled and chopped

1 inch fresh ginger root, minced

3 tablespoons fresh lemon juice

3 tablespoons soy sauce

3 tablespoons light brown sugar

2 teaspoons sesame oil or olive oil

Salt and freshly ground black pepper

3–4 SERVINGS

1. Place the meat in a resealable plastic bag. Whisk together the onion, ginger, lemon juice, soy sauce, brown sugar, 1 teaspoon of the oil, and salt and pepper to taste in a small bowl, then pour into the bag with the meat. Seal the bag and refrigerate for 1 to 2 hours, turning the bag over at least once.

2. Remove the meat from the marinade, and sprinkle with salt and pepper to taste. Heat the remaining oil in a large skillet over medium-high heat, or prepare a grill to medium, and cook meat for about 2½ minutes. Do not cook through — meat should be warm red inside. Serve immediately.

6 Maple Syrup and Honey

MAPLE FACTS

It takes about 40 years for a maple tree to grow large enough to tap. A tree 10 inches in diameter is considered minimum size for one tap.

It takes approximately 40 gallons to produce one gallon of syrup.

The normal maple season lasts 4 to 6 weeks, sometimes starting as early as February in southern Vermont and lasting into late April in northern Vermont.

Vermont has a strictly enforced maple grading law that controls standards of density, flavor, and color. The grade of maple syrup must be plainly and correctly marked on each container, along with the name and address of the producer.

There are four grades of Vermont Maple Syrup for consumers and one commercial grade.

"Vermont Fancy"
Light Amber color, delicate maple bouquet
Delightfully mild maple flavor, excellent on ice cream or on foods that permit its subtle flavor to be appreciated

"Grade A Medium Amber"
Medium Amber color, pronounced maple bouquet
Characteristic maple flavor; popular for table and all-around use

"Grade A Dark Amber"
Dark Amber color, robust maple bouquet
Heartier maple flavor; also very popular for table and all-around use

"Grade B"
The strongest and darkest table-grade maple syrup
Some people prefer this syrup for the table, and its stronger maple flavor makes it the best grade for cooking

Vermont law requires syrup to be free from any preservatives or other additives. Pure Vermont maple syrup is an excellent source of organic sugar.

Vermont maple syrup is made into maple sugar, maple cream, and maple candies. These pure maple products are made by evaporating more water from pure maple syrup and controlling the crystallization process during cooling.

The tourist industry has had a very positive impact on maple marketing, and maple products are presently being shipped to countries all over the world.

Vermont is the largest producer of maple syrup in the United States, producing about 37 percent of the total U.S. crop in 2000. Every county in Vermont produces some maple syrup. It is estimated that there are around 2,000 maple producers in the state.

In 2000, those producers made an estimated 460,000 gallons of maple syrup, with a value of approximately $13,340,000.

Production varies from year to year, with the weather playing an important role.

Honey-sweetened Tropical Fruit Salad

As the founder of the Southern Vermont/Northshire Beekeepers Association, Maddie Sobel attends conferences and seminars to learn more about the health benefits of honey and other products that come from her hives, including propolis, royal jelly, and bee venom. She also creates unique recipes using the various honeys available at different times of the harvest season.

This recipe works well with a light, early-season honey, but use whatever you have. The layered flavors in this sparkling summer fruit salad bring all the ingredients to life. The fruit compote can be served over a lemon coconut sorbet or on a bed of mesclun greens and garnished with toasted coconut and almonds.

MAKES 6–8 SERVINGS

1 cup sweetened flaked coconut

2 teaspoons plus 3 tablespoons honey

1 cup slivered, blanched almonds

Juice of 1 orange

Juice of 1 lime

1 teaspoon almond extract

¼ cup light rum

6 cups mixed tropical fruit, such as strawberries, mango, pineapple, assorted berries, melon, cut into bite-size pieces

1 head Bibb or red leaf lettuce, washed, dried, and torn into bite-size pieces

2 cups mesclun greens, washed and dried

½ sweet red onion, peeled and thinly sliced

1. Preheat the oven to 300°F. Toss the coconut with 2 teaspoons of the honey in a bowl and add a touch of water to help blend evenly. Spread the coconut on a baking sheet, and spread the almonds on another baking sheet. Toast both in the oven for about 10 minutes or until lightly browned, stirring occasionally. Remove from the oven and turn out onto a flat tray to cool completely.

2. Shake orange juice, lime juice, almond extract, rum, and 3 tablespoons honey in a mason jar to blend into a dressing. Combine fruit in a large bowl and add one half of the dressing, tossing gently to coat.

3. Arrange lettuce and mesclun on salad plates or a large platter. Garnish edges with onion, and top with the fruit mixture. Drizzle the salad with the remaining dressing, sprinkle with coconut and almonds, and serve.

THE MIDDLEBURY INN

The Middlebury Inn has been open to guests since 1827 and is registered as a national historic hotel with a full-service restaurant. Their food is purchased only through Vermont purveyors, with an emphasis on the use of seasonal, local ingredients. The kitchen purchases fruit from Stevens Orchard, known for their Honeycrisp apples, and Champlain Valley Apiaries has been doing business with the inn for decades. The flavor of their honey changes with the weather, and is another small reminder of the march of the seasons.

The inn does its best to use whatever local producers may have to offer, always keeping in mind that buying directly from the farmers enables these suppliers to realize a better profit. The Middlebury Inn enjoys supporting these hardworking Vermonters.

Smoked Salmon, Goat Cheese, Apple, and Watercress Salad with Honey Vinaigrette

This vinaigrette is a delicious all-purpose dressing you will love experimenting with at home. Throw in a little dried lavender, some fresh mint or tarragon, or even some toasted pecans. You can vary it to match almost any salad.

4 SERVINGS

- ½ cup white distilled vinegar
- 1 tablespoon Dijon mustard
- 4 tablespoons honey, preferably locally harvested
- 1 garlic clove, peeled and minced
- ¼ teaspoon orange zest
- Red pepper flakes
- Freshly ground black pepper
- ¼ teaspoon kosher salt
- ¾ cup canola oil
- 2 apples, such as Honeycrisp (Stephen's Orchard), Fuji, Pink Lady, or McIntosh, cut into thin, matchstick strips
- 4 ounces watercress, cleaned and dried (about 2 cups)
- 4 ounces smoked salmon
- Fresh goat cheese to taste, crumbled

1. Whisk together the vinegar, mustard, honey, garlic, zest, red pepper flakes and pepper to taste, and salt in a mixing bowl, combining well. Whisking constantly and vigorously, very slowly drizzle in the oil until well combined.

2. Combine the apples, watercress, a little vinaigrette, and salt and pepper to taste. Gently toss the ingredients.

3. Place salmon evenly on a platter. Place the apple and watercress salad on top and drizzle the vinaigrette around the plate. Garnish with goat cheese on top. Serve at once.

Champlain Valley Apiaries Balsamic Salad Dressing

Honeygar is 50 percent apple cider vinegar and 50 percent honey. To make honeygar, use good apple cider vinegar and fresh, local honey. (If you're in Vermont, try honey from Champlain Valley Apiaries.) The easiest way to make honeygar is to take half a jar of apple cider vinegar and top it off with honey. Allow it to sit, and shake the jar occasionally until the solution solidifies. Honeygar is an old Vermont health remedy that was promoted by the famous Vermont practitioner Dr. Jarvis. To use, simply mix a small amount of honeygar with cold or hot water and drink.

2 tablespoons honeygar

¾ cup balsamic vinegar

1 cup extra-virgin olive oil

1 garlic clove, peeled

⅛ teaspoon salt, or to taste

⅛ teaspoon freshly ground black pepper, or to taste

1 teaspoon fresh oregano, or to taste

1 teaspoon fresh sage, or to taste

1 teaspoon fresh basil, or to taste

ABOUT 2 CUPS DRESSING

Place all ingredients in a food processor or blender and blend until ingredients are completely combined. Adjust seasonings with salt and pepper.

Roasted Beets with Baby Greens, Maple Mustard Vinaigrette, and Vermont Goat Cheese

The sweetness of the beets and the roasted crunch of the pumpkin seeds combine with the mild tang of the Vermont goat cheese to make this a flavorful and delicious dish.

2 pounds (about 6) small beets, red and yellow

½ cup fresh orange juice

¼ cup extra-virgin olive oil

1 teaspoon fennel seeds

Salt and freshly ground black pepper

2 ounces white wine vinegar

1 tablespoon whole grain mustard

Juice of ½ lemon

4 ounces pure maple syrup, preferable Vermont-made

1 cup plus 2 tablespoons canola oil

½ cup pumpkin seeds

6 ounces mesclun salad mix

2 ounces fresh goat cheese, crumbled

6 SERVINGS

1. Preheat oven to 350°F. Arrange beets in a 7- by 11- by 2-inch baking dish.

2. Whisk the orange juice, olive oil, fennel seeds, and salt and pepper to taste in a medium bowl, and pour over the beets. Cover the pan with aluminum foil and roast the beets in the oven until they are fork tender, about 60 minutes. Remove the beets from the pan, reserving the roasting liquid. Let the beets slightly cool, then peel and cut each beet into wedges.

3. Make the maple mustard vinaigrette: Whisk the vinegar, mustard, lemon juice, and maple syrup in a medium bowl, combining well. Slowly but vigorously whisk in the canola oil, combining all the ingredients well. Adjust seasonings with salt and pepper to taste.

4. Toast the pumpkin seeds: Preheat oven to 350°F. Spread the seeds in a single layer on a baking sheet pan, and bake in the oven until golden, about 5 minutes, stirring occasionally. Remove from the oven and transfer to a plate and allow to slightly cool.

5. Assemble the salad: Place the mesclun in a medium bowl, pour a few tablespoons of the vinaigrette over the top, and gently toss the salad to coat all ingredients well. Arrange the greens on salad plates, with the beet wedges on the side, and drizzle beets with the reserved roasting juice. Top with goat cheese, and season with salt and pepper to taste. Sprinkle some toasted pumpkin seeds on top and serve at once.

Note: The vinaigrette makes more than needed for this recipe, but it's a delicious salad accompaniment, so you will be very happy to have an extra supply on hand. Store tightly covered in the refrigerator for up to 5 days.

The von Trapp family began welcoming guests to their farmhouse in Stowe, Vermont, in 1948. When the family settled in Stowe in the 1940s they ran their property as a working farm complete with livestock, gardens, and maple sugaring. As the farmhouse grew into a lodge, they developed relationships with local farmers to keep up with the supplies needed for their guests. Since then, it has grown into a 96-room hotel with 100 guesthouses and 12 villas and all the amenities and services of a first-class resort.

Today, Executive Chef Juergen Spagolla works with the Vermont Fresh Network and has an ongoing relationship with many local farmers and purveyors who provide him with native ingredients such as eggs and rabbits. In addition, a limited supply of herbs, edible flowers, cabbages, and raspberries are grown in the Trapp Family Lodge gardens.

The 2,700-acre mountaintop property offers sweeping views and 100 kilometers of trails for cross-country skiing, snowshoeing, and hiking. Other activities include horse-drawn wagon and sleigh rides, garden tours, concerts in the meadow, and nightly musical entertainment. The lodge continues to be owned and operated by the von Trapp family, who were the inspiration for the movie *The Sound of Music*.

BUTTERNUT MOUNTAIN FARM

Butternut Mountain Farm is unique among maple suppliers in that it is devoted almost entirely to the maple industry. It is also homegrown and locally owned. The farm was started in 1973 by David Marvin on the slopes of Butternut Mountain in Johnson, Vermont, and has become one of the state's premiere producers, packagers, and distributors of maple syrup. From managing forest lands (their own and that of area landowners) to packaging and distributing maple syrup, Butternut Mountain Farm strives to connect their work from the tree to the table. They have long and well-established relationships with many local chefs who appreciate the quality products and service that the farm offers. David loves to see his products featured in tasty meals at local restaurants, where they are enjoyed by Vermonters and visitors alike.

Grilled Maple-marinated Portobello Mushrooms

Serve these sweet, smoky, and meaty mushrooms on a roll with your favorite sandwich dressing.

⅓ cup pure maple syrup, Vermont Grade B

⅓ cup soy sauce

⅓ cup maple vinegar, cider vinegar, or rice wine vinegar

4 large portobello mushrooms

Salt and freshly ground black pepper

4 SERVINGS

1. Whisk together the maple syrup, soy sauce, and vinegar in a medium bowl until well combined.

2. Remove and discard the gills and stems from the mushrooms, and place them in a resealable plastic bag. Pour the marinade over mushrooms, seal the bag, and refrigerate for 1 to 6 hours turning the bag over at least once.

3. Prepare a grill to medium-high.

4. Remove mushrooms from marinade, reserving marinade for basting. Pat mushrooms dry with paper towels, and sprinkle with salt and pepper to taste.

5. Grill mushrooms for 3 to 4 minutes on each side, basting with reserved marinade as necessary.

Mixed Baby Greens with Maple Dressing, Cranberries, and Apples

This bright, colorful salad combines the sweetness of the maple sugar with a hint of tartness from the Granny Smith apples and dried cranberries.

4–6 SERVINGS

⅓ cup extra-virgin olive oil

1 garlic clove, peeled and halved

3 tablespoons maple vinegar or cider vinegar

⅓ cup maple sugar

Salt and freshly ground black pepper

2 Granny Smith apples, peeled, cored, and cut into thin strips

1 tablespoon fresh lemon juice

8 cups mixed baby greens, lightly packed

½ cup dried cranberries

½ cup toasted, chopped walnut halves or pecans

3 ounces goat cheese, crumbled

1. Make the maple dressing: Drizzle a little of the oil into a large wooden bowl. Add the garlic and mash it into a fine paste using a wooden spoon. Whisk in the vinegar and sugar until well combined. Whisk in the remaining oil in a slow stream until completely incorporated. Adjust seasonings with salt and pepper.

2. In a medium bowl, toss apples with lemon juice to prevent from browning.

3. Add the apples, greens, cranberries, and half the walnuts to the bowl with the dressing, and toss to coat well. Divide the salad among plates or bowls and sprinkle with the remaining walnuts. Top with goat cheese and serve at once.

Hemingway's Honey Balsamic Vinaigrette

Serve this vinaigrette with Hemingway's Fallen Soufflé of Vermont Goat and Cheddar Cheeses on page 124. Its sweetness is a natural foil for the acidity in the soufflé. For that reason, this vinaigrette is wonderful with any dish that needs a little added sweetness. Try it in place of your standard vinaigrette on salads, or as a light sauce with fish or shellfish. Similar to honey mustard, it can also be used on sandwiches instead of plain mustard.

1½ tablespoons minced shallots

1 tablespoon Dijon mustard

¼ cup honey

⅓ cup dark balsamic vinegar

1 cup salad oil or vegetable oil

Salt and freshly ground black pepper

1 ½ CUPS VINAIGRETTE

Whisk the shallots, mustard, honey, and vinegar in a medium bowl until well combined. Slowly and vigorously whisk in the oil to create an emulsion. Adjust seasonings with salt and pepper to taste.

Honey Apple Chutney

The Vermont Beekeepers Association is one of the oldest agricultural groups in Vermont. The members take a great deal of pride in the honey they harvest, promoting and marketing it as a Vermont-grown gourmet product. This delicious chutney is a great accompaniment to savory dishes — try it with grilled pork chops.

2 apples, cored and chopped

¾ cup currants

¾ cup chopped onion

½ cup chopped green bell pepper

½ cup chopped dates

2 garlic cloves, peeled and finely chopped

1 cup honey

¾ cup apple cider vinegar

½ teaspoon ground cinnamon

1 teaspoon red pepper flakes

ABOUT 2 ½ CUPS CHUTNEY

Put all ingredients in a medium skillet, and bring to a boil over medium-high heat. Reduce heat to a simmer and cook for about 40 minutes, stirring occasionally. Cool and refrigerate.

Fresh Spinach Salad with Basil Maple Vinaigrette

Valley Dream Farm is owned and operated by the Tisbert family: Joe, Anne, Jay, Ashley, Becky, Jon, and Zippy the Wonder Dog! Most of their business is done from their farm stand or with CSA farm members. In addition, they are members of the Deep Root Organic Co-op in Johnson, Vermont, where they are able to sell their organic produce wholesale. Their products are shipped throughout Vermont and to several organic chains along the East Coast. They currently ship wholesale pumpkins, field cucumbers, squashes, and sweet corn.

The farm stand opens in late June, offering consumers deliciously fresh organic vegetables. In mid-July, Valley Dream also invites customers to visit their cut-your-own field-flower garden. Spring bedding plants, hanging baskets, and custom window boxes are available. They also provide educational school tours in May and June.

This vinaigrette is the perfect way to showcase farm-fresh ingredients.

4–6 SERVINGS

½ cup coarsely chopped basil leaves

2 tablespoons minced onion

2 tablespoons chicken stock

4 tablespoons vinegar

1 tablespoon Dijon or yellow mustard

2 tablespoons pure maple syrup

Salt to taste

1 cup extra-virgin olive oil

2 spinach bunches (10–12 ounces each), washed, dried, stemmed, and torn into bite-size pieces

2 cups cherry tomatoes, or to taste, halved

4 strips of bacon, cooked and crumbled (about ¼ cup)

1. Make the vinaigrette: Combine the basil, onion, stock, vinegar, mustard, maple syrup, and salt, in a food processor or blender, mixing well.

2. Continue to process, and slowly add the oil a little at a time until all the oil is used and fully incorporated. The dressing should have a smooth and satiny texture.

3. Toss the spinach, tomatoes, and bacon bits in a large salad bowl. Add the dressing a ¼ cup at a time, gently tossing, until you have reached desired taste. Divide salad among chilled salad plates or bowls, and serve.

Maple Nut Muffins

Two kinds of maple give these muffins a deep, rich sweetness that goes well with the nuts.

2 cups all-purpose flour

¼ cup maple sugar

1 tablespoon baking powder

½ teaspoon salt

1 egg

1 cup whole milk

½ cup (1 stick) butter, melted and slightly cooled

⅔ cup pure maple syrup, preferably Vermont medium or dark amber

1 cup pecans, butternuts, or walnuts, chopped

10 MUFFINS

1. Preheat oven to 350°F. Grease a muffin pan or line with paper muffin cups.

2. Mix flour, maple sugar, baking powder, and salt in a medium bowl. Whisk the egg, milk, butter, and maple syrup in another medium bowl. Add the milk mixture to the flour mixture, stirring until almost combined. Gently fold in the nuts.

3. Spoon the batter into the prepared muffin pan. Bake muffins in the oven until they are golden brown and firm to the touch, about 20 minutes.

4. Transfer to cooling rack. Serve warm with maple butter or maple cream.

7 Desserts and Other Baked Goods

Recipe from VERMONT MYSTIC PIE COMPANY

Laura's Maple Pumpkin Pie

David Barash's love of pies goes back to the 1960s when, as a boy, he spent many happy hours helping his mother make pies from scratch. Dave has made his pie dream a reality. His company, Vermont Mystic Pie, sells apple pie, blueberry apple pie, and pie shells to small country stores in the Northeast and various independent stores and chains around the country.

For Laura Ann Nedich, the head pastry chef at the Vermont Mystic Pie Company, pumpkin pie was a family Thanksgiving tradition. Her mother always made it with canned pumpkin and Cool Whip, but Laura has updated it with fresh local pumpkins, cream, a dab of Vermont maple syrup, and Vermont Mystic's pie shells.

1 Vermont Mystic Pie Shell, unbaked, or other prepared (9-inch) pie shell in pie plate

1 cup fresh pumpkin (from 1 small pie pumpkin)

2 eggs

¼ cup pure maple syrup, preferably Vermont-made

¼ cup brown sugar

1 teaspoon ground ginger

1 teaspoon ground cinnamon

½ teaspoon nutmeg

⅛ teaspoon cloves

¼ teaspoon kosher salt

⅓ cup heavy cream

⅓ cup whole milk

¼ teaspoon maple extract

MAPLE WHIPPED CREAM

¼ cup heavy cream

1–2 tablespoons pure maple syrup

1 (9-INCH) PIE

1. Preheat oven to 400°F.

2. Cut the pumpkin in half, scoop out the seeds, and place face down on baking sheet with ¼ cup water. Bake pumpkin in the oven until soft, about 45 minutes. Remove from oven. Scrape pulp away from skin, discard skin, and purée pulp in a food processor. Set aside.

3. In a large bowl whisk together the eggs, maple syrup, sugar, ginger, cinnamon, nutmeg, cloves, salt, and pumpkin until smooth. Slowly whisk in the cream, milk, and maple extract until smooth. Strain mixture into a separate large bowl through a fine mesh strainer to avoid lumps.

4. Pour mixture into the pie shell. Transfer to the freezer and freeze overnight.

5. Preheat oven to 300°F. Place frozen pie onto a baking sheet. Bake for 40 to 50 minutes or until pies are completely set.

6. Transfer to a cooling rack and let cool.

7. Make Maple Whipped Cream: 30 minutes before making the whipped cream, place a medium stainless steel bowl and the whisks from your electric handheld mixer in the freezer. (This will speed up the whipping process.)

8. Pour heavy cream and maple syrup into the bowl and whisk with the mixer on medium speed until cream forms soft peaks. Place a generous spoonful on top of each piece of pumpkin pie, and serve.

Recipe from VERMONT BUTTER & CHEESE COMPANY

Pumpkin Pie Topped with Candied Ginger and Crème Fraîche

This is a fabulous pie — easy to make because of the premade shell and canned purée, but very flavorful and light. The crème fraîche/ginger topping is brilliant.

1 (9-inch) unbaked pie shell in pie plate

1 cup sugar

¼ teaspoon salt

1¼ teaspoons ground cinnamon

½ teaspoon ground ginger

¼ teaspoon ground nutmeg

¼ teaspoon ground cloves

1½ cups canned pumpkin purée

1 teaspoon pure maple syrup, preferably Vermont-made

3 farm-fresh eggs, separated

16 ounces (2 cups) crème fraîche, preferably Vermont-made

2 tablespoons chopped candied ginger (available as "crystallized" in the Asian section of market)

1 teaspoon honey, preferably locally harvested

1 (9-INCH) PIE

1. Preheat oven to 450°F.

2. Prick the pie shell all over with a fork and bake until golden brown, 10 to 15 minutes, or if store bought, cook according to package directions. Remove shell from the oven to cool and reduce heat to 350°F.

3. Combine ½ cup of the sugar, salt, cinnamon, ginger, nutmeg, and cloves in a double boiler. Stir in the pumpkin purée and maple syrup.

4. Beat the egg yolks in a medium bowl and stir into the pumpkin mixture. Add 1 cup of the crème fraîche and mix well. Cook pumpkin mixture over simmering water (not boiling) until slightly thickened, stirring constantly, about 6 minutes.

5. Meanwhile, prepare an ice bath. Transfer the bowl with the pumpkin mixture to the ice bath and let the custard cool, stirring occasionally, about 7 minutes.

6. Beat the egg whites in a medium bowl until soft peaks form. Gradually beat in the remaining ½ cup sugar. Gently fold into the pumpkin mixture. Pour filling into the cooled crust (you may have more than you need; don't overfill), smooth top, and bake for 45 minutes, until filling has set and the top has browned. Cool pie to room temperature, about 2 hours.

7. While the pie is baking, prepare the topping: Mix the remaining cup of crème fraîche with the candied ginger and honey. Refrigerate topping mixture. Spread evenly over the top of the cooled pie or place a dollop of topping mixture on top of each pie slice.

Strawberry Rhubarb Pie

The Lilac Inn in Brandon is a renovated 11,000 square foot Historic District mansion, built in 1909. It sits amid two acres of beautifully manicured gardens. The inn offers the services and amenities one expects to find at a small luxury hotel. There are nine tailored guest rooms designed to suit each visitors needs. Many weddings, corporate retreats, visitors to Middlebury College, and Green Mountain recreation enthusiasts have enjoyed its ambience.

Throughout the year, the Lilac Inn's menu showcases the freshest native ingredients whenever possible. Many of their recipes rely on the superb flavors of Vermont cheeses, maple syrup, and cider, as well as locally grown game and produce. This strawberry-rhubarb pie is an old Maryland recipe that Shelly has used since she and her husband, Doug, got married in 1970. It is a special reminder of the couple's home state. Even when they lived as far away as England, this pie brought them a taste of home.

3 cups hulled and halved fresh
   strawberries

1½ cups sugar

3 tablespoons cornstarch

3 cups trimmed and diced rhubarb

2 tablespoons all-purpose flour

1 tablespoon cold unsalted butter,
   cut into pieces

2 (9-inch) premade pie shells,
   1 in pie plate, 1 rolled out

1 egg

1 tablespoon milk

Confectioners' sugar

1 (9-INCH) PIE

1. Preheat oven to 450°F.

2. Place strawberries in a medium saucepan. Add ½ cup of the sugar and mash strawberries slightly to extract juice. Combine the cornstarch with a little bit of cold water in a cup and stir until smooth. Add to the strawberries, and cook over medium heat until the juice is thickened, stirring occasionally.

3. Distribute the rhubarb over the pie shell in pie plate. Sprinkle with flour and remaining 1 cup sugar. Dot with butter. When the strawberry mixture is slightly cooled pour over the rhubarb.

4. Cover with the rolled out pie shell and crimp the edges with your fingers or a fork to seal. Slit the top in a few places. Whisk the egg and milk and brush over the top shell. Place the pie on a baking tray with sides to catch any juice overflow.

5. Bake in the oven for 10 minutes. Reduce heat to 350°F and bake until crust is golden brown and juices are bubbling, about 30 minutes. Remove from oven and cool. Garnish with a light dusting of confectioners' sugar and serve as is or with a scoop of vanilla ice cream, if desired.

Rhubarb Custard Kuchen

Guests at Liberty Hill Farm adore this recipe, even if they always thought they hated rhubarb! The farm's owner grew up loving rhubarb and the many dessert possibilities for this often misunderstood plant.

CRUST

1¾ cups all-purpose flour

½ teaspoon baking powder

⅛ teaspoon salt

¾ cup unsalted butter

1 egg, beaten

1 tablespoon whole milk

FILLING

1½ pounds rhubarb, trimmed and cut into ½-inch pieces (about 4 cups)

1 egg, beaten

¾ cup whole milk

1 teaspoon pure vanilla extract

1 cup sugar

1 teaspoon cinnamon

2 tablespoons all-purpose flour

12 SERVINGS

1. Preheat oven to 400°F.

2. Sift the flour, baking powder, and salt in the bowl of a food processor and process until well combined. Cut in the butter. Add the egg and milk and continue to process until the mixture resembles coarse meal, about 2 minutes. Gently press the mixture into the bottom of a 9- by 13-inch pan.

3. Fill the kuchen: Spoon the rhubarb into the pan.

4. Whisk together the egg, milk, and vanilla in a small bowl, and pour evenly over the top of the rhubarb.

5. Combine the sugar, cinnamon, and flour in a medium bowl, and sprinkle evenly on top of the rhubarb mixture.

6. Bake in the oven until the top is golden brown and juices are bubbling, about 45 minutes.

Vermont Mystic Apple Pie

To find the best apple pie recipe, Dave Barash searched Vermont's hills and valleys. He went to county fairs to seek out the blue-ribbon winners of pie-baking contests. He ate a lot of pies and reviewed a lot of recipes. He sought the advice of Vermont's best pie makers. Assisted by The New England Culinary Institute (NECI), Dave even held a statewide contest of his own to find the best recipe. Through it all, Dave tasted many pies and learned a great deal about pie making, but he still didn't have the recipe that he wanted: an all-natural pie with a flaky butter crust, a flavorful combination of Vermont apple varieties, and subtle seasonings.

The final decision meant going back to the drawing board to develop an original recipe. With the help of Jeff Hammelman (Master Baker at King Arthur Flour) the perfect crust was finally developed. After lots of experimentation, Dave settled on the best apple variety and the tastiest spice mixture. Here is the result.

DOUGH

1 (9-INCH) PIE

½ cup plus 2 tablespoons pastry flour, chilled

½ cup plus 2 tablespoons all-purpose flour, chilled

1 stick plus 1 tablespoon unsalted butter, chilled

1 teaspoon kosher salt

¼ cup cold water

1. Make the dough: Place the pastry flour, all-purpose flour, and butter in the bowl of an electric mixer. Using a paddle attachment, mix on low speed until the butter forms almond-size pieces. Mix the salt into the water. Add the salt water to the flour-butter mixture, and mix until just combined. Wrap the dough in plastic and let rest in the refrigerator for at least 30 minutes or overnight.

2. Divide the dough in half, one for the top and one for the bottom crust. On a lightly floured work surface, roll out each piece of dough slightly larger than 9 inches. Line a 9-inch pie plate with one of the dough rounds.

3. Make the filling: Mix the sugar, cinnamon, allspice, nutmeg, flour, and salt in a medium bowl until combined. Add the apples and toss to coat, then add lemon juice and stir to combine. Fill the lined pie plate with the apples. Place the second dough round on top of the apples and crimp the edges by hand. Transfer to the freezer and freeze the pie for 1 hour.

4. Preheat oven to 450°F. Line a baking sheet with foil. Place the baking sheet on bottom rack of the oven to heat.

FILLING

½ cup granulated sugar

¼ teaspoon ground cinnamon

⅛ teaspoon ground allspice

⅛ teaspoon ground nutmeg

2 tablespoons all-purpose flour

⅛ teaspoon kosher salt

4 Empire apples, peeled, cored, and cut into large slices

2 Cortland apples, peeled, cored, and cut into large slices

1 teaspoon freshly squeezed lemon juice

EGG WASH

1 egg

1 tablespoon whole milk

5. Take pie out of freezer and cut 4 air vents in the top. Whisk together egg and milk to make egg wash. Brush the top of the pie with egg wash.

6. Place on warm baking sheet and bake in the oven for 15 minutes. Reduce temperature to 400°F, and bake until the top is golden brown and the juices are bubbling, another 45 to 50 minutes. Remove from oven and set aside for at least 30 minutes before cutting to allow juices to thicken.

Note: If the crust begins to brown too quickly, cover it with foil.

Grandma's Dutch Apple Torte

The crust for this fast, never-fail family standard is similar to shortbread. It's just delicious! This is the recipe of Cape Cod resident Barbara Soller, grandmother of Champlain Orchard's owner, Bill Suhr.

1 cup all-purpose flour

2 teaspoons baking powder

¼ teaspoon salt

⅛ teaspoon nutmeg

2 tablespoons sugar, plus more for the apples

1½ tablespoons butter, plus more for the apples

1 egg, beaten

1 teaspoon pure vanilla extract

2 tablespoons whole milk

7 apples, peeled, cored, and sliced

Ground cinnamon

1 (9-INCH) PIE

1. Preheat oven to 375°F. Lightly butter a 9-inch pie plate, and set aside.

2. Mix the flour, baking powder, salt, nutmeg, and sugar in a large bowl. Cut in the butter with a pastry blender. Mix the egg, vanilla, and milk in a small bowl and add to the flour mixture. Blend with a fork until mixture begins to form a soft dough; press evenly into the pie plate.

3. Toss apples with cinnamon and sugar to taste. Mound apples into the crust. Sprinkle apples and edges of crust with sugar. Dot with butter, and bake for 40 minutes until bottom is golden brown. Cover with foil if the top browns too quickly. Cool slightly. Serve with vanilla ice cream.

Variations:

- To make a 10-inch torte, increase the crust recipe by 50 percent.
- You can also add ground nuts to the dough for added crunch; it's nice with almonds.
- Try this with peaches or plums or berries: Add about a tablespoon of flour or cornstarch to the fruit, and also mix some flour and sugar and spread the mixture on top of the crust before filling the pie with fruit. If you're making a blueberry torte, when you remove it from oven, immediately sprinkle a small handful of large perfect berries on top of the hot pie.

Apple Crumb Pie with Crème Fraîche

This recipe is based on a true French "Tarte aux Pommes," with an American touch added. The crème fraîche filling gives a refreshing and smooth texture that is reminiscent of a crème brulée, while the pecan crumble topping adds a crunchy contrast.

1 (10-inch) prepared pie shell

5 large apples, such as Northern Spy or Rhode Island Greening

1½ cups crème fraîche, preferably Vermont-made

1 tablespoon pure vanilla extract

¾ cup all-purpose flour

1 farm-fresh egg

¾ cup sugar

½ cup dark brown sugar

½ cup cultured butter, preferably Vermont-made, cold and cut into pieces

1 cup chopped pecans

1 (10-INCH) PIE

1. Preheat oven to 450°F. Fit pastry into a 10-inch pie plate, flute edges, and refrigerate for 30 minutes or longer.

2. Peel, core, and slice apples into ¼-inch slices. Arrange in the chilled pie shell.

3. Combine the crème fraîche, vanilla, ¼ cup of the flour, egg, and sugar in a medium bowl. Beat until smooth and pour over the apple slices. Bake in the oven for 10 minutes at 450°F, then reduce heat to 350°F and bake for another 30 minutes.

4. Mix the remaining ½ cup flour, brown sugar, and cultured butter together in a small bowl until the mixture is crumbly. Fold in the pecans and sprinkle over the baked pie. Return the pie to the oven and continue baking for 15 minutes or until top is golden brown.

VERMONT BUTTER & CHEESE COMPANY

In the late 1970s Allison Hooper, an American college student in France, began writing letters to local organic farmers; in return for room and board she would work around the farm. A farmer in Brittany answered her letter and soon she was hard at work learning the art of artisanal cheese-making in the European tradition.

Bob Reese, marketing director of the Vermont Department of Agriculture, was a colleague of Allison's in the 1980s, when she had returned to Vermont and was working as a state dairy lab technician. Bob had invited a French chef to prepare an upcoming special state dinner, and he needed fresh goat cheese, which was scarce in Vermont at that time. Bob knew that Allison had spent time in France and had acquired cheese-making skills there. He also knew that she kept goats on her Vermont farm. So he asked her for help. Her chèvre was a huge success and a cheese-making partnership was born.

The Vermont Butter & Cheese Company, launched in 1984, is based in Websterville, Vermont. Twenty local family farmers supply all the fresh milk for the company's products. Allison and Bob promote sustainable agriculture, but they know that the farmer must realize a profit to make the system feasible. They work with farmers on goat's milk pricing, farm management, and developing a larger market for premium goat's and cow's milk cheeses. Vermont Butter & Cheese is also working with the University of Vermont's Center for Sustainable Agriculture with the goal of keeping the company's milk supply sustainable.

Vermont Butter & Cheese Company has gained an outstanding reputation for its mild goat's milk cheese, which is available in its classic form or blended with ingredients such as Divina olives, roasted red peppers, herbes de Provence, or fresh garlic. There is also a Vermont feta crafted in the traditional Greek style. Cow's milk is used for their crème fraîche and European-style butters. Fromage blanc, a light addition to uncooked dishes, and Quark, a German-style cheese, as well as mascarpone, the smooth, thick main ingredient in tiramisu, are all on the list of company products. Each product was developed to meet the requests and needs of the country's talented chefs who wanted only the finest, freshest ingredients to use in their restaurants and recipes.

Flip-over Apple Cake

Serve this cake warm or at room temperature. It is tasty with a favorite topping such as whipped cream, ice cream, or yogurt, but it is just as delicious plain. Garnish with a sprig of mint.

½ cup (1 stick) unsalted butter, plus more for the pan

4 medium apples, preferably Northern Spy or Rhode Island Greening

1 tablespoon ground cinnamon

1 cup plus 1 tablespoon sugar

1 cup unbleached all-purpose flour

1 egg, lightly beaten

1½ cups coarsely chopped walnuts

Mint sprigs

1 (9-INCH) ROUND CAKE

1. Preheat oven to 350°F. Generously grease the bottom and sides of a 9-inch round cake pan with butter and set aside.

2. Melt ½ cup butter in a medium saucepan over medium heat. Set aside to cool to room temperature.

3. Peel, core, and cut the apples into ¼-inch slices. Place the apples in a bowl and toss to coat with cinnamon and 1 tablespoon of the sugar. Place apple slices in overlapping concentric circles on the bottom of the prepared pan. Make a second layer if necessary.

4. Sift the remaining 1 cup of sugar and the flour in a large mixing bowl. Whisk in the egg and melted butter just until combined (do not overmix). Fold in the walnuts and continue to mix until smooth. Pour batter evenly over fruit, and smooth top with a rubber spatula.

5. Place on the center rack of the oven and bake until the cake is golden brown and a cake tester or toothpick inserted into the center comes out clean, about 40 to 45 minutes.

6. Remove cake from oven and place on a wire rack to cool, about 15 minutes. When the pan is cool enough to handle, run a knife around the edge and invert the cake onto a serving plate.

7. Serve warm or at room temperature, plain or with a favorite topping such as whipped cream, ice cream, or yogurt. Garnish with mint sprigs.

Village Inn Apple Cake

Moist and delicious, this is always a favorite of the inn's guests.

6 medium apples, such as Northern Spy or other tart, crisp apples, peeled, cored, and thinly sliced

⅓ cup plus 1½ cups sugar

2 teaspoons ground cinnamon

4 eggs

1½ teaspoons pure vanilla extract

1 cup canola oil

½ cup freshly squeezed orange juice

3 cups all-purpose flour

½ teaspoon salt

1 tablespoon baking powder

½ teaspoon baking soda

Confectioners' sugar

1 (10-INCH) CAKE

1. Preheat oven to 350°F. Grease a 10-inch tube pan with removable bottom. Set aside.

2. Toss the apples, ⅓ cup of the sugar, and 1½ teaspoons of cinnamon in a large bowl, mixing well.

3. Beat the remaining 1½ cups sugar and the eggs in a large bowl using an electric mixer for about 2 minutes at medium speed or until the mixture is pale yellow. Add the vanilla and mix until well combined.

4. Whisk the oil and orange juice together in a small bowl. Combine the flour, salt, baking powder, baking soda, and remaining ½ teaspoon cinnamon in a separate medium bowl. Add a third of the dry ingredients to egg mixture and beat until just combined. Add half of the oil and juice mixture to the egg mixture and beat until just combined. Repeat process in the same manner until flour mixture and oil and juice mixture are done. Do not overmix.

5. Pour half of the batter into prepared pan. Layer half of the apples over batter. Top with the remaining batter, and then finish with remaining apples. Pour any accumulated juices from the apples over the top of the cake.

6. Bake in the oven for about 1 hour 15 minutes, or until a tester inserted into the cake comes out clean. Garnish with a light dusting of confectioners' sugar.

Apple-topped Cheesecake

Tina Wood, owner with her husband, Willis, of Wood's Cider Mill, has always loved making cheesecakes. One of her fondest memories is the cheesecake her mother made for book club gatherings. Tina and her sisters would stay awake until after their parents had gone out and then they would polish off what was left after the book club had met. Tina's mom's cheesecake was covered with a thick, gooey cherry sauce, but Tina prefers the delicacy and flavor of apples.

4 medium apples, such as Cortland, peeled, cored, sliced ⅛-inch thick

½ cup cinnamon cider syrup, preferably Wood's Cider Mill

6 tablespoons unsalted butter, softened

⅓ cup plus ½ cup sugar

1 cup all-purpose flour

Salt

2 (8-ounce) packages cream cheese, softened

½ teaspoon pure vanilla extract

3 eggs

¼ cup sliced almonds

1 (9-INCH) CHEESECAKE

1. Preheat oven to 350°F.

2. Arrange apple slices in a single layer in a shallow baking dish. Drizzle ¼ cup of the cinnamon cider syrup evenly over the apples.

3. Cover with foil and bake in the oven for 15 minutes. Remove from oven and set aside.

4. Cream the butter and ⅓ cup of the sugar in a large bowl using an electric mixer at medium speed, until light and fluffy. Add the flour and a pinch of salt and continue to combine until the mixture becomes crumbly, then gently press it into the bottom of a 9-inch springform pan, and set aside.

5. Combine the cream cheese, remaining sugar, a pinch of salt, and vanilla in a large bowl of an electric mixer. Cream until smooth and fluffy, scraping the bowl as necessary. Mix in the eggs, one at a time, until well combined, scraping the bowl each time. Spread the cheese filling evenly over the crust.

6. Arrange the warm apples in a circular design over the top of the filling. Evenly drizzle the remaining ¼ cinnamon cider syrup over the apples, and sprinkle almonds over the top. Bake in the oven until golden brown, about 40 minutes.

7. Remove from oven and transfer to a cooling rack. Once cooled, place on a serving platter and carefully loosen springform sides. Remove and place in the refrigerator to chill for at least 4 hours before serving.

FLAG HILL FARM

Located in the foothills of the Green Mountains, in the town of Vershire, Flag Hill Farm has been growing apples and making international award–winning cider since 1984. The owners, Sabra Ewing and Sebastian Lousada, use only organic fruit to make two varieties of hard cyder — sparkling and still. Flag Hill spells their cyder with a "Y" to distinguish their handmade, farmhouse product from sweet apple cider and carbonated apple wines.

The farm grows many of the apple varieties used in their hard cyder and supplements their supply with local unsprayed and wild apples from neighboring farms. Flag Hill Farm's hard cyder is bottled in limited release and packaged in hand-numbered bottles, available only in Vermont. The farm has also begun producing apple and pear brandies.

Flag Hill's founders met the chef/owners of Hemingway's Restaurant, Linda and Ted Fondula, at a Vermont Fresh Network evening event. Sabra and Sebastian were pouring their champagne-method hard cyder and dry, still, hard cyder at the event. Ted, who had studied to be a sommelier, gave them great feedback and invited them to serve it at Hemingway's during a special fall dinner to celebrate Vermont Fresh Network producers. Each course of the special dinner was paired with a Vermont wine; Flag Hill served their chilled Vermont sparkling cyder before dinner in Hemingway's elegant bar. The guests enjoyed a full evening of local specialties and informative talk from local farmers and producers.

Recipe from HEMINGWAY'S RESTAURANT

Hemingway's Late Summer Cyder Soup with Orange Sorbet

Hemingway's wanted to create a dessert that featured a unique Vermont product and was "clean" — that is, a dessert with no fat. This nonfat offering has become a perennial staple on Hemingway's dessert menu.

SIMPLE SYRUP

1½ cups granulated sugar

1½ cups water

SORBET

½ bottle sparkling hard cider (such as Flag Hill Farm Cyder) or plain dry French apple cider

1 cup orange juice

Zest from 1 orange

Juice and zest from 1 lime

SOUP

1 cup Gewurztraminer wine

1½ cups simple syrup, cooled

½ cup white or red table grapes

½ cup fresh cherries, such as Bing, pitted

3 fresh plums, pitted

1 3-inch cinnamon stick

Zest from 1 orange

1 fresh mint sprig

Sparkling hard cider

2 ripe plums, pitted, sliced, and fanned

2 ripe peaches, pitted, sliced and fanned

1 ripe kiwi, peeled and diced

½ cup raspberries

1 cup fresh cherries, pitted and cut in half

8 SERVINGS

1. Make the simple syrup: Whisk together the sugar and water in a small saucepan, and bring to a boil over medium-high heat, whisking constantly until sugar has dissolved and mixture has become translucent, about 20 seconds. Remove saucepan from heat and allow to cool completely before using.

2. Make the sorbet: Combine cider, orange juice, orange zest, lime juice, and lime zest in a medium bowl. Add 1½ cups of simple syrup. Transfer the mixture to an ice cream maker, and process according to the manufacturer's instructions. Store in the freezer.

3. Make the soup: Simmer the wine, 1½ cups simple syrup, grapes, cherries, plums, cinnamon, orange zest, and mint in a large heavy-bottom saucepan until tender, about 30 minutes. Remove from heat. Discard cinnamon stick and mint. Purée the mixture with a handheld immersion blender or in a regular blender (in batches if necessary) until the texture is smooth. Strain the mixture through a fine sieve or strainer, and then chill in the refrigerator.

4. Ladle ¼ cup of the chilled soup into a soup bowl. Add a splash of hard cider. Fan the plums and peaches around the upper portion of the bowl. Place the cherries, raspberries, and kiwi in the center of the bowl. Top with a scoop of orange sorbet.

CHERRY HILL FARM

Cherry Hill Farm is located one and a half miles uphill from the old downtown of Springfield. It is a former dairy farm of about 100 acres that looks west across to the Green Mountains. The owners, Peter and Victoria Hingston, were attracted to the area while on holiday from England and brought their English fruit-growing skills to Vermont.

Peter and Vicky grow black, red, and white currants, along with red and black raspberries on Cherry Hill Farm. Currants were chosen as a crop supplement to keep the fields open using a fruit other than raspberries. None of the fruit is sprayed for insects, and pesky Japanese beetles are removed by hand. The bushes are very hardy, and do not suffer from many growing problems, enabling the Hingstons to use earth-friendly methods.

The currant — a unique little berry — has an established place at Cherry Hill. Peter and Vicky cannot say enough good things about the health value of this berry, explaining that it boasts high levels of antioxidants and four times the vitamin C of oranges, as well as the highest levels of potassium found in fruits. Currants are a bit tart, somewhat like cranberries. Peter has developed a number of delicious ways to combine tart currants with sweet ingredients. Apple and black currant smoothies, fruit iced tea, jams and jellies, even pie filling are all lovely ways to enjoy the under-appreciated berries.

In early July, the farm opens for pick-your-own berries, drawing customers from far and wide. The Hingstons also manage a summer farm stand and sell their products at farmers' markets in Bellow's Falls and Lebanon. They sell black currant purée, frozen berries, and preserves, which they make in a converted milk room of the former dairy farm.

Jason Tostrup, the chef at the Inn at Weathersfield, is a fan of the Hingstons' produce and products and has used both fresh berries and the farm's black currant purée in his recipes. Recently, Cherry Hill Farm was featured as a partner of the Inn at Weathersfield at the annual Farmers' Dinner.

Warm Berry Compote

This quick summer compote can be served either hot or cold. It is delicious on its own or as a topping for ice cream, yogurt, or pancakes. It will keep in the refrigerator for two to three days or in the freezer for three months.

4 SERVINGS

1 pound assorted summer berries, preferably a mix of black, red, or white currants, and red or black raspberries

⅓ cup granulated sugar, or to taste

1 teaspoon freshly squeezed lemon juice

1 (3-inch) cinnamon stick (see Note)

Vanilla ice cream, preferably Vermont-made

Note: *A vanilla pod split lengthwise, seeds scraped, or 2 to 3 fresh sprigs of mint may be substituted for the cinnamon stick.*

1. Combine the berries, 2 to 3 tablespoons of water, sugar, lemon juice, and cinnamon stick in a large saucepan over medium heat. Bring to a boil, gently stirring occasionally. Reduce to a simmer and cook until the fruit is soft and the sugar dissolves, about 15 minutes. Taste the berries as they cook, adding more sugar if needed. Remove the cinnamon stick.

2. Scoop ice cream into dessert bowls and top with 1 or 2 spoonfuls of warm compote.

Raspberry Almond Thumbprint Cookies

A good-for-you cookie that really tastes great, these thumbprints are one of most popular offerings at the Butterfly Bakery. The sweetness of the jam plus the nuttiness of the cookie makes this treat a hit with everyone.

2 cups almonds

2 cups rolled oats

2 cups whole spelt flour, or 1 cup whole wheat flour and 1 cup all-purpose flour, combined

¼ teaspoon salt

1 cup pure maple syrup

1 cup sunflower oil

2 (10-ounce) jars of raspberry jam

ABOUT 30 COOKIES

1. Preheat oven to 350°F. Line 3 baking sheets with parchment paper or aluminum foil, and set aside.

2. Grind the almonds in a food processor until they start to clump, then transfer to a large bowl. Place the rolled oats in the same food processor and pulse until they are fine, but not yet flour, and add to the almonds. Add the spelt flour and salt to the almond mixture. Mix until well combined.

3. Make a well in the center of the dry ingredients and combine the maple syrup and sunflower oil in the well. Mix together the wet and dry ingredients until a smooth dough forms.

4. Roll the dough into 1½-inch balls and place them about 1½ inches apart on the prepared sheet pans. Press your thumb into each to make a good-size indentation. With a spoon, fill each indentation with a small spoonful of jam.

5. Bake in the oven for 15 to 20 minutes, or until the cookies can be gently lifted off the baking sheets with a spatula without crumbling. If you used aluminum foil make sure to remove the cookies to a cooling rack while they are still warm.

Variations: This is a great recipe to experiment with — it works with any nut-jam combination. Switch your favorite nut for the almonds and your favorite jam for the raspberry.

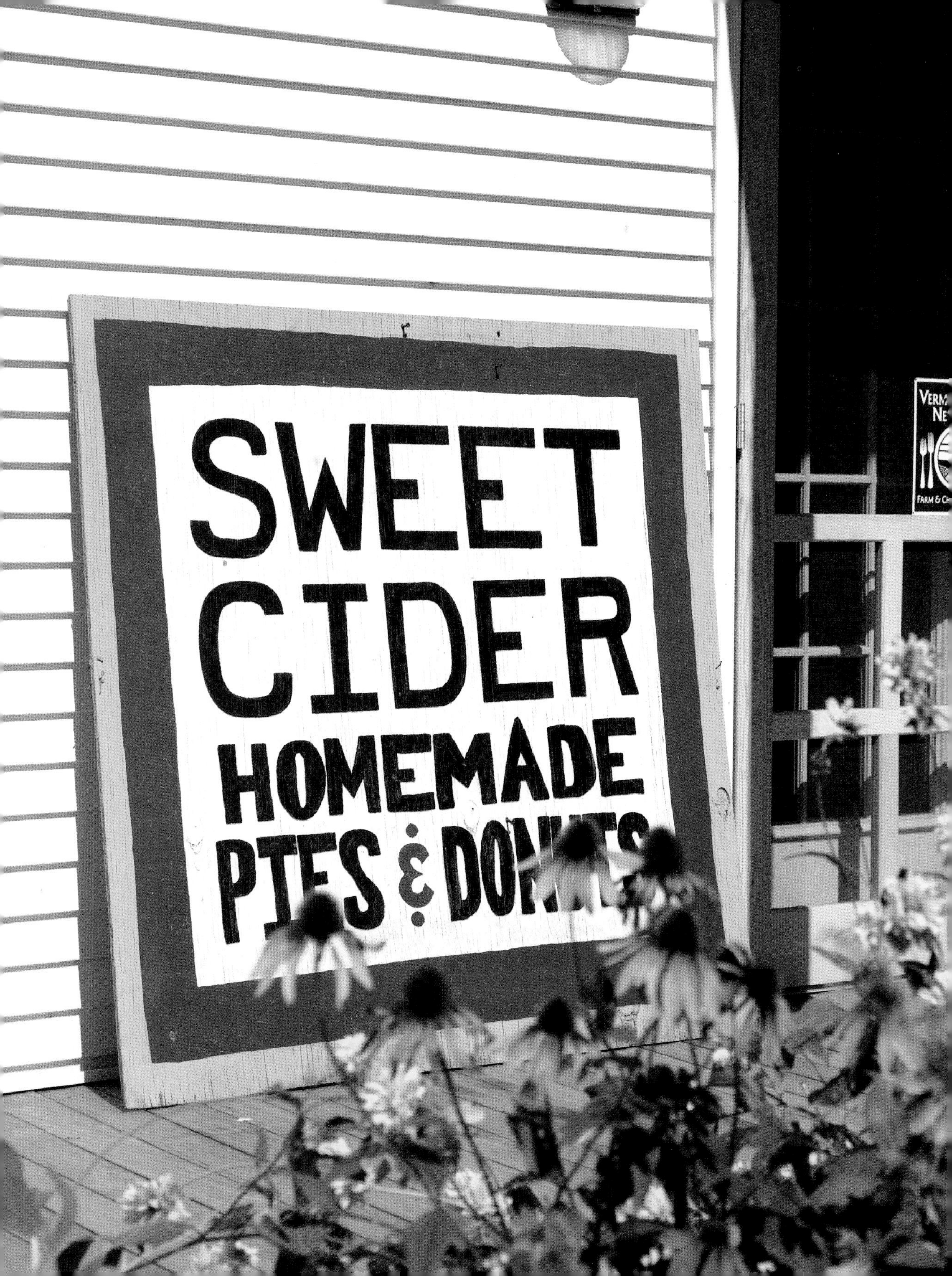
SWEET
CIDER
HOMEMADE
PIES &

Blueberry Bread Pudding with Warm Blueberry Sauce

In October of 1958, David French purchased a farmhouse with a carriage house and a barn in Wilmington. He turned it into a ski lodge and named it the Nutmeg Inn after his home state of Connecticut. The property has changed hands since then and is now run by Susan and Gerald Goodman. They call the property the Nutmeg Country Inn & Bakery.

Innkeeper and Executive Chef Susan Goodman's bakery is known for its seasonal fresh fruit pies and desserts. People come from all over to sample the pies and other goodies made from the juicy-sweet offerings of local farmers and growers.

This recipe was created when Goodman worked as the pastry manager at Steamer's Grill in Los Gatos, California. It became so popular that customers started calling in their orders well in advance to make sure they had one order to eat for dessert and one to go!

8 SERVINGS

1 cup whole milk

3 cups heavy cream

2 vanilla beans, split lengthwise and seeds scraped

12 eggs yolks

1¼ cup granulated sugar

1 pinch freshly ground nutmeg

1 loaf of brioche, cut into 1-inch cubes

4 cups fresh blueberries

1 tablespoon coarse sugar (see Note), or to taste

1 teaspoon freshly squeezed lemon juice

¼ tablespoon fresh lemon zest

¼ teaspoon ground cinnamon

Note: *Coarse sugar, also called decorating sugar, crystal sugar, and sugar crystals, has granules about four times larger than those of regular granulated sugar.*

1. Lightly butter a 9½- by 13½- by 2-inch glass baking dish, and set aside.

2. Bring the milk and cream to simmer in a large saucepan over medium heat. Remove pan from heat and add the vanilla seeds and pods. Cover and let sit for 10 minutes to infuse flavors.

3. Combine egg yolks and 1 cup of the granulated sugar in a large bowl, and whisk until light yellow. While whisking constantly, temper the yolks with a small amount of the warm cream mixture. Continue to pour all of the milk mixture very slowly into the yolk mixture, whisking constantly until completely combined. Pour mixture through a fine mesh strainer, and discard the vanilla pods. Add the nutmeg and combine well.

4. In a large bowl, gently but thoroughly toss the brioche and 2 cups of the blueberries, and pour into the prepared dish. Add half of the cream mixture to the brioche and let sit for 10 minutes. Press the bread gently to submerge it into the liquid. Pour in the remaining mixture, making sure all of the bread is soaked, and sprinkle the top with the coarse sugar. Allow the pudding to stand for 30 minutes. Meanwhile, preheat oven to 300°F.

5. Bake pudding uncovered in a water bath in the oven for 1¼ hours or until pudding is set and bread is puffed and lightly browned.

6. Meanwhile, make the sauce: Combine the remaining 2 cups blueberries, remaining ¼ cup sugar, ½ cup water, lemon juice, lemon zest, and cinnamon, in a medium saucepan, and bring to a boil over medium heat. Boil for 1 minute and remove from heat. Transfer mixture to a blender or food processor and purée until smooth. Strain and cool.

7. To serve, cut the warm pudding into squares and place in the center of a plate. Top with warm blueberry sauce, letting it drizzle down the sides to puddle on the plate.

Cranberry Almond Squares

This recipe can be prepared a day ahead and served as an anytime snack.

1½ cups sugar

2 eggs

¾ cup (1½ sticks) unsalted butter, melted and cooled slightly

¾ teaspoon almond extract

¼ teaspoon ground cinnamon

1 pinch ground nutmeg

½ teaspoon salt

1½ cups all-purpose flour

1½ cups fresh cranberries, preferably Vermont-grown

½ cup sliced almonds

16 SQUARES

1. Preheat oven to 350°F. Lightly butter a 9- by 9-inch or 11- by 7-inch baking pan, and set aside.

2. Beat the sugar and eggs in a large bowl using an electric mixer, until slightly thickened. Beat in the melted butter, almond extract, cinnamon, nutmeg, and salt.

3. Stir in the flour. Fold in the cranberries and almonds with a rubber spatula.

4. Pour the batter into the prepared pan and bake in the oven for about 55 minutes, or until a toothpick inserted into the center comes out clean. Transfer to a rack and cool completely. Cut into 16 squares.

Cranberry Apple Crisp

Ye Olde Tavern in Manchester is a circa-1790 colonial inn. It is not difficult for modern-day visitors to imagine arriving by stagecoach as guests did in the eighteenth century. The tavern is the perfect firelit refuge, a place where road-weary travelers can find a warm welcome and an extraordinary meal. The menu features regional New England and continental fare, highlighting a wealth and diversity of Vermont-grown ingredients and products. They use Vermont dairy, cheese, pheasant, ice cream, coffee (grown somewhere else, but roasted by Green Mountain Coffee), apples, fiddleheads, rhubarb, mushrooms, and a variety of other seasonal products. An award-winning wine list enhances the dining experience.

Serve this simple dessert with a scoop of vanilla bean ice cream, preferably from Wilcox Ice Cream Stand, made right in Manchester Center. A dollop of whipped cream and a light dusting of cinnamon add a delicious finishing touch.

1 pound tart apples, such as Granny Smith, peeled, cored, and sliced (about 4 cups)

2½ cups cranberries

¾ cup sugar, or to taste

½ cup all-purpose flour, preferably King Arthur

½ cup kettle or rolled oats

¾ teaspoon ground cinnamon

¾ teaspoon ground nutmeg

2 tablespoons pure maple syrup, preferably Vermont-made

5 tablespoons cold unsalted butter, cut into small pieces

6–8 SERVINGS

1. Preheat oven to 375°. Butter an 8- by 8- by 2-inch square pan, and set aside.

2. Combine the apples, cranberries, and sugar in a large bowl, then spread into the prepared pan.

3. Combine flour, oats, cinnamon, and nutmeg. Stir in the syrup and cut in butter until coarse meal forms. Spoon over fruit to cover.

4. Bake in the oven until juices are bubbling, apples are tender, and the top is golden brown, about 30 minutes.

Broiled Apples with Maple and Pomme de Vie

Imagine this quick dessert with a scoop of cold, rich vanilla ice cream (Vermont's Strafford Creamery makes a wonderful version). You will love the caramelized apple flavor of this sophisticated tart, made without the hassle or calories of a crust.

2 tablespoons unsalted butter, softened

4–6 firm medium apples, such as organic Jonagold, Northern Spy, or Cortland

Juice of 1 lemon

4 tablespoons sugar

⅓ cup pure maple syrup

3 tablespoons Pomme de Vie (Vermont-made apple brandy)

Vanilla ice cream

4–6 SERVINGS

1. Preheat broiler. Grease a cookie sheet or shallow baking pan with the butter, and set aside.

2. Peel, core, and cut apples into fat ¼-inch-thick slices. Evenly sprinkle the lemon juice and 2 tablespoons of the sugar over apples.

3. Place the apples in a single layer on the prepared pan and broil about 6 inches from the heat, until apples are golden, about 7 to 10 minutes. Remove pan from oven and sprinkle the remaining 2 tablespoons sugar evenly over the apples. Return to the oven and continue to broil until the edges just begin to darken or slightly char.

4. Meanwhile, in a small saucepan bring the maple syrup to a boil over medium-high heat. Add the brandy and cook for 3 minutes, stirring frequently. Spoon hot apples and sauce over ice cream and serve immediately.

Easy Banana Cake with Low-fat Dessert Sauce

Willie T's Good Food Bakery is located on Tylord Farm in Benson. Willie T uses Vermont-grown, Vermont-milled organic wheat and pure Vermont maple syrup with other quality whole food ingredients to make a unique selection of desserts without eggs or hydrogenated oil. Fruit breads — easy to make and lower in fat and sugar — are a healthful, delicious dessert alternative to traditional cakes.

Fresh berries and a simple yogurt sauce really make this banana cake special. For a vegan alternative to the yogurt sauce try a drizzle of honey or maple syrup on the plate.

1 LOAF

2 cups whole wheat pastry flour

½ cup Sucanat sugar (see Note)

1 teaspoon baking soda

⅛ teaspoon salt

¾ cup apple juice

1 teaspoon pure vanilla extract

4 tablespoons pure maple syrup

2 cups chopped ripe bananas

½ cup chopped walnuts or raisins, or both, optional

1 cup nonfat yogurt

Blueberries, raspberries, or blackberries, optional

Note: *Sucanat sugar can be found at most co-ops. It is a natural sweetener made from dehydrated fresh sugar cane juice. It has a taste similar to molasses or sugar.*

1. Preheat oven to 350°F. Grease an 8- by 4-inch loaf pan, and set aside.

2. Sift the flour, sugar, baking soda, and salt into a medium mixing bowl. Add the apple juice and ½ teaspoon of the vanilla extract and 3 tablespoons of the maple syrup, stirring until almost combined. Fold in the bananas with a rubber spatula, and then the nuts or raisins, if desired.

3. Pour the batter into the prepared bread pan. Bake in the oven until bread is golden brown and firm to the touch, about 50 minutes.

4. Meanwhile, make the dessert sauce: Combine the yogurt, the remaining 1 tablespoon maple syrup, and the remaining ½ teaspoon vanilla extract in a small bowl until well combined.

5. To serve, drizzle the sauce on a plate and place a slice of cake on top. Garnish with berries, if desired.

Recipe from BUTTERFLY BAKERY OF VERMONT

Carrot Cake with Cream Cheese Frosting

Claire Fitts, owner of the Butterfly Bakery of Vermont, believes in keeping her local economy healthy by purchasing as many regionally produced ingredients as possible. The bakery uses flour from King Arthur and Champlain Valley Mills and butter and sour cream from Cabot Creamery. The bakery's cookies and bars are made with Hillsboro Sugarworks organic, pure Vermont maple syrup. Claire enjoys her interactions with these small business people; mutual support is a very important part of the bakery's philosophy.

This amazingly moist carrot cake can be made using a combination of whole wheat and all-purpose flour, but Claire loves to use whole spelt flour. The mellow nutty flavor of spelt is what really makes the carrot cake great. Look for spelt in natural and health food stores.

1 cup vegetable oil

2¼ cups pure maple syrup

4 tablespoons arrowroot or cornstarch dissolved in 4 tablespoons of water

2 cups whole spelt flour, or 1 cup whole wheat flour and 1 cup all-purpose flour combined

2 teaspoons baking soda

2 teaspoons baking powder

2 teaspoons cinnamon

½ teaspoon salt

4 cups shredded carrots

1 cup chopped walnuts plus additional for decoration, optional

2 (8-ounce) packages cream cheese, at room temperature

1 tablespoon pure vanilla extract

1 (9-INCH) CAKE

1. Preheat oven to 350°F. Lightly grease two 9-inch cake pans, and set aside.

2. Whisk the oil, 1½ cups of the maple syrup, and arrowroot in a large bowl until well combined.

3. Mix the spelt flour, baking soda, baking powder, cinnamon, and salt in a separate, large bowl. Then add the dry mixture to the wet mixture and whisk until smooth.

4. Fold in the carrots and walnuts, if using, with a rubber spatula, mixing thoroughly. Pour the batter into the prepared pans and transfer to the oven.

5. Bake for about 1 hour or until the cake has pulled away from the sides of the pans. Transfer to a cooling rack.

6. Meanwhile, make the frosting: Beat together the cream cheese, the remaining ¾ cup maple syrup, and the vanilla in a food processor until smooth. Transfer to a bowl and store in the refrigerator until the cake is ready for frosting.

7. When the cakes have cooled completely, hold one pan at an angle and give it a nice hard tap against the counter to loosen the cake from the pan. Then invert the cake onto a cake plate.

8. Remove cream cheese frosting from the refrigerator and frost the top and sides of the layer. Loosen the second cake and gently invert it onto the first. (It should be noted that these cakes crumble easily, so don't try to hold the cake in your hands.) Frost the whole cake and cover the sides with walnuts, if desired.

Gingerbread Cupcakes with Orange Cream Cheese Frosting

Richly dark and dense, these cupcakes refresh the traditionally spicy flavor of old-fashioned gingerbread with a cool and creamy orange frosting. It is one of the house favorites at Izabella's Eatery.

1¼ cups pastry flour

1½ teaspoons ground ginger

1 teaspoon cinnamon

¼ teaspoon ground cloves

½ teaspoon allspice

¼ teaspoon salt

6 tablespoons unsalted butter, softened

½ cup granulated sugar

½ cup unsulfured molasses

1 egg, lightly beaten

1 teaspoon baking soda

1 (8-ounce) package cream cheese, softened

1½ cups confectioners' sugar

½ teaspoon pure vanilla extract

1 teaspoon freshly grated orange zest

1 tablespoon fresh orange juice

Candied ginger, optional

Candied orange, optional

12 CUPCAKES

1. Preheat oven to 350°F. Line a 12-cup muffin tin with paper muffin cups. Set aside.

2. Mix the flour, ginger, cinnamon, cloves, allspice, and salt in a large bowl.

3. Combine 4 tablespoons of the butter with the granulated sugar in a separate bowl, and beat until fluffy using an electric mixer. Add the molasses and egg and continue to beat until the mixture is smooth — the mixture may appear slightly curdled.

4. In a small bowl whisk together the baking soda and ½ cup of boiling water until the baking soda has dissolved. Add the baking soda mixture into the molasses mixture, whisking until combined. Add the molasses mixture to the flour mixture, whisking until combined.

5. Divide the batter among the prepared muffin cups. Bake muffins for about 20 minutes, until they are golden brown and firm to the touch, or until a toothpick inserted into the center comes out clean. Transfer cupcakes to a rack and cool completely.

6. Meanwhile, combine the cream cheese and the remaining 2 tablespoons butter, the confectioners' sugar, and vanilla in a medium bowl. Beat with an electric mixer until fluffy and smooth. Add the orange zest and orange juice, and continue to beat until smooth and well combined.

7. Transfer to the refrigerator for approximately 30 minutes.

8. When cupcakes are cool, spread the frosting evenly on the cupcakes, and sprinkle with candied ginger or candied orange or a little of both, if desired.

Chocolate Porter Cake

This dense, mildly sweet cake is balanced by a rich frosting that also complements the pint of beer baked into every cake!

1 (10-INCH) CAKE

2 cups Stovepipe Porter from Otter Creek Brewery, or other porter

1 pound plus 3 tablespoons unsalted butter

1½ cups unsweetened cocoa powder

4 cups all-purpose flour, plus more for cake pans

1 tablespoon baking soda

1½ teaspoons salt

4 cups granulated sugar

4 eggs

1⅓ cups sour cream

12 ounces semisweet chocolate chips

1 cup plus 2 tablespoons whipping cream

4¼ cups confectioners' sugar

1 tablespoon pure vanilla extract

1. Preheat oven to 350°F. Lightly coat two 10-inch cake pans with cooking spray and flour.

2. Bring beer and 1 pound of the butter just to a boil in a medium saucepan. Sift in the cocoa and whisk until smooth. Remove from heat.

3. Sift the flour, baking soda, and salt in a large bowl, then whisk in the granulated sugar and set aside.

4. Combine the eggs and sour cream in a large bowl. Beat with an electric mixer until smooth, scraping bowl as necessary. Add the beer mixture and continue to combine briefly, then fold into the flour mixture.

5. Divide the batter into the prepared pans and bake in the oven for 50 minutes, or until the sides of the cakes have pulled away from the pans and the tops are firm. Cool at room temperature for 15 minutes.

6. Meanwhile, make the frosting: Place the remaining 3 tablespoons of butter and the chocolate chips in a double boiler over low heat, whisking constantly until melted and combined. Add the cream and quickly whisk to combine before the chocolate dries out or breaks. Remove from the heat, and stir in the confectioners' sugar a handful at a time, whisking until smooth and free of lumps. Add vanilla and whisk to combine well.

7. Pour the frosting into a metal bowl and transfer to the refrigerator. Stirring occasionally, allow frosting to cool enough to spread, about 1 hour.

Chocolate Cake

If you use soy milk, this is a great vegan cake that tastes not-so-vegan, especially with the dark ganache frosting. It is important to note that you should use a high-quality dark chocolate. This cake looks absolutely beautiful if you cover the sides with chocolate shavings, broken chocolate, or cacao nibs.

3½ cups soy milk or 1½ cups milk and 2 cups heavy cream

2½ cups pure maple syrup, preferably Vermont-made

¾ cup vegetable oil

3 tablespoons arrowroot or cornstarch dissolved in 3 tablespoons water

1 tablespoon pure vanilla extract

2¾ cups all-purpose flour or whole spelt flour

1 cup plus 2 tablespoons cocoa powder

2¼ teaspoons baking powder

2¼ teaspoons baking soda

1½ teaspoons salt

1½ cups hot coffee or boiling water

1 pound dark chocolate or chocolate chips

1 (8-INCH) CAKE

1. Preheat oven to 350°F. Lightly grease three 8-inch cake pans.

2. Whisk together 1½ cups of the soy milk, the maple syrup, oil, arrowroot, and vanilla in a medium bowl.

3. Sift the flour, cocoa powder, baking powder, baking soda, and salt in a separate large bowl. Slowly whisk the wet ingredients into the dry ingredients until all the liquid is added and the batter is smooth — the batter will be very thin.

4. Whisk the coffee into the batter and immediately pour into the prepared cake pans. Bake in the oven for about 45 minutes or until a toothpick inserted in the centers comes out clean and the cakes pull away from the sides of the pans. Cool on a rack.

5. Meanwhile, make the frosting: Scald the remaining 2 cups soy milk in a medium saucepan over medium-low heat, making sure not to burn the liquid. Break up the chocolate into ¼-inch pieces and place in a medium bowl with high sides. Pour the hot milk over the chocolate pieces and whisk until the chocolate melts into a smooth mixture. Cool to room temperature, pour into a bowl, and cover with plastic wrap. Place the ganache in the refrigerator to set.

6. Once the cake layers are completely cooled and the ganache is thickened but spreadable, about 4 hours, invert the cakes onto separate plates. Frost the top of each layer and layer the cakes. Then frost the sides.

Note: If the frosting becomes too thick, let stand at room temperature to soften; if it's too thin, beat with an electric mixer until it thickens

Mascarpone Chocolate Fondue

This is one of the best "Chocolate Lover" desserts; all you need is a good, intense dark chocolate that will balance the creamy and rich texture of the mascarpone cheese when melted. Then, let the accompaniments set the tone.

6–8 SERVINGS

1 (8-ounce) container mascarpone, preferably Vermont-made

1 cup strong dark chocolate chips

⅓ cup milk

2–3 tablespoons Kahlùa, espresso, or other flavored liqueur or syrup

Salt

Sliced bananas, strawberries, apples, marshmallows, and/or cubed pound or angel food cake

1. Combine mascarpone, chocolate, milk, Kahlùa, and a pinch of salt in a small saucepan. Cook over medium-low heat, stirring constantly, until the mixture is melted and smooth.

2. Transfer mixture to a ceramic fondue pot and keep warm over a canned heat burner or candle. Serve with fruit, marshmallows, and cubed cake.

Whole Wheat Pastry Flour Brownies

When the Gleasons taste the nutty flavor of these brownies, they really appreciate the fact that the flour is the secret ingredient to their success. The secret is not only the flavor of the whole wheat pastry flour, but the fact that Ben and Theresa planted the seeds, watched the wheat grow, and harvested and milled the flour themselves. That intimacy with the ingredients really makes you appreciate what you're eating.

4 eggs, beaten

½ cup (1 stick) unsalted butter, melted

1 teaspoon pure vanilla extract

1 cup whole wheat pastry flour, plus additional for dusting

½ cup cocoa powder

2 cups sugar

½ teaspoon salt

½ cup bittersweet chocolate chips, best quality (optional)

½ cup coarsely chopped pecan halves (optional)

15–20 BROWNIES

1. Preheat oven to 325°F. Butter and lightly flour a 9- by 13-inch baking pan, and set aside.

2. Combine the eggs, butter, and vanilla in a medium bowl, and blend using an electric mixer.

3. Combine the flour, cocoa powder, sugar, and salt in a medium bowl. Add to the egg mixture and blend well. Fold in chocolate chips and pecans with a rubber spatula, if desired.

4. Pour batter into the prepared pan, and bake in the oven until the top is just firm to the touch, 35 to 40 minutes. Remove from the oven and let cool in the pan, then cut into small squares to serve.

GLEASON GRAINS

Ben and Theresa Gleason each spent part of their childhoods on family farms. Ben's family grew potatoes and milked Guernsey cows in Connecticut. Theresa's family raised grain, hogs, and cattle in Indiana. Ben has been growing organic grains and milling flour for the Middlebury Natural Foods Co-op and artisan bakeries since 1982.

Very few families make their living on small farms in the United States today. Much of our food is produced on corporate farms, where the farmer is primarily a manager. Ben and Theresa love the familiarity with the land that comes with running a small farm. The farmer knows every inch of the land, feels the soil in his hands every day, and smells the rain in the air. The knowledge gained from this stewardship creates a better product and a healthier economy. The Gleasons love their land and the living it provides their family.

Gleason Grains is small enough for Ben and Theresa to know their customers. They enjoy delivering their flour and talking to bakers. Because their flour is not blended with flours from other farms, as is most commercial flour, it retains the special characteristics of place, or terroir. Bakers tell them they love the distinctive flavor! And the Gleasons love knowing that their friends are nourishing themselves with wheat that they have carefully tended. Ben and Theresa wish you happy baking!

Recipe from WOLAVER'S ORGANIC ALES

Wolaver's Chocolate Stout Fondue

Beer and chocolate? You bet! The espresso notes in Wolver's Oatmeal Stout blend beautifully with chocolate, while the soft hop character complements the fresh fruits used for dipping. This dessert is interesting, unique, and delicious.

2 cups roughly chopped semisweet chocolate or chocolate chips

⅔ cup roughly chopped milk chocolate or chocolate chips

1 (12-ounce) bottle Wolaver's Organic Oatmeal Stout, or other stout (you can use more or less, depending on desired consistency)

1 teaspoon pure vanilla extract

1 tablespoon unsalted butter (optional)

Sliced fruit, such as pears, strawberries, kiwi, and/or apples

4–6 SERVINGS

1. Combine chocolates and stout in the top of a double boiler. Cook over medium-low heat, stirring constantly, until the mixture is melted and smooth. Remove fondue from stovetop and mix in vanilla extract and butter, if using.

2. Transfer mixture to a ceramic fondue pot and keep warm over a canned heat burner or candle. Serve with sliced fruit for dipping.

Variation: If you enjoy peanut butter, melt some and add it to the mixture for a peanut butter–chocolate stout concoction.

Maple Nut Cake

This moist and flavorful maple nut cake is very easy to make. Just combine the ingredients in a large bowl and fold in some walnuts — that's all there is to it. Cut the cake into squares and serve warm with a scoop of vanilla ice cream.

1⅔ cups all-purpose flour

1 cup packed light brown sugar

1 teaspoon baking soda

½ teaspoon salt

⅔ cup pure maple syrup

⅓ cup vegetable oil

1 teaspoon vinegar

½ cup coarsely chopped walnuts

Confectioners' sugar for sprinkling

16 BROWNIE-SIZE SERVINGS

1. Preheat oven to 350°F. Lightly grease an 8-inch square baking pan, and set aside.

2. Combine the flour, sugar, baking soda, salt, maple syrup, ⅓ cup of water, vegetable oil, and vinegar in a large bowl. Mix with an electric mixer until smooth scraping bowl as necessary. Fold in the walnuts.

3. Pour batter into the prepared pan. Bake in the oven for 35 to 40 minutes, or until a toothpick inserted into the center of the cake comes out clean. Transfer to a rack and cool, then cut into small squares and sprinkle the tops with confectioners' sugar. Serve with a scoop of vanilla ice cream.

HONEY FACTS

The 1868 U.S. agriculture survey showed Vermont as being the leading honey-producing state in New England, with 12,000 to 15,000 hives producing from 400,000 to 1,000,000 pounds of honey annually. Although production has fallen, Vermont is still #1 in New England with 6,000 hives producing about 500,000 pounds of honey in 2005.

The average honey crop in Vermont is 50 to 60 pounds (five gallons) per hive.

Honeys differ in color and taste depending on the blossoms visited by the honeybees. Honey can be enjoyed in several forms: comb honey, liquid honey, and whipped honey.

Store honey at room temperature. It does not need to be refrigerated.

From the Vermont Beekeepers Association

Recipe from HONEY GARDENS APIARIES, INC.

Laura's Mom's Honey Cake

For years, Honey Gardens had a very productive bee yard on the land that belongs to Christophe and his family (of Christophe's on the Green Restaurant) in Vergennes. They have been very supportive of Honey Gardens over the years and also use their elderberry honey on the restaurant's menu. Honey Gardens offers unfiltered Apitherapy honey, which is totally raw and retains beneficial traces of pollen, propolis, and beeswax, which contribute healthful minerals, vitamins, enzymes, amino acids, and carbohydrates to the honey.

Working with approximately 1,100 colonies of honeybees, Honey Gardens' vision is to connect people to their environment through the healing power of plants and the work of the bees.

Laura Sideman, the creator of this recipe, joined the team at Honey Gardens after working at Shelburne Farms. This honey cake recipe is inspired by the Jewish tradition of eating honey to welcome in a sweet New Year. The fact that Laura's Mom's entire neighborhood now bakes this cake is testament to its deliciousness.

⅛ teaspoon ground cloves

⅛ teaspoon ground nutmeg

⅛ teaspoon allspice

1 teaspoon ground cinnamon

½ teaspoon salt

⅛ teaspoon baking soda

2 teaspoons baking powder

4½–5 cups all-purpose flour, plus additional for dusting pan

5 farm-fresh eggs

1 pound honey

1½ cups sugar

2 cups freshly brewed strong coffee, cold

¾ cup vegetable oil

1 teaspoon pure vanilla extract

1 (10-INCH) CAKE

1. Preheat oven to 300°F. Grease and lightly flour a 10-inch tube pan or angel food cake pan. Set aside.

2. Sift the cloves, nutmeg, allspice, cinnamon, salt, baking soda, baking powder, and flour in a large bowl. Set aside.

3. Beat the eggs in a separate medium bowl using an electric mixer. Add the honey, sugar, coffee, oil, and vanilla and mix until blended well. Add to the flour mixture and beat until fairly smooth.

4. Pour the batter into the prepared pan and bake in the oven until the top is golden brown and a toothpick inserted into the center of the cake comes out clean, about 1 hour and 20 minutes.

5. Remove from oven and transfer pan to a cooling rack. Invert onto a cake plate or stand.

Gingerbread Ice Cream Sandwiches with Cider Maple Ice Cream

This signature dessert from the Cliff House features the New England flavors of apple, maple syrup, and ginger. At the Cliff House, the cookies are cut with a scallop-edge cookie cutter, then layered with a scoop of cider maple ice cream. For presentation, the sandwiches are packaged in brown butcher paper, wrapped to resemble small gifts.

To vary the dessert's presentation, the cookies may be cut in half and stacked on top of each other (with ice cream between each layer). A drizzle of reduced cider is used to garnish the final dish.

CIDER MAPLE ICE CREAM

1 quart cider

½ cup milk

2 cups heavy cream

1 vanilla bean, split

½ cup sugar

¼ cup pure maple syrup, preferably Vermont-made

5 egg yolks

GINGERBREAD

2¼ cups all-purpose flour

½ teaspoon baking soda

¼ teaspoon baking powder

1 tablespoon ground ginger

1 tablespoon ground cinnamon

½ teaspoon salt

½ cup (1 stick) butter

⅓ cup packed dark brown sugar

1 egg

6 tablespoons molasses

6–8 SERVINGS

1. Make the ice cream: Reduce the cider from 1 quart to 1 cup in a medium saucepan over medium-high heat.

2. Combine the milk, cream, vanilla bean, sugar, maple syrup, and reduced cider in a medium saucepan and bring to a boil over medium-high heat. Remove from heat and set aside for 10 minutes. Meanwhile, prepare an ice bath and set aside.

3. Beat the yolks until uniform and thick. Stir ¼ cup of the cream mixture in a slow stream into beaten egg to temper it. Continue adding the cream mixture in the same fashion, stirring continuously with a wooden spoon or rubber spatula. When the cream mixture has been completely incorporated into the yolks, transfer the bowl to the prepared ice bath and let the custard cool completely, stirring occasionally.

4. Transfer mixture to an ice cream maker, and process according to the manufacturer's instructions. Store in the freezer.

5. Meanwhile, make the gingerbread: In a medium bowl, sift the flour, baking soda, baking powder, ginger, cinnamon, and salt. Cream the butter and brown sugar in a separate large bowl with an electric mixer until smooth and fluffy, scraping bowl as necessary. Add the dry ingredients and mix until just combined. Beat in the egg and molasses until well combined and a soft dough forms.

6. Divide the dough into 2 balls and flatten into 2 disks. Wrap each disk in plastic wrap and transfer to the refrigerator. Let the dough chill until firm, about 4 hours.

7. Preheat oven to 350°F.

8. Roll out the dough onto a clean, floured work surface to about ¼-inch thickness. Cut out the cookies using a scallop-edge cookie cutter, dipping cutter in flour between cuts. Transfer the cookies to a nonstick baking sheet, about ½-inch apart and transfer to the oven. Bake until crisp and golden on the bottom, about 12 minutes. Remove from the oven and set cookies to cool completely on a rack.

9. Assemble the sandwiches: Scoop the ice cream on half of the ginger-bread cookies. Top each with another cookie and gently press to form a sandwich.

Maple Moose

The inn's location in the Moosalamoo Region of the Green Mountain National Forest, plus the innkeeper Olya's affection for the moose who visit the yard from time to time, inspired her to create something appropriately "moose." The result is this authentic Vermont recipe that produces a refreshing and unusual mousse. It has become a popular "no sugar added, but far from sugar free" dessert that is sometimes a breakfast request. For the most intense flavor use dark syrup (Grade B rather than the lightest grade). Garnish with walnuts if desired.

1 egg white, at room temperature

¾ cup pure maple syrup, preferably Vermont-made, heated

1 cup well-chilled heavy cream

Chopped walnuts (optional)

6 fresh mint sprigs (optional)

6 SERVINGS

1. Lightly grease and flour 6 giant or Texas-size muffin tins (see Note) or mini bundt pans.

2. Beat the egg white in a medium bowl with an electric mixer on medium-high speed until soft peaks form. Add the hot syrup in a slow stream and continue to beat until the egg white is stiff, forming a thick meringue.

3. In a separate, well-chilled bowl, whip the cream until mixture holds soft peaks. Gently fold the whipped cream into the maple meringue with a rubber spatula. Spoon carefully into prepared tins.

4. Transfer to the freezer and freeze for 3 hours. Release from the molds and garnish with walnuts and mint, if desired.

Note: A giant or Texas-size muffin cup is approximately 3½-inches in diameter and holds about ⅝ cup batter.

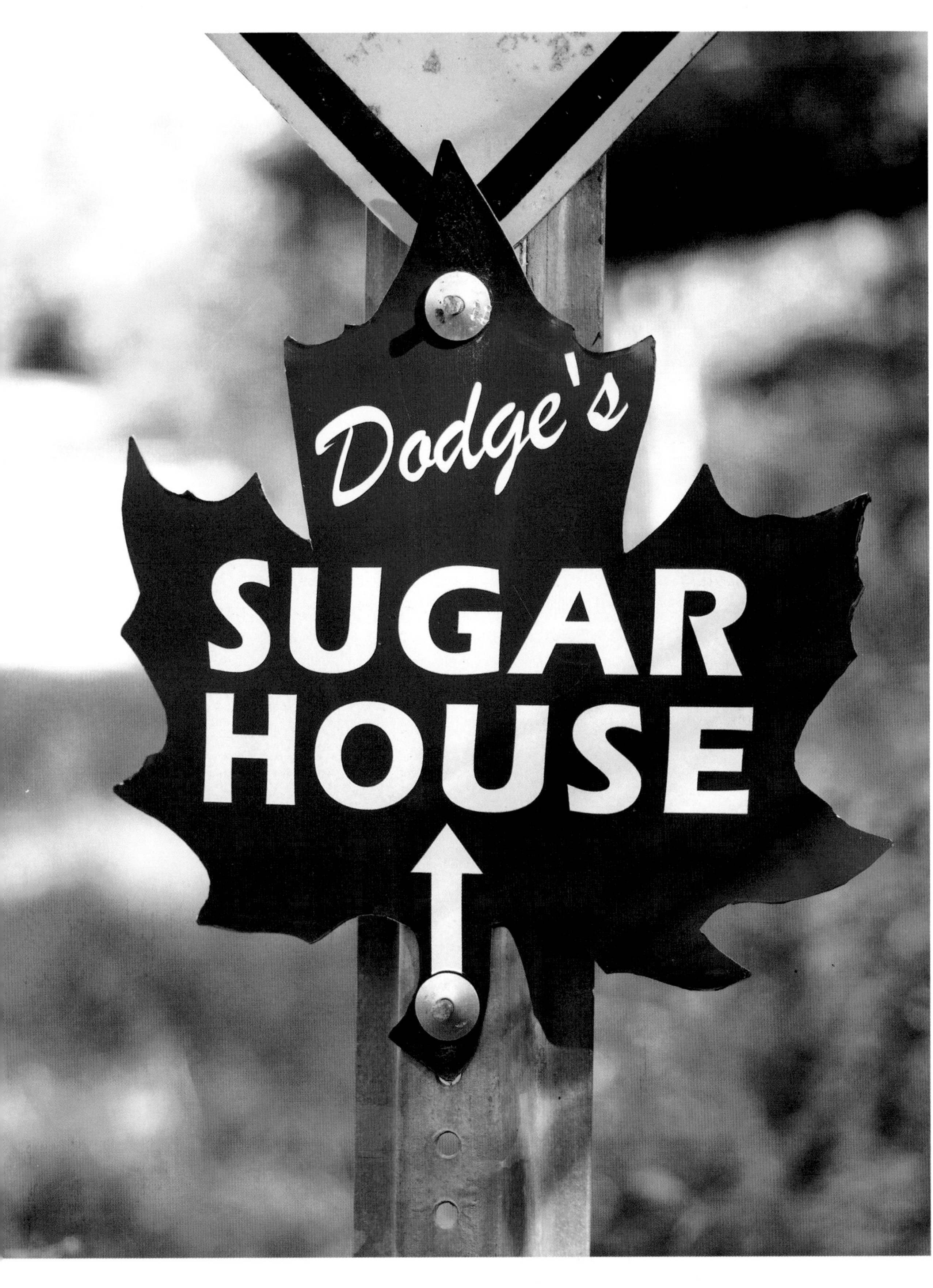
Dodge's
SUGAR
HOUSE

Maple Crème Caramel

Maple Grove Dining Room & Cottages welcomes guests year-round to their cozy farmhouse restaurant and seasonally in the cottages. Whenever possible the restaurant uses locally grown ingredients. The dining room offers tender steaks and fresh seafood, tempting pastas, and house favorites such as Vermont Cordon Bleu and baked stuffed shrimp. Desserts include chocolate mousse cake and banana and blueberry crumble made from scratch by the owner. Oatmeal chocolate chip cookies serve as the after-dinner mint. There is fireside dining in the winter, indoor and deck dining in the summer and fall.

This rich dessert may be served with whipped cream and fresh blueberries, if desired.

½ cup pure maple syrup, preferably Vermont-made

⅓ cup pure maple syrup, Vermont Grade B

5 farm-fresh egg yolks

1 teaspoon pure vanilla extract

1 teaspoon ground cinnamon

2 cups whipping cream

6 SERVINGS

1. Preheat oven to 275°F. Lightly butter 6 (¾-cup) ramekins and set aside.

2. Simmer ½ cup maple syrup in a small saucepan over medium heat for about 10 minutes, until syrup is reduced to a thick pouring consistency. Don't overcook or you will make candy. Immediately pour caramel into prepared ramekins, swirling ramekins to coat sides with some of the caramel. Set aside.

3. Make the custard: Whisk Grade B maple syrup, egg yolks, vanilla, and cinnamon in a medium bowl to combine.

4. Heat the cream in a medium saucepan until just boiling. Gradually whisk hot cream into yolk mixture, then divide the mixture among the prepared ramekins.

5. Set the ramekins into a baking pan and fill the pan with hot water halfway up the sides of the ramekins. Cover the baking pan with foil, carefully transfer to the oven, and bake for 50 minutes. During the last 10 minutes of baking, check custards to make sure the center is set and a little wiggly but not totally cooked.

6. Remove custards from the water and chill uncovered in the refrigerator until cold, at least 4 hours. Custards can be made one day ahead but make sure to cover once they are cold. Keep refrigerated.

7. To serve, run a knife around edges of ramekins to loosen custards, and invert onto dessert plates.

Butternut Squash Ravioli with Apples and Pears

Putney Pasta began making fresh-frozen, all-natural premium pastas in 1983 in a tiny renovated barn in Putney, Vermont. The owners were committed right from the start to using the finest and freshest ingredients they could find, adding no preservatives or additives of any kind. They drove their VW Rabbit all over the region, delivering pastas to local co-ops, general stores, and restaurants. Today the business is thriving; the VW has been retired and replaced by tractor trailer trucks that deliver the pastas to natural food stores, co-ops, and grocery stores in all 50 states.

Who says you can't have pasta for dessert? Expand your pasta world with this unique recipe that combines many Vermont flavors. Fruits, nuts, and ice cream, along with the sweet ravioli stuffing, make this an unusual and memorable dessert.

2 (9-ounce) packages Putney Pasta Butternut Squash & VT Maple Syrup Ravioli (see Note)

4 tablespoons butter

2 apples, such as McIntosh, cored, unpeeled, and thinly sliced

2 ripe pears, such as Bartlett or Bosc, cored, unpeeled, and thinly sliced

½ teaspoon ground cinnamon

¼ teaspoon ground nutmeg

1 tablespoon sugar

½ cup walnut pieces

1 pint rum raisin ice cream

4–6 sprigs fresh mint

Note: *Putney Pasta is widely available, but if you cannot find it, substitute another squash- or pumpkin-filled ravioli.*

4–6 SERVINGS

1. Cook ravioli according to package directions, drain, and set aside.

2. Melt the butter in a large skillet over medium heat. Add the apples, pears, cinnamon, nutmeg, and sugar and sauté until fruit is fork tender, 3 to 5 minutes, stirring occasionally.

3. Add the walnuts and ravioli and continue to cook until heated through.

4. To serve, divide the pasta mixture into plates or pasta bowls. Garnish each dish with rum raisin ice cream and a sprig of fresh mint. Serve at once.

RED HEN BAKING COMPANY

Red Hen Baking Company in Duxbury, was started in 1999 by husband-and-wife team Randy George and Eliza Cain. They still operate the business with the help of 17 dedicated employees. Every day of the year they bake and deliver more than a dozen different types of long-fermented, certified organic breads.

The company has a strong sense of community, regularly buying their ingredients from three local farmers. Ben Gleason, from Gleason Grains of Bridport, supplies all their whole wheat flour; Tony Lehoullier, of Foote Brook Farm in Johnson, grows all the Yukon Gold potatoes used in their potato bread; and the maple syrup for their sticky buns comes from the von Trapp farm in Waitsfield. These business relationships are mutually beneficial — Randy and Eliza are able to speak with Tony when he delivers the potatoes and discuss how the crop is progressing. He in turn keeps close track of their usage and is able to be more responsive than most distributors could afford to be. They all benefit from the economic efficiency of making a direct sale. In the years that Tony has been supplying Red Hen Baking, he has refined his storage methods to the point where he is able to keep potatoes for the entire year with no sprouting and very few blemishes.

The company's relationship with Ben Gleason began in 2000, after they had been in business for a year. The couple hired a baker who told them about the great locally grown whole wheat flour he had used in a bakery in the Middlebury area. Randy contacted Ben and was very excited to learn that he grew mostly hard red winter wheat — the type generally most suitable for the breads Red Hen Baking makes. Ben's refined techniques, and his flat land east of Lake Champlain (the closest thing that Vermont has to plains), have yielded consistently high-quality wheat for many years. The pictures of Ben that hang in the retail shop never cease to interest customers. They are amazed to see Ben working the fields — "just over the hill" — that produce Red Hen's whole wheat flour. Ben pays Randy and Eliza a visit every three weeks or so, his station wagon loaded with 1,000 pounds of his freshly milled flour. Randy and Eliza have built a relationship with Ben and his family and have made the trip to see his fields of amber waves. It is a gratifying, and very rare, phenomenon in this day and age for a baker to have such a close relationship with the farmer who grows his wheat.

The von Trapp Farm in Waitsfield is a small dairy farm owned and operated by Martin and Kelly von Trapp. Although the trend in agriculture in recent years, in Vermont and throughout the United States, has been toward greater specialization, the von Trapps abide by the old Vermont tradition of supplementing their farm income by making maple syrup every spring. Eliza grew up less than a mile from the von Trapp farm and has known Martin and Kelly all her life, so it was natural for her to look to them for syrup when the bakery developed their maple-glazed sticky buns (a specialty sold only at farmers' markets and their retail shop). The bakers visit Martin and Kelly at the farm about once a month to pick up five gallons of Grade C syrup. Usually they combine that trip with their weekly milk run; Randy and his wife fill their jars with fresh milk that Eliza makes into yogurt. Often they trade some of their day-old bread, which the von Trapps feed to their cows, for the milk. There is a veritable web of connections in this relationship!

French Miche

The miche is a French bread that was repopularized by the late Lionel Poilane, who became famous for his 2-kilo miche, now shipped (at great expense!) around the world. But Poilane's most valuable export was inspiration, and it is that commodity that is the main ingredient in this loaf from Red Hen. In keeping with Poilane's emphasis on fine ingredients that, along with the baker's hands, come together to give the bread terroir, this miche uses whole wheat from Ben Gleason, who grows and mills organic wheat on his farm in Bridport, near Middlebury.

This bread should be formed into a large, round loaf. It should be baked very dark to allow all of the flavors to be released in the crust and to fully bake the interior. Although it may look burned, if made properly, this bread will have a slightly sweet and nutty crust with no burned flavor whatsoever. Because of the size of the loaf (and the resulting high ratio of crumb [or interior] to crust) and the very wet dough that it is made from, a great deal of moisture is released from the interior and through the crust as the bread cools. This keeps the crust from getting too hard in spite of being so dark. Note that the ingredients for the natural starter and the final dough must be at room temperature (about 75°F).

Before embarking on this recipe, be aware that this is a naturally leavened bread. This means that it uses the method employed for centuries before baker's yeast was isolated in a laboratory and brought to the marketplace. Although in this country we often refer to naturally leavened breads as "sourdough," the flavor connotation in that term really doesn't accurately describe the earthy, slightly sweet and mildly sour flavor of this bread. The flavor and texture of a good naturally leavened bread cannot really be imitated with baker's yeast. You should be forewarned that creating the starter (or "chef," the French word for "chief," also sometimes referred to as "seed" or "mother" in this country) for this bread takes at least a week, but once you have a healthy starter, it can be stored for up to a week and revived with a few feedings (described below). Although bread of this type is beyond the ambitions for many home bakers, there are an increasing number of serious home bakers who have found themselves obsessed with perfecting delicious naturally leavened breads at home. In the hopes that a few more people will "catch the bug," the recipe is included here.

A NOTE ON STARTER TERMINOLOGY

For the sake of consistency and to reduce confusion, the miche recipe uses the following terms for the natural starter. Chef: Literally "chief" in French. We use this term to refer to the flour and water combination, which has a healthy population of wild yeast and beneficial bacteria and is the active ingredient in the levain. There are usually two to three feeding cycles of chef performed before it is ready to be used in a levain. A piece of the chef must always be set aside and refrigerated or fed to perpetuate a healthy culture. Levain: Literally "natural leavening" in French. We use this term to refer to the final stage of a natural starter — the one that will be used directly in the final dough.

CHEF (MOTHER STARTER)

½ cup whole rye flour (about 75°F)

Unbleached wheat flour, as needed

MICHE STARTER

¼ cup ripe "chef" (mother starter)

3 tablespoons restored germ wheat flour

1 cup fine ground whole wheat flour, preferably Gleason's

¼ cup whole rye flour

FINAL DOUGH

Miche Starter from above

1⅓ cups fine ground whole wheat flour, preferably Gleason's

⅝ cup restored germ wheat flour, or ⅔ cup wheat flour and ⅙ cup wheat germ

¾ cup whole rye flour

6 cups unbleached wheat flour

2 tablespoons salt

1. For the chef, or mother starter, mix a slurry of the rye flour and ¾ cup 80°F water together in a nonmetallic container with a loose-fitting lid. This should be a thin, pancake-batter consistency (if it is not, add more rye flour or water to achieve this consistency). Leave this mixture in a room that is between 75 and 80 degrees.

2. After 24 to 36 hours, the mixture should have some bubbles and a subtly sweet aroma. At this point, add ½ cup 75°F water and ½ cup unbleached wheat flour. After another 24 to 36 hours, the mixture should be bubbling more vigorously than before. Discard half of the mixture and add another ½ cup of wheat flour and ½ cup 75°F water. At this point, the time it takes for the mixture to become active should be down to 12 to 15 hours. When it has reached a point where it will get frothy in 12 hours, pour off all but ¼ cup of the starter and add ¾ cup wheat flour and ½ cup 75°F water. This will make it a little thicker. Repeat this last step a few times if necessary until the starter becomes frothy after 12 hours. Once it has reached the point at which it will become frothy after 12 hours, you have a chef that can be used to feed the miche starter.

3. The key to a good, vigorous starter is keeping it between 75 and 80°F (room and starter temperature). If you're not going to use it right away and cannot feed it every 12 hours, you can store the chef in the refrigerator for 1 week, where it will become dormant. If you refrigerate your chef, you should "refresh" (feed) it at least three times (mix ¾ cup wheat flour and ½ cup 75°F water with ¼ cup of the chef) to "wake it up" before using it.

A Healthy Chef

The chef should consist of a 2 to 1 (by volume) ratio of unbleached wheat flour to water. A chef can be kept in the refrigerator for up to one week, but the longer it is stored under refrigeration, the more feedings it will require to get it back to a healthy state. After refrigeration, the chef should be left at room temperature for 6 hours before giving it two (or more) feedings. A healthy and vigorous chef is bubbly and sweet, not overly sour and not flavorless. Usually it will reach this state 8 to 10 hours after its last feeding. The chef is really the soul of this loaf and, as fans of natural fermentation know, the resulting flavor and texture of the loaves make it worth going through the trouble of continually feeding your chef every 12 hours.

Prepare the miche levain about 4 hours before making the final dough: Combine 1 cup of 75°F water with ¼ cup of the chef, the wheat germ, wheat flour, and rye flour in a container with a loose-fitting lid and enough room for the starter to double in volume. The mixture should be the consistency of pancake batter. Leave in a container with a loose-fitting lid and enough room for the starter to double in volume. Let it sit in a room that is between 75 and 80°F for 4 to 5 hours.

Make the dough: Combine 2½ cups of 75°F water, the miche starter, the whole wheat flour, germ wheat flour, the rye flour, and the wheat flour in a large bowl. Mix with a wooden spoon, then switch to your hands when using a spoon becomes too difficult. You want to incorporate all of the dry ingredients into the wet, so that no dry spots are visible. When this is done, cover the bowl with a towel and let the dough rest, or "autolyse," for 20 minutes (see "Methods Rather than Recipes," page 268).

After the autolyse, dimple the dough with your fingers all over the top. Pour ¼ cup of 75°F water over this and sprinkle the salt into the water. Now incorporate these ingredients by hand with a punch and fold motion. When there is no water leaking from the dough, use a plastic scraper to transfer the dough to a wooden or stone kneading board. Knead the dough just until it is smooth. It should feel quite wet. Lightly coat a large bowl with oil and transfer the dough to it.

This dough should get four folds. To do this, pull all of the dough from the outside to the inside and flip the whole mass over so that it is in a tight, smooth ball. The first fold should happen about 20 minutes after transferring the dough back to the bowl, then the next three should happen at one-hour intervals. With each fold, the dough should feel slightly more elastic and gassy.

One hour after the last fold, divide the dough into two equal pieces and form into round loaves. Place the loaves upside down into a well-floured basket that will allow the bread to increase in volume by at least a third. Let the loaves sit, or "proof" in the baskets for at least one hour, or until a light fingerprint will not spring back.

Meanwhile, place a baking stone on the bottom rack of the oven, and preheat oven to 475°F. When the loaves are proofed, transfer them to a bread peel or a cookie sheet lightly dusted with fine cornmeal or semolina flour. Quickly slice a series of light scores into the top of the loaf with a razor blade and slide each loaf rapidly off the peel onto the baking stone in the oven. Immediately toss about half a cup of water into the oven chamber (be very careful to avoid the oven light — it may shatter if water contacts it) and bake the loaves for about 40 minutes or until they take on a deep brown color. Remove from oven and cool on a rack for at least 2 hours before slicing.

Methods Rather than Recipes: Bread-making Tips from Red Hen Baking Company

People often assume that we must have a treasure trove of secret recipes for our breads. In fact, we willingly share our recipes with anyone who is interested, but the real trick to making our breads is in the process. When you're dealing with a living thing like bread dough, there is no painting by number. A printed recipe gives you, at most, only a very basic outline of the many things that you need to be attentive to as you go through the process of making bread.

If you're interested in advancing your bread skills, or are hung up on a certain issue with your bread-making, come by and visit us at the bakery on Route 100. We love to show people what we do — there are no secrets here!

Until you get a chance to visit us, here are a couple of tips that we find helpful for people who are experienced with home baking but are still working on perfecting artisan breads.

Don't overwork yourself kneading the dough.

One of the most important techniques that we employ at the bakery (even though we have a machine mixer that could mix 300 pounds of dough for 30 minutes if we wanted it to) is called an autolyse. This is the French term for giving the dough a rest. It is the way bakers did things before the days of mixers and it actually yields better results than an extended kneading period does. To do a proper autolyse, mix up a dough with all the flour your recipe calls for and just 90 percent of the total water amount called for. Leave out the salt, 10 percent of the water, and the leavening agent (unless your recipe employs a wet starter, in which case you will need to add the leavening). Combine it just enough so that there are no more dry clumps of flour (it will still be shaggy and not particularly stretchy). Cover this in a bowl and let it sit for 20 minutes. When you come back to the dough after the autolyse, you will find that in this short time, the water has absorbed into the flour and the dough is much more pliable than it first was . . . and you didn't even sweat to make that happen! Now you are set up for employing the next two tips.

Don't be afraid to make a wet dough.

One of the critical characteristics of a good artisan bread is an interior (or "crumb") that is moist and has irregularly sized holes in it — we call this "an open crumb." The single biggest thing that you can do to get this kind of crumb is to make a dough that is much wetter than most recipes call for. After the autolyse step that we describe above, you can slowly add the remaining water along with the salt and leavening. Keep adding small amounts of water while kneading the dough between additions. Don't be afraid to add even more water than your recipe calls for. To achieve the kind of crumb that we're after, you want to end up with a dough that, when put into a bowl, will flatten out rather than doming up. When you have achieved this level of "hydration," knead it just until it is smooth and no wet spots are visible. Now you're ready for the next step.

Fold your dough as it rises.

For this step to work properly, you want your dough and room temperatures and leavening amounts to be set so that the total rising time that you'll need

will be between 3 and 4 hours. During this long, slow rising time, a wet dough needs to be turned, or folded. This should not be a punching down like some recipes call for. The folding process is really an extension of the kneading process. It's a passive method of dough development (like the autolyse is) because it builds strength through a combination of your work and the work of all the microorganisms that are thriving in the dough. We fold our doughs by essentially turning them inside out. We take the sides and fold them to the middle completely, until the mass of dough can be turned over in a tight ball. The first fold should be done 20 minutes after mixing. Thereafter, the folds can be gradually spaced out as the fermentation continues to do the work for you. By the end of the process, you will have done four to

six folds depending on how wet your dough was, and with each fold your dough will get stronger. By the end of this process, you will have a dough that has increased in volume and is domed on the top from the increased strength imparted by the folds. Between 45 minutes and 1 hour after the last fold, it will be ready for shaping.

Now you know some of the secrets that are really more critical to making good bread than the formulas themselves. Learning to work with the dough in this way takes experience and continual attention. Remember that there are no complete failures. Every bake has something to teach you!

Once again, we are happy to show you some of the above processes in action at the bakery. Go ahead and try these tips and observe the differences!

RECIPES BY CATEGORY

RECIPE CONTRIBUTORS AND SUPPLIERS

A

The Alchemist Pub and Brewery
23 South Main Street
Waterbury, VT 05676
802-244-4120
www.alchemistbeer.com
*Celeriac and Green Apple Salad,
page 33*

Annie's Naturals
564 Gateway Drive
Napa, CA 94558
800-288-1089
www.anniesnaturals.com
*Goddess Primavera Pasta Salad,
page 30*

Applecheek Farm
567 McFarlane Road
Hyde Park, VT 05655
802-888-4482
www.applecheekfarm.com
*Emu Steaks with Soy Ginger Sauce,
page 198*
Maple Nut Cake, page 253

B

**Bailey's Restaurant at Bolton Valley
Resort**
4302 Bolton Valley Access Road
Bolton, VT 05477
802-434-3444
www.boltonvalley.com
Blueberry Mint Relish, page 86
Goat Cheese Bread Pudding, page 126
Rosemary-seared Lamb Loin, page 159

Birdseye Diner
590 Main Street
Castleton, VT 05735
802-468-5817
Spinach Vichyssoise, page 38

Birds Nest Inn
5088 Waterbury-Stowe Road
Waterbury Center, VT 05677
800-366-5592
www.birdsnestinn.com
*Maple Apple Waffles with Ben & Jerry's
Ice Cream, page 76*

Bittersweet Farm B&B
1 Jim Drier Road
Bristol, VT 05443
802-453-3828
*Blueberry-stuffed French Toast,
page 79*
*Grilled Marinated Venison Loins,
page 165*

Black River Produce
P.O. Box 489
North Springfield, VT 05150
800-228-5481
www.blackriverproduce.com
Supplier of produce and dairy

Blueberry Hill Inn
1307 Goshen Ripton Road
Goshen, VT 05733
802-247-6735
www.blueberryhillinn.com
*Apple-stuffed Chicken Breast with
Calvados Jus, page 182*

Bowman Road Farm
P.O. Box 267
Barnard, VT 05031
802-763-7454
Hungarian Goulash, page 136
New England Pot Roast, page 135

Butterfly Bakery of Vermont
87 Barre Street
Montpelier, VT 05602
802-310-1725
www.butterly-bakery.com
*Carrot Cake with Cream Cheese Frost-
ing, page 244*
Chocolate Cake, page 248
*Raspberry Almond Thumbprint
Cookies, page 234*

Butternut Mountain Farm
37 Industrial Park Drive
Morrisville, VT 05661
800-828-2376
www.moosewoodhollow.com
*Grilled Maple-marinated Portabella
Mushrooms, page 209*
*Mixed Baby Greens with Maple
Dressing, Cranberries, and Apples,
page 210*

C

Cabot Creamery
1 Home Farm Way
Montpelier, VT 05602
888-792-2268
www.cabotcheese.com
Winter Squash Gratin, page 129

Café Provence
11 Center Street
Brandon, VT 05733
802-247-9997
www.cafeprovencevt.com
*Beet Salad in Puff Pastry Layers,
page 24*

Cavendish Game Birds, Inc.
190 Paddock Road
Springfield, VT 05156
800-772-0928
www.cavendishgamebirds.com
Supplier of quail and pheasant

Champlain Orchards
2955 Route 74 West
Shoreham, VT 05770
802-897-2777
www.champlainorchards.com
*Awesome Pear or Apple Pancake,
    page 75*
*Apple, Blue Cheese, and Walnut Pizza,
    page 92*
*Field Greens with Candied Apples,
    Roasted Walnuts, and Apple Vinai-
    grette, page 87*
Grandma's Dutch Apple Torte, page 223

Champlain Valley Apiaries
P.O. Box 127
Middlebury, VT 05753
800-841-7334
www.champlainvalleyhoney.com
*Champlain Valley Apiaries Balsamic
    Salad Dressing, page 204*

Champlain Valley Rabbitry
1725 Route 22 A
West Haven, VT 05743
802-265-8276
www.vermontqualityrabbits.com
On the Farm Rabbit, page 167

Cheese Outlet Fresh Market
400 Pine Street
Burlington, VT 05401
800-447-1205
www.cheeseoutlet.com
*Root Vegetable Chowder with Vermont
    Maple Smoked Cheddar, page 117*

Cherry Hill Farm
409 Highland Road
Springfield, VT 05156
802-885-5088
www.cherryhillfarmvt.com
*Cherry Hill Farm's Very Fruity Iced Tea,
    page 80*
Warm Berry Compote, page 233

Churchill House Inn
3128 Forest Dale Road
Brandon, VT 05733
800-320-5828
www.churchillhouseinn.com
*Churchill House Cottage Cheese
    Pancakes, page 99*
Maple Moose, page 258
Strawberry Soup, page 90

Circle W Rabbitry
2A Rabbit Run
Underhill, VT 05489
802-899-4438
Supplier of rabbit meat

**Cliff House at Stowe Mountain
    Resort**
5781 Mountain Road
Stowe, VT 05672
800-253-4754
www.stowe.com
Ale-braised Beef Short Ribs, page 133
*Gingerbread Ice Cream Sandwich with
    Cider Maple Ice Cream, page 256*
Vermont Croque Monsieur, page 153

Kristina Creighton
www.kristinakitchen.com
*Curried Carrot and Sweet Potato Soup,
    page 39*

Crowley Cheese Factory
14 Crowley Lane
Healdville, VT 05758
800-683-2606
www.crowleycheese.com
Crowley Eggs au Gratin, page 106

D
Deep Root Organic Cooperative
P.O. Box 248
Waterbury Center, VT 05656
802-635-7616
www.deeprootorganic.com
*Acorn Squash with Wild Mushroom
    Cranberry Stuffing, page 66*

Dish Catering
266 Locust Hill
Shelburne, VT 05482
802-863-0547
www.dishcateringvt.com
*Crostini with Fresh Figs, Blue Cheese,
    Sage, and Balsamic Vinegar, page 121*
Moroccan Vegetable Tagine, page 72
*Yucatan Pork Tenderloin with Jicama,
    Avocado, and Red Onions, page 147*

Does' Leap Farm, LLC
1703 Route 108 South
East Fairfield, VT 05448
802-827-3046
*Mini Frittatas with Zucchini, Goat
    Cheese, and Tomatoes, page 114*

The Dorset Inn
On-The-Green
8 Church Street
Dorset, VT 05251
877-367-7389
www.dorsetinn.com
*Brie-stuffed Chicken Breast in Pear
    Sauce, page 180*
*Roast Rack of Pork Stuffed with Sage,
    Apple, and Onion, page 148*

E
EastEnder Restaurant
Gallery Place
442 Woodstock Road
Woodstock, VT 05091
802-457-9800
www.eastendervt.com
*Tortellini alla Farmstead Bolognese,
    page 143*

F
The Farmer's Diner
5573 Woodstock Road
Quechee, VT 05059
802-295-4600
www.farmersdiner.com
Vermont-style Hush Puppies, page 122

Fat Rooster Farm
354 Morse Road
South Royalton, VT 05068
802-763-5282
www.fatroosterfarm.com
Maple-glazed Chicken with Roasted
  Garlic and Lemon Purée, page 174

Flag Hill Farm
P.O. Box 31
Vershire, VT 05079
802-685-7724
www.flaghillfarm.com
Broiled Apples with Maple and Pomme
  De Vie, page 241
Normandy Chicken with Apples and
  Cream, page 172

G
The Gables Inn
1457 Mountain Road
Stowe, VT 05672
800-422-5371
www.gablesinn.com
Stuffed French Toast, page 98

Gleason Grains
2076 East Street
Bridport, VT 05734
802-758-2476
Whole Wheat Pastry Flour Brownies,
  page 250

Grafton Village Cheese Company
533 Townshend Road
Grafton, VT 05146
800-472-3866
www.graftonvillagecheese.com
Caramelized Onion, Grafton Cheddar,
  and Apple Tart, page 113
Grafton Cheddar Ale Soup, page 116
Grafton Squash Casserole, page 57
Scott Fletcher's Cheese Dream Sand-
  wich, page 112

H
Half Pint Farm
P.O. Box 8835
Burlington, VT 05402
802-316-6073
www.halfpintfarm.com
Pan-cooked Summer Greens, page 49
Roasted Summer Vegetables, page 50

Healthy Living Natural Foods Market
222 Dorset Street
South Burlington, VT 05403
802-863-2569
www.healthylivingmarket.com
Healthy Living Café Meat Loaf,
  page 144

Hemingway's Restaurant
4988 US Route 4
Killington, VT 05751
802-422-3886
www.hemingwaysrestaurant.com
Hemingway's Cream of Garlic Soup,
  page 37
Hemingway's Fallen Soufflé of Vermont
  Goat and Cheddar Cheeses, page 124
Hemingway's Honey Balsamic Vinai-
  grette, page 211
Hemingway's Late Summer Cyder Soup
  with Orange Sorbet, page 231

Hen of the Wood Restaurant
92 Stowe Street
Waterbury, VT 05676
802-244-7300
www.henofthewood.com
Roasted Rabbit with Parsnip Purée,
  Pete's Red Cabbage, and Sage Jus,
  page 168

Honey Gardens Apiaries
2777 Route 7
Ferrisburgh, VT 05456
802-877-6766
www.honeygardens.com
Laura's Mom's Honey Cake, page 255

Hope Farm
P.O. Box 164
1984 Hudson Road
East Charleston, VT 05833
802-723-4283
hopefarm@surfglobal.net
Hope Farm's Corn and Cheese
  Chowder, page 118
Lamb Curry, page 164

I
The Inn at Weathersfield
1342 Route 106
Perkinsville, VT 05151
802-263-9217
www.weathersfieldinn.com
Grilled Quail Salad with Maple Vinai-
  grette and Scallions, page 188

Izabella's Eatery
351 West Main Street
Bennington, VT 05201
802-447-4949
www.izabellaseatery.com
Apple, Pickle, and Sweet Pepper Tuna
  Salad, page 32
Gingerbread Cupcakes with Orange
  Cream Cheese Frosting, page 246
Heirloom Split Pea Soup, page 40

J
JDC'S Just Delicious Catering
Applecheek Farm
567 McFarlane Road
Hyde Park, VT 05655
802-888-4482
www.applecheekfarm.com
Emu Steaks with Soy Ginger Sauce,
  page 198
Maple Nut Cake, page 253

K
Killdeer Farm
55 Butternut Road
Norwich, VT 05055
802-649-2916
www.killdeerfarm.com
Black Trumpets and Sweet Corn in
  Tarragon Cream Sauce, page 55
Melon Salsa, page 81
Petit Pois à la Français, page 52

L

La Panciata
7 Belknap Street
Northfield, VT 05663
802-485-4200
www.lapanciata.com
Smoked Salmon à la Cream Cheese,
page 120
Stuffed Focaccia, page 152

LedgEnd Farm
1288 Munger Street
Middlebury, VT 05753
802-388-8979
legendeer@comcast.net
Supplier of venison

Let's Pretend Catering
57 Commerce Avenue, Suite #3
South Burlington, VT 05403
802-651-1081
www.letspretendcatering.com
Apple–Butternut Squash Soup,
page 88
Tomato and Arugula Salad, page 20

Liberty Hill Farm
511 Liberty Hill Road
Rochester, VT 05767
802-767-3926
www.libertyhillfarm.com
Cheese Scones, page 102
Maple Nut Muffins, page 214
Rhubarb Custard Kuchen, page 219

The Lilac Inn
53 Park Street
Brandon, VT 05733
800-221-0720
www.lilacinn.com
Strawberry Rhubarb Pie, page 218

Livewater Farm
1289 Westminster West Road
Westminster West, VT 05346
802-387-4412
Sweet and Sour Vermont Cheeseburger
with Attitude, page 145

M

Maple Grove Dining Room &
Cottages
1246 Franklin Street
Brandon, VT 05733
802-247-6644
www.maplegrovecottages.com
Maple Crème Caramel, page 261

Maple Wind Farm
1045 Carse Road
Huntington, VT 05462
802-434-7257
www.maplewindfarm.com
Moroccan Lamb, page 155
Organic Roast Chicken, page 178

Michael's on the Hill
4182 Waterbury-Stowe Road; Route
100 North
Waterbury Center, VT 05677
802-244-7476
www.michaelsonthehill.com
Roasted Cavendish Quail with Celery
Root Purée, page 193

The Middlebury Inn
14 Court Square
Middlebury, VT 05753
800-842-4666
www.middleburyinn.com
Pepper-seared Filet Mignon with a
Maple Balsamic Sauce, page 132
Sautéed Pork Medallions with Honey
Rosemary Butter and Apple Salsa,
page 146
Smoked Salmon with Goat Cheese,
Apple, and Watercress Salad with
a Honey Vinaigrette, page 203

Monument Farms Dairy
2107 James Road
Weybridge, VT 05753
802-545-2119
Fresh Asparagus Soup, page 45

The Mountain Top Inn & Resort
195 Mountain Top Road
Chittenden, VT 05737
800-445-2100
www.mountaintopinn.com
Hot Chicken Salad in Lavash Bread
Bowls, page 187
Lump Crab Cakes with Vermont Sweet
Peppers, page 31
Potato, Bacon, and Egg Tart, page 109

N

New England Culinary Institute
Mark Molinaro, Executive Chef
56 College Street
Montpelier, VT 05602
877-223-6324
www.neci.edu
Eggplant Caponata, page 51

Nola's Secret Garden
P.O. Box 153
Ripton, VT 05766
802-388-6107
Tabbouleh Salad, page 23

Nutmeg Country Inn & Bakery
153 Route 9 West
Wilmington, VT 05363
800-277-5402
www.nutmeginn.com
Blueberry Bread Pudding with Warm
Blueberry Sauce, page 236

O

Olivia's Crouton Company
1423 North Street
New Haven, VT 05472
888-425-3080
www.oliviascroutons.com
Olivia's Caesar Salad, page 27
Vermont Asparagus with Parmesan
Pepper Crumbs, page 46

Osteria Pane e Salute
61 Central Street, 2nd Floor
Woodstock, VT 05091
802-457-4882
www.osteriapaneesalute.com
Sausages with Black Grapes, page 151

Otter Creek Brewing
793 Exchange Street
Middlebury, VT 05753
800-473-0727
www.ottercreekbrewing.com or
    www.wolavers.com
Otter Creek Vermont Lager Stew, page
    138
Wolaver's Chocolate Stout Fondue,
    page 252

P

Penny Cluse Café
169 Cherry Street
Burlington, VT 05401
802-651-8834
www.pennycluse.com
Swiss Chard Pie, page 60

The Perfect Wife Restaurant &
    Tavern
2594 Depot Street
Manchester Center, VT 05255
802-362-2817
www.perfectwife.com
Rond de Nice Squash Stuffed with
    Potato "Risotto," and served with
    Red and Yellow Tomato Sauces,
    page 64

Pete's Greens
266 South Craftsbury Road
Craftsbury, VT 05826
802-586-2882
www.petesgreens.com
Creamy Braising Greens Soup, page 34

The Putney Inn
P.O. Box 181
Putney, VT 05346
800-653-5517
www.putneyinn.com
Baked Macaroni and Cheese, Vermont
    Style, page 127

Putney Pasta
28 Vernon Street, Suite 434
Brattleboro, VT 05301
800-253-3683
www.putneypasta.com
Butternut Squash Ravioli with Apples
    and Pears, page 262

R

Red Brick Grill
28 Depot Street
Poultney, VT 05764
802-287-2323
Long-braised Moroccan-spiced Lamb
    Shanks, page 162

Red Hen Baking Company
961B US Route 2
Middlesex, VT 05602
802-223-5200
www.redhenbaking.com
French Miche, page 264

Rhapsody Natural Foods
28 Main Street
Montpelier, VT 05602
802-229-6112
www.rhapsodynaturalfoods.org
Basic Pan-fried Tempeh with Onions
    and Garlic, page 62

Riverview Café
36 Bridge Street
Brattleboro, VT 05301
802-254-9841
www.riverviewcafe.com
Goat Cheese Cakes with Crab Apples
    and Cardamom Sauce, page 123

Riverside Emus
179 Scott Road
Newbury, VT 05051
802-866-5648
Supplier of emu meat

S

Seyon Lodge State Park
2967 Seyon Pond Road
Groton, VT 05046
802-584-3829
www.vtstateparks.com/htm/seyon.cfm
Beet Gnocchi with Roasted Garlic
    Butter Sauce, page 58

Shelburne Vineyard
6308 Shelburne Road
Shelburne, VT 05482
802-985-8222
www.shelburnevineyard.com
Poached Salmon Fillets with Baby
    Spinach and Herbs, page 70

Simon Pearce Restaurant
The Mill
1760 Quechee Main Street
Quechee, VT 05059
802-295-1470
www.simonpearce.com
Cheddar Cheese Quiche, page 108
Sesame Chicken with Spicy Dipping
    Sauce, page 184
Shepherd's Pie, page 142

Maddie Sobel
President of the Southern Vermont/
    Northshire Beekeepers Association
maddiefarm@aol.com
Honey-sweetened Tropical Fruit Salad,
    page 201

Squash Valley Produce, Inc.
2547 Waterbury-Stowe Road
Waterbury, VT 05672
802-244-1290
Creamy Vermont Winter Pumpkin Soup,
    page 42

Stevens Orchard
188 Stevens Orchard Road
Orwell, VT 05760
802-948-2292
www.honeycrispvt.com
Fantastic Apple Sauce, page 86
Flip-over Apple Cake, page 226

The Stowe Inn & Tavern
123 Mountain Road
Stowe, VT 05672
802-253-4030
www.stoweinn.com
Shiitake and Oyster Mushroom Tortellini with Sherry Cream Sauce, page 68

T
Taylor Farm
825 Route 11
Londonderry, VT 05148
802-824-5690
www.taylorfarmvermont.com
Smoked Gouda, Sun-dried Tomato, and Parsley Muffins, page 105

Tucker Hill Inn
65 Marble Hill Road
Waitsfield, VT 05673
800-543-9841
www.tuckerhill.com
French Toast à la Tucker Hill, page 100

Three Mountain Inn
Route 30
Jamaica, VT 05343
800-532-9399
www.threemountaininn.com
Creamy Polenta, page 130
Grilled Cavendish Quail, page 195

Trapp Family Lodge
700 Trapp Hill Road
P.O. Box 1428
Stowe, VT 05672
800-826-7000
www.trappfamily.com
Cabot Cheddar Mashed Potatoes, page 56
Crispy Mushroom Strudel with Pheasant, Fresh Herb Cream Sauce, and Cranberries, page 196
Rack of Lamb with Maple Walnut Crust, Green Beans, and Merlot Pan Jus, page 156
Roasted Beets with Baby Greens, Maple Mustard Vinaigrette and Vermont Goat Cheese, page 206

Two Brothers Tavern
86 Main Street
Middlebury, VT 05753
802-388-0002
www.twobrotherstavern.com
Chocolate Porter Cake, page 247
Venison Stew, page 170

Tylord Farm/Willie T's Good Food Bakery
3608 Route 22 A
Benson, VT 05743
802-537-2613
www.prettyhealthyandtasty.com
Easy Banana Cake with Low-fat Dessert Sauce, page 243

V
Valley Dream Farm, LLC
5901 Pleasant Valley Road
Cambridge, VT 05444
802-644-6598
Fresh Spinach Salad with Basil Maple Vinaigrette, page 212

Vermont Agency of Agriculture, Food & Markets
116 State Street
Montpelier, VT 05620
802-828-2416
www.vermontagriculture.com
Apple facts

Vermont Beekeepers Association
www.vtbeekeepers.org
Honey Apple Chutney, page 211
Honey facts

Vermont Butter & Cheese Company
40 Pitman Road
Websterville, VT 05678
800-884-6287
www.butterandcheese.net
Apple Crumb Pie with Crème Fraîche, page 224
Mascarpone Chocolate Fondue, page 249
Pumpkin Pie Topped with Candied Ginger and Crème Fraîche, page 217

Vermont Herb & Salad Company
1204 Money Hole Road
Benson, VT 05743
802-537-2006
Fax: 802-537-2007
Mâche Salad with Carrots, Dried Cranberries, and Walnuts, page 29

Vermont Maple Foundation
www.vermontmaple.org
Maple facts

Vermont Mystic Pie Company
The Grist Mill
92 Stowe Street
Waterbury, VT 05676
877-588-7437
www.vermontmysticpie.com
Laura's Maple Pumpkin Pie, page 216
Vermont Mystic Apple Pie, page 220

Vermont Quality Meats Cooperative
28 Allen Street
Rutland, VT 05701
802-747-5950
www.vtqualitymeats.com
Cavendish Quail with Maple Onion Glaze, page 191
Lamb Loin Chops with Mustard Butter, page 161

The Village Inn of Woodstock
41 Pleasant Street
Woodstock, VT 05091
800-722-4571
www.villageinnofwoodstock.com
Butternut Squash Bisque, page 41
Cranberry Almond Squares, page 239
Village Inn Apple Cake, page 227

W
Wellspring Farm CSA
182 Lafiria Place
Marshfield, VT 05658
802-426-3361
www.wellspringcsa.com
Eggplant Caponata, page 51

Whitford House Inn
912 Grandey Road
Addison, VT 05491
800-746-2704
www.whitfordhouseinn.com
Strawberry Jam, page 83

Wood's Cider Mill
1482 Weathersfield Center Road
Springfield, VT 05156
802-263-5547
www.woodscidermill.com
*Harvest Stuffed Squash with Apples
   and Cranberries, page 96*
Apple-topped Cheesecake, page 228

Y
Ye Olde Tavern
5183 Main Street
Manchester Center, VT 05255
802-362-0611
www.yeoldetavern.net
Cranberry Apple Crisp, page 240

INDEX